EVERYTHING IS POA

EVERYTHING IS POA

ONE MAN'S SEARCH FOR PEACE AND PURPOSE IN EAST AFRICA

JAMEY GLASNOVIC

RMB

First Edition

For information on purchasing bulk quantities of this book, or to obtain media excerpts or invite the author to speak at an event, please visit rmbooks.com and select the "Contact" tab.

RMB | Rocky Mountain Books Ltd.
rmbooks.com
@rmbooks
facebook.com/rmbooks

Cataloguing data available from Library and Archives Canada
ISBN 9781771604543 (softcover)
ISBN 9781771604550 (electronic)

Copy editor: Peter Enman
Proofreader: Peter Midgley
All photographs are by Jamey Glasnovic unless otherwise noted.
Printed and bound in Canada

We acknowledge the financial support of the Government of Canada through the Canada Book Fund and the Canada Council for the Arts, and of the province of British Columbia through the British Columbia Arts Council and the Book Publishing Tax Credit.

This one is for Brian, Jesse, Audra, Scott,
Haley, Anna, Bob, Chris and Sue.
Family.

AUTHOR'S NOTE

As this book comes to print it has been five years since my trip to Africa. COVID-19 first emerged about a year after getting back to Canada and has been a deadly and destructive chapter in our collective experience. Writing a book about travel hardly seems important in the context of navigating a global pandemic, but doing the work helped me wade through what was a difficult period for us all. As this project eventually emerged from a limbo of disrupted lives and uncertain futures, the temptation was to tinker with the manuscript, or at the very least update the information gathered and the conclusions rendered. Instead I have left it largely as is, with the hope of capturing a collection of moments that reflect what in hindsight now feels like a more innocent time.

CONTENTS

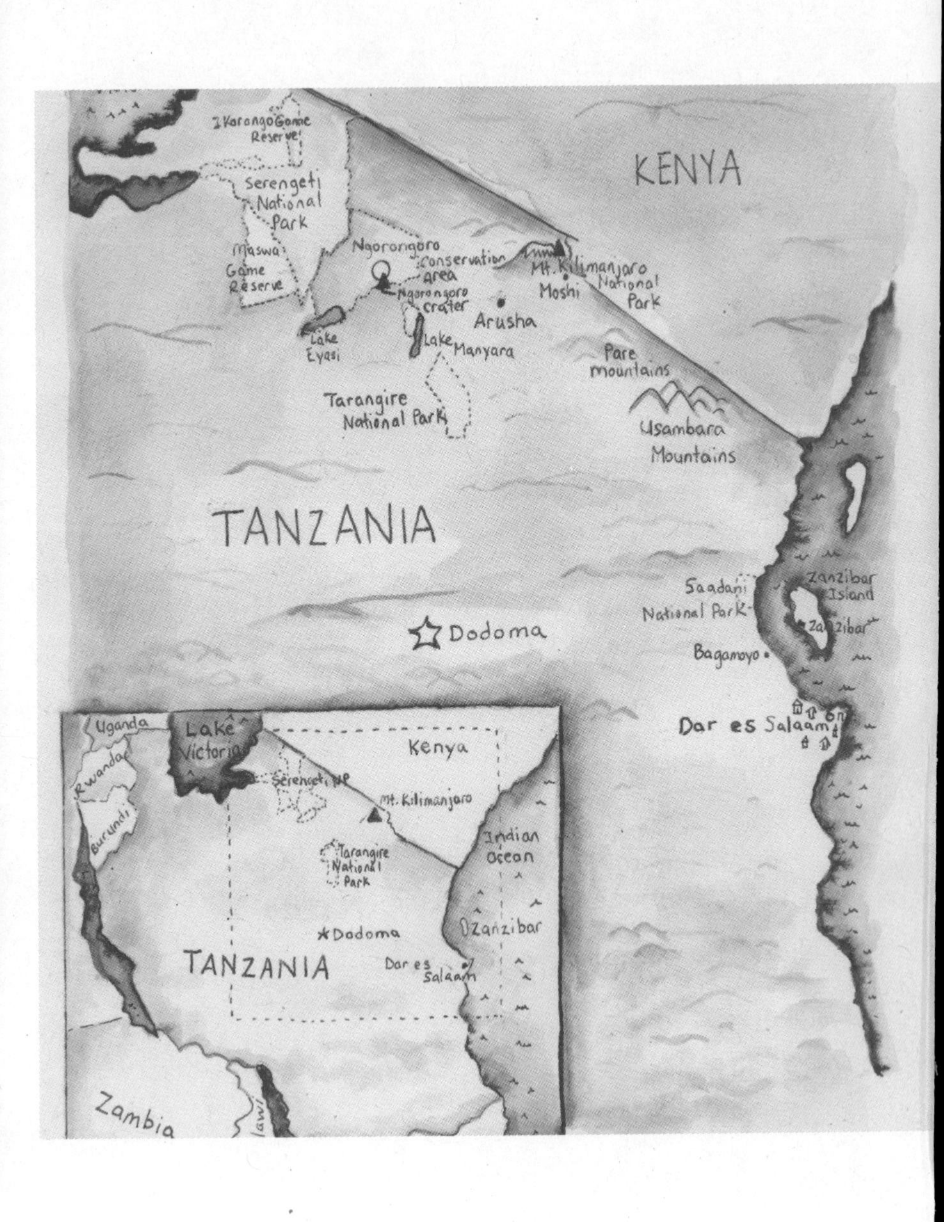
Ikorongo Game Reserve
Serengeti National Park
Maswa Game Reserve
Ngorongoro Conservation Area
Ngorongoro crater
Lake Eyasi
Lake Manyara
KENYA
Mt. Kilimanjaro National Park
Moshi
Arusha
Pare mountains
Tarangire National Park
Usambara Mountains
TANZANIA
Saadani National Park
Zanzibar Island
Zanzibar
Dodoma
Bagamoyo
Dar es Salaam
Uganda
Lake Victoria
Rwanda
Burundi
Serengeti NP
Kenya
Mt. Kilimanjaro
Tarangire National Park
Indian Ocean
Zanzibar
Dodoma
TANZANIA
Dar es Salaam
Zambia

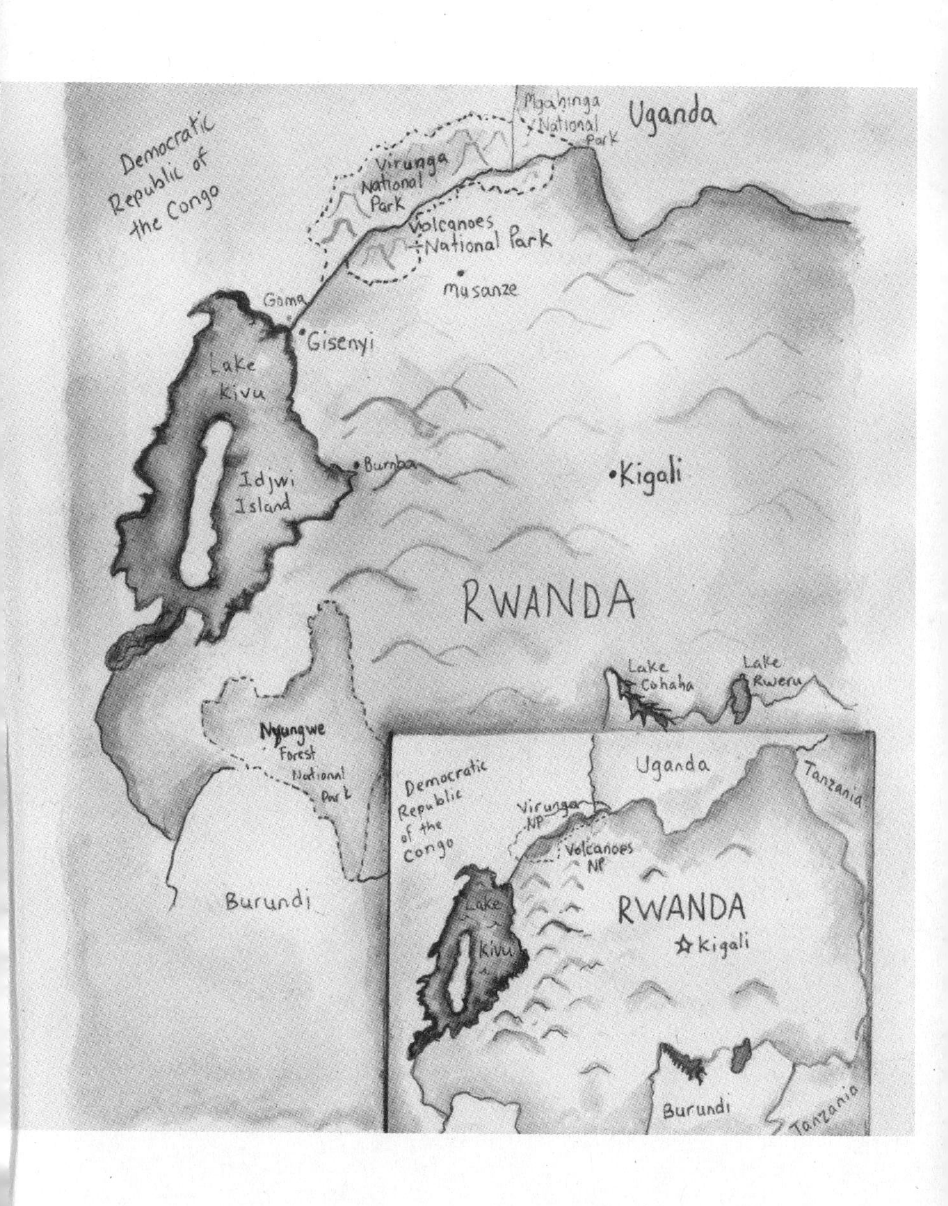

Democratic Republic of the Congo
Mgahinga National Park
Uganda
Virunga National Park
Volcanoes National Park
Musanze
Goma
Gisenyi
Lake Kivu
Idjwi Island
Bumba
Kigali
RWANDA
Lake Cohaha
Lake Rweru
Nyungwe Forest National Park
Burundi
Uganda
Tanzania
Democratic Republic of the Congo
Virunga NP
Volcanoes NP
RWANDA
Kigali
Lake Kivu
Burundi
Tanzania

PART ONE

THE VIRUNGA MASSIF

1

GORILLAS, NO MIST

It's official: I'm the luckiest man on earth.

I say this because Isano, a mature male mountain gorilla, is on the move. When a silverback gorilla decides on a destination there isn't much that can stand in his way, and my exact positioning in this moment could easily be called into question.

I'm in Volcanoes National Park, in the East African country of Rwanda, and although the mid-morning sun is beating down it won't start getting hot until after noon here on the far western edge of Mount Sabyinyo. Isano had been surveying his sunny domain from the top of a small clearing until 30 seconds ago. A regal and imposing figure set firmly on all fours, the silver-white fur of his lower back visible from the angle I happen to be standing at rippling in a light but gusty breeze. He's clearly ready to help defend the group should any trouble arise, but for the moment all is calm. A 400-pound gorilla, looking quite serious in his duties barely ten metres away, is something to be keenly aware of. The problem is, there's a lot going on.

From just about every direction, the sound of breaking branches and rustling underbrush dominates the senses. These are not noises of an aggressive nature but simply the soundtrack to mountain gorillas feeding and playing before naptime. Off to my left and partially obscured from view, a subadult, two juveniles and a baby are wrestling around and using two hanging vines as a makeshift jungle gym. To my right, deep in the underbrush, two or three members of the group are making a fair ruckus as they forage on leaves and shoots. In a stand of mature bamboo out of sight beyond the top of the clearing, some kind of forest demolition project is well underway.

Like I said, a lot going on.

The Agashya group of gorillas currently has 23 members, including three silverbacks. They are part of a larger program of conservation and protection that includes monitored tourist visits. Here on the southeastern slopes of the Virunga massif the gorilla population is thriving because a healthy percentage of the dollars spent goes to habitat management and reclamation, and educating tourists and locals about the animals, as well as to anti-poaching patrols. There is also a gorilla tracking program across the border in the Democratic Republic of the Congo (DRC), and in neighbouring Uganda as well.

The defining feature of the Virunga massif is its volcanoes. There are eight of them within a roughly 8000 square kilometre area, and the rich volcanic soil coupled with an abundance of rain supports close to 900 plant species. It is a veritable Garden of Eden. In the dry season the gorillas can travel up to five kilometres a day in search of food. In the wet season, when plant growth is at its peak – and let's face it, the motivation to get out of a comfortable nest in the pouring rain is minimal – the distance is half of that.

Which brings me to my point. Isano is on the move and I have not seen him coming. There is a seven-metre proximity limit imposed on visiting tourists, for the protection of gorilla and tourist alike, but the gorillas don't always adhere to the guidelines. In my distraction Isano has halved the distance between us in a handful of lumbering-yet-somehow-graceful strides. Walking on all fours, he has moved diagonally across the clearing. After a brief pause, a course adjustment turns him on a downhill vector to avoid a clump of underbrush.

Squared up, his shoulders and head are massive, and the longer hair that grows down the animal's forearms accentuates what is without a doubt devastating upper body strength. After three more casual strides toward me, Isano takes a hard left around the end of the bushes he has chosen to avoid and disappears into the deeper undergrowth a few seconds later.

At the turn there is a brief glance directly at me that is simply part of the continuing scan of the surrounding environment. This is a big part of a silverback's job, to keep an eye on things. As patently indifferent as the look is, I'm still proud I haven't peed my pants. Glancing over at David, the New Zealander standing next to me, I see we are both at a loss for words. In fact, it takes a couple of minutes to regain my composure and focus again on the clearing and surrounding forest. I am in a daze of sensory overload and stunned awe, and the loud crack of snapping bamboo is what eventually brings me back.

Regulations dictate you only get an hour with the gorillas before leaving them alone for the rest of the day. Eight tourists per gorilla group, times 12 habituated groups, for a maximum of 96 people spread out across the park on any given morning. When you arrive at park headquarters you can't help but feel the time will be too short, especially after laying out US$1500 for the privilege. In reality the intensity of the encounter makes it just about right. Thirty minutes of trying to find your footing on a steep slope covered in trampled-down brush is exhausting enough, and after 30 more minutes of awkward gawking, the eight of us turn downhill with our guides Fidel and François and begin our journey back to the vehicles parked at the trailhead.

Along the way there is excited conversation about what we have just seen. A Canadian, a Kiwi, two Americans and four Belgians, thrust together by circumstance to share in a profound life experience. That Isano decided against ripping my face off, I realize as I'm walking along, is not down to luck. For the most part gorillas are peaceful animals who resort to aggression only in rare circumstances, and almost always amongst themselves in those moments when the social hierarchy needs adjusting, or when in contact with other gorilla groups in the area. These particular animals are used to human visitors. A tourist has never been seriously harmed by a habituated gorilla.

The miracle here is that these incredible, beautiful creatures have decided, despite a shameful history on our part, that we're okay. *Homo sapiens* are tolerable company in small doses. We're the odd, largely hairless cousins who thankfully don't stay for dinner. It appears, against all odds, that we humans are welcomed back into the Garden for an hour each day, if we behave ourselves.

For this I am truly lucky. And profoundly grateful.

PART TWO

THE STEAMY COAST AND EASTERN ARC MOUNTAINS

2

WELCOME TO AFRICA, MZUNGU

It's time for a new adventure.

For about a decade now I have been obsessed, there is simply no other word for it. I try and tell myself the unrelenting fascination with mountain ranges is more love affair than fixation, but the margins are slim. One thing is certain: multiple trips in the Canadian Rockies and Nepal Himalaya by bicycle and on foot suggest something other than simple interest. The first two books I wrote were about this complicated mountain dynamic. My home, my preoccupations, my frustrations and the things I loved most dearly were all bashing up against the walls of my mind as I attempted to make sense of the larger implications. I spent ten years trying to reconcile my affection for both the Bow Valley and the Khumbu Valley with the rapid change mass tourism brings to sacred places. I was compelled to explore. Driven to understand. Desperate to come to grips with sense of place. I was obsessed.

In my experience the Bow Valley in western Canada and the Khumbu Valley in northeastern Nepal are one and the same. Different in detail, no question, but the same in spirit. After a few years' worth of concentrated attention they began to grow all too familiar, and yet also managed to stay fresh with every change in the weather or new viewpoint discovered. These were landscapes hopelessly stuck in my craw that continuously shouted for further examination. I did the best I could to understand the complicated dynamics at play, and learned a lot along the way about culture, geography, geology, history and commerce. But even the most powerful attractions eventually wane. I'm hoping a fresh perspective can help clarify an incomplete vision that persists.

With that in mind, I find my gaze drawn to a new horizon. It's time for a new adventure. A new experience. A new place of amazement and wonder. For a long time now, Africa has been lurking in the back of my mind, held in check by my North American and Asian fixations. Now there is an opportunity to expand my experience and look at things from a different frame of reference, but with a land mass of 30 million square kilometres, or 20 per cent of the earth's total land area, I have to at least narrow the search. The Eastern Arc Mountains of Tanzania and Kenya seem like an appropriate introduction to the continent, given my attraction to undulating landscapes.

East Africa itself is hard to define. As currently understood – according to my Lonely Planet Guide, anyway – it is made up of five countries: Tanzania, Kenya, Uganda, Rwanda and Burundi, but the boundaries have at times been fluid, and strict classification depends not only on the source cited but also the parameters of the search. According to Wikipedia, these five countries, in addition to South Sudan, make up the East African Community, an intergovernmental organization initiated to facilitate trade and explore the feasibility of one day creating a single sovereign state. Rwanda and Burundi are sometimes considered part of Central Africa, and historically, the colonial British East Africa Protectorate, and before that German East Africa was considered to be the area now defined as Tanzania, Kenya and Uganda. Geographically,

Djibouti, Eritrea, Ethiopia and Somalia could easily be included.

Furthermore, the United Nations Statistics Division scheme of geographic regions includes 20 territories in its East African designation, including all of the above and Madagascar and Mozambique, among others. As intriguing as this vast tract of land is to the romantic adventurer in me, for logistical and practical reasons I plan to contain my exploration to the five countries described in my guide. No need to bite off more than one can chew right out of the gate. Besides, I simply don't have the time or the money to see it all in one go.

It's important to mention here that first impressions can be powerful once a destination has been chosen. The imprint first impressions leave on memory goes a long way to shaping a lasting picture of a place. Sometimes it works that way. Other times the drudgery of the journey to get there dulls the senses and erodes attention. Coming into a new city on a new continent after dark certainly doesn't help. After an airport shuttle, two planes, 28 hours, nearly 20,000 indirect kilometres, and 11 time zones, the only thing that strikes me about Dar es Salaam, Tanzania, at 10:45 p.m. on a Tuesday night, is that it's hot. It's really freaking hot. And muggy. For some reason I hadn't anticipated this to any reasonable degree.

Clearing customs and collecting my luggage is notable only for the fact that I'm already sweating, and I've been in the country less than 30 minutes. And I've been standing still most of that time. Hardly a high-intensity activity worthy of this physiological response. Some arrival paperwork that will immediately be binned or buried in a box in a warehouse somewhere, a quick photo and fingerprint scan, and US$50 for a 90-day visa is a series of procedures conducted with reasonable efficiency with only one flight arriving at this late hour. Landing in a strange country late at night can be unnerving, but the entire airport has a heavy, subdued feel to it, and finding a taxi to the hotel is simple enough given there are about 20 guys standing around waiting for a fare.

The ride downtown is similarly unremarkable. Some idle chit-chat with the driver in a spanking new, spacious and air-conditioned SUV is companion to a straight shot on a direct motorway to the city centre. Insufficient and inefficient lighting does lend an element of minor excitement to the scene. Underpowered three-wheel tuk tuks labour along as motorcycles bob and weave through the relatively light traffic, with the occasional heavy truck with no running lights adding a measure of startled surprise to the vehicle flow. Coming up fast on a bicyclist who is all but invisible until the last minute makes me question the wisdom of bringing my own bicycle with me on this trip, but I won't be riding at night under any circumstances, so the concern quickly fades into the surrounding darkness.

After arriving at the hotel without traffic incident, check-in is fast and efficient, but despite being tired and disoriented I'm not ready to just go to bed. An exploration of the surrounding neighbourhood is probably pointless at this late hour, but it would be nice to have a couple of beers and celebrate the first stage of any adventure, which is simply getting to the start of it. The hotel restaurant is already closed for the night, and doesn't have a liquor licence in any case, so I dump my bags and quickly explore the room before heading back down to the lobby.

"Is everything all right with the room?" the manager, Nadeem, asks as I exit the elevator into the blessed air-conditioned cool of the lobby.

"Yes, it's perfect," I reply with genuine appreciation. Air conditioning, satellite TV with hundreds of channels, and a small safe for my camera and lenses will make sojourns out into the city to get oriented less cumbersome. It's also a touch swankier than I'm used to. For 36 bucks American, it's way more than I expected.

"But I was wondering if there was somewhere nearby I could get a beer?"

"There is a locals bar, but it's late," Nadeem says, with notable hesitation. "I would make sure you don't have anything valuable with you."

I like the idea of a locals bar as opposed to a hotel bar, which can be comparatively sterile and uninteresting, but Nadeem seems reluctant to just send me out there into the dark and steamy city. Directions don't sound entirely straightforward either, up the block and over a block but through an alley and around a corner to get there, so my excitement for the outing diminishes somewhat. Nadeem's concern also strikes me as a bit strange, or at least exaggerated. This is not Syria or Afghanistan, or even the DRC, which is in a bit of turmoil at present. Sure, Dar es Salaam is a city of four million people and visiting any big city carries with it an element of personal risk, but is it more dangerous here after dark than Toronto or Chicago or Oakland? I wonder.

The United Republic of Tanzania is, in fact, one of the safest countries in Africa. According to the website answersafrica.com, Tanzania rates fifth on its top ten list of safe countries, although the site does not offer much in the way of statistics to back the rankings, citing only that western media coverage often accentuates muggings, carjackings and petty theft in their stories, a narrative that is by no means pervasive across the entire continent. That focus also insinuates a desperate and destitute populace, an impossible generalization when talking about 1.2 billion people. But we find it difficult to resist applying labels to things we have not experienced first-hand, and so the false impression continues.

Truth be told, getting physically mugged is not a big concern. At six-foot-two and 240 pounds I like to think I can handle myself, and if the situation reaches a tipping point, handing over my wallet and my camera would suck, but I'm not going to get beaten up or killed over it. Having a skilled pickpocket lift my money or belongings would also annoy the shit out of me, but again, not the end of my world. This terrorism thing, however, is a different deal altogether. Getting shot or blown up in an act of random intimidation that serves some nutbar's – sorry, misguided soul's – demented agenda, well, that is deeply unsettling, which is probably why terrorism is an effective tool of disruption that continues to be used.

Before I leave the African continent the DusitD2 hotel and business complex in neighbouring Kenya will be attacked. The BBC will report that the Nairobi bombing and subsequent exchange of gunfire with militant forces will leave 21 dead, including the five extremists involved. This is why there are armed guards at all banks, and metal detectors and X-ray machines at all major malls, and in the swankier hotels here in Dar, no doubt.

Another example of this unpleasant reality is that five days from now a man armed with a gun and a knife will shoot up a popular Christmas market in Strasbourg, France, killing five and injuring 11 more.

It is the random nature of these events that gives them so much power, and it happens all over the world, in Africa, in Asia, in South America and in Europe. But for pure random threat I didn't need to leave my home continent. In 2018, 323 mass shootings occurred in the United States of America, according to Wikipedia. Over 1600 people were shot, and 387 of them died. In Toronto, Canada's biggest city, Global News reported 228 incidents involving firearms in the first half of 2018, resulting in 308 people being injured or killed.

It is worth noting here that I have not identified any of the perpetrators involved in these desperate acts. This is intentional, because the reality is that extremism is an affliction, not an identity. It is perpetrated by individuals of many races, who have any number of different religious or political affiliations that they use to justify their actions. It is also worth mentioning that not all of these incidents are terror related. Many of the incidents in Toronto were undoubtedly petty crimes or arguments gone wrong in a big way, or the collateral damage from gang violence, but once you start digging, you find all kinds of scary shit going on out there in the world.

All of this is beyond the scope of tonight's challenge, however, which is to settle into a relaxing beer after a long journey. After some deliberation Nadeem decides the best course of action is to walk me over to the pub. I am sleep deprived and disoriented in my new surroundings, so I accept the escort, but even as my apprehension grows I'm left wondering, "What am I missing here?"

The road fronting the hotel is a minor thoroughfare, but traffic is light at this hour. After crossing to the opposite side, we make it a few doors up the street before Nadeem engages in a conversation with a handful of guys hanging out on the front stoop of a building. One of the guys is a security guard armed with a billy club. After some brief chit-chat in Swahili we are pointed to the correct door and I am led down a nondescript hallway to an equally nondescript interior doorway. One thing is for sure, I wouldn't have been likely to find this place on my own, even though it's less than a block away.

Whereas Nadeem has been attentive and accommodating, my bartender is the height of indifference. A young woman in her late 20s or early 30s, she's doing inventory and probably wants to go home as soon as possible, but she agrees to serve me, so I settle in at the far end of the six-stool brick-fronted bar. Ambience is not the order of the day. There's no music playing, and the TV is off. It occurs to me this is the breakfast room for a budget hotel and not the locals bar previously mentioned, but after a 28-hour travel day I'll take what I can get. This will do in a pinch.

Looking around while I wait for my change, I see the six four-top tables are bathed in the muted glow of blue, red and green pot lights. Behind the bar there are three pop fridges stocked with Coca-Cola, Fanta and beer, as well as a chest freezer for ice and who knows what else, but no proper back bar. A few simple shelves display a small selection of scotch, as well as Konyagi, the notorious local liquor. Deciding against a headlong plunge into the local moonshine, I settle for a quart bottle of Safari lager, followed up quickly by another quart bottle. At 3,000 Tanzanian shillings each, or about $1.75 Canadian, I can get into enough trouble with just the beers, thank you very much.

My bartender doesn't say a single word during the visit beyond quoting a price, and it's like pulling teeth getting the change back from my beers, but it's nice to settle in with my notebook and the prospect of the coming months. My mind is flying now. Recalling small details from the previous 28 hours and formulating a plan for getting acquainted with this new environment, I'm trying to capture the essence and excitement of it all before the exhaustion and beer catch up to me. Midway through beer number two an African businessman comes in to get some takeaway alcohol. A mickey of Konyagi as it turns out, and the bartender is equally indifferent in facilitating an efficient exchange of product and service for cash. I'm glad I'm not the only one she doesn't care about.

Out on the street 15 minutes later, the bright Chelsea Hotel signage is a shiny oasis in the dusty gloom, but I'm still not inspired to call it a night. With a couple of big beers in me I'm more relaxed. Not drunk exactly, but slightly braver than I was an hour ago. Staring over at the building and then looking up and down the street for inspiration, I'm experiencing the first defining moment of the trip: What do I do now?

Travel is a series of choices made in unfamiliar surroundings based on previous experience and hopeful anticipation. When I left home in Canmore, Alberta, it was minus six degrees Celsius and snowing lightly, while here, a few blocks from the Indian Ocean, it's 25 degrees in the middle of the night. I'm in a new city and have a desire to find out what this place is all about. How is a man supposed to resist the idea of a walkabout in these circumstances? The short answer is, he can't.

I may be feeling brave, but I'm not reckless. The walkabout is on main streets only, no dark alleys to start, and as it turns out, the similarities to the neighbourhood surrounding the tourist district of Thamel in Kathmandu are noteworthy. Kathmandu is the most recent major foreign city I've visited, and the unexpected familiarity is immediate, and strangely comforting. The encroaching buildings and narrow street layout look much the same in the dark.

The rough and inconsistent pavements a near-perfect match. The shuttered shops and overabundant signage are close enough to draw my notice. The one big difference is there are no stray dogs here, just a few scrawny cats.

Overall, it's quiet and it's mostly men who are still out and about. Some of them sleeping outside to avoid the heat of stuffy apartments, a couple of others manning small takeaway shops selling soda pop and simple snacks. I am surprised to find a few of the sanitation workers and security guards on the night shift are women, and a couple of cabbies offer up a hello in anticipation of me needing a ride, but mostly I'm ignored. As if a white guy wandering around this neighbourhood at one a.m. is a perfectly normal occurrence. Even the four teenagers, loud and energetic in their distracted wandering down the street, pay me no mind.

Hardly the sketchy situation I had begun to imagine based on Nadeem's cautionary attitude. In an era of growing divisiveness and hateful rhetoric this is good, because as a curious traveller, being afraid of the world would be inconvenient.

Twenty minutes of zigzagging through the neighbourhood within a few blocks of the hotel confirms I have landed in an environment far removed from my small mountain town in the Canadian Rockies. Here I am, on a continent I have imagined visiting for decades but couldn't find the time or the courage to engage with. The jet-lagged and confused emotional roller coaster I'm riding is on the upswing again. Exploration and adventure awaits. In the 18th century, mzungu, translated as "someone who roams around," began to be used to describe early European explorers in the Great Lakes Region of Central Africa. Now it is common to use the word to refer to foreign travellers throughout East Africa. If tonight is any indication I will be roaming around with only a vague idea of what I hope to find, so the appellation fits.

Welcome to Africa, mzungu.

• • •

The first couple of days of an extended journey are often the hardest. Leaving the comforts of home behind, getting acquainted with new surroundings, and not being tied to a rigid routine are all disruptive to a soul that has grown complacent. A new destination, while exciting, is a shock to the system and does require a period of adjustment. This happens to me every time, and still I'm caught by surprise when it does, but the restaurant at the Chelsea Hotel is a couple of storeys above the street and has floor to ceiling windows that offer a clear view down Uhuru Street toward the city centre if I sit facing east. An enjoyable start to the day is to drink milk tea, have breakfast and watch the city wake up.

Down below, people are already walking to work or setting up shop, without any idea they're secretly being watched. The Jakaya Kikwete Youth Park, a sprawling complex of outdoor sports fields, is only a couple of blocks away, and inevitably a group of teenage footballers (soccer players to us North Americans) will jog casually past as part of their morning training regimen. Toward downtown the Mnazi Mmoja bus stand spits out aging buses and beaten-up old tuk tuks that come slaloming up the street, and all of it is framed by the modern high-rises of the central Kisutu district a couple of blocks away.

Dodoma, 450 kilometres inland, is the capital of Tanzania, but Dar es Salaam is the economic and cultural centre of the country. East Africa's second largest port, the city of four million people enjoys a mix of African, Arabic and Indian influence. Working my way out from the hotel on progressively more ambitious excursions over the last couple of days, I've started to get a feel for it all.

The Kariakoo Market nearby has a central hub, but it unofficially radiates out for blocks in every direction. Filling the streets and sidewalks with vendors selling housewares and watches and fruit and clothing and toys, while also making travel in a vehicle an unenviable proposition. Stop and go that's mostly stop. Near the bus stand vendors are also set up beneath tarps and giant umbrellas, trying without much success to beat the oppressive heat. And constantly on the make, mobile vendors sell fruit and nuts and clothing and shoes, many of them clicking small flat stones together between their fingers as they walk to remind the inattentive they are open for business. With all the competition, I can't help but think being an open-air vendor would be a hard, hot way to make a living.

Shuffling through the local neighbourhoods I also can't help but be intrigued by the remarkable diversity of people who call Dar home, not so much from their physical appearance as from their manner of dress. I don't care who you are, the first time you see a Maasai tribesman walking down a busy city street wearing a kikoi (a type of sarong worn by the Maasai near the coast), along with simple sandals with old motorcycle tires for soles, while carrying a herding stick – well, that's going to stop you short.

The average young city slicker will be in jeans and a t-shirt, and older businessmen will be in slacks and collared shirts, just like everywhere, but many Tanzanian women still wear a kanga, a brightly coloured and intricately patterned rectangular swatch of cloth, worn like a wrap. What I was least expecting (once I get used to the

Maasai, that is) is the niqab worn by the local Muslim women. Yesterday, I ceded a narrow sidewalk to three women coming in the opposite direction, covered from head to toe in black cloth with only their eyes exposed. Silly me, I assumed that type of outfit would shelter a timid soul, but they owned the sidewalk, and one of the women had the most intense, penetrating stare I've ever come across. It said, "Out of the way, mzungu."

Yes, ma'am. Right away, ma'am.

This is how I begin to make sense of a place – short forays designed to get the lay of the land while I calibrate my confidence and ambition. Inevitably, important details about the local environment emerge. Sipping my tea, I can't help but wonder what I might come across today. Once I rally the motivation to get moving, that is.

It is a sad fact, but I'm never as fit or as organized as I would like to be when I set out on a big adventure. Work and trip planning are a time-consuming and wearying prelude to buying some freedom from the metaphorical hamster wheel. It always takes a week or two to properly settle into the new lifestyle. But I'm partway in now. I've shaken the worst of the jet lag and am starting to feel better, or more stable in my emotional response to so much change, at least. With each passing hour I'm feeling better prepared to ride out the waves of doubt that are an inevitable part of suddenly finding yourself alone and a long, long way from the comfort and familiarity of home.

Out on the street after breakfast it's hot. It's always hot. From recent experience I know that within five minutes small damp patches of sweat will begin to grow and spread across my t-shirt. First in my armpits, then in the middle of my chest a few minutes later. Then finally across my back, where a few irritating drops will inevitably, and in an oh-so-charming fashion, drip down the crack of my backside. Don't ever let anyone tell you foreign travel isn't at times glamourous and exotic – it surely is – but remember it's also often uncomfortable, and occasionally gross.

As I stand and contemplate my options for the morning, a young man has come up on me. Not aggressively, but certainly with a ton of confidence. He has approached in a way that will make it impossible to ignore his presence. Seeing as I'm going to have to engage, I try and get out on the front foot.

"Hello, how are you?" I ask.

"Good. I am good. How are you?"

"I'm good, thank you."

"My name is Mishi," he says. "What are you doing today?"

During the beginning of the exchange there are casual hand slap handshakes and fist bumps, as if we have been friends for years. I've noticed Mishi a couple of times over the course of the last few days, hanging out on the street in front of the hotel. It's clear he's angling for me to hire him, as a tour guide for the morning, or maybe to escort me to a local gallery, where larger versions of the street art I've seen around are for sale. The oil-on-canvas paintings of Maasai village scenes and African wildlife are both colourful and beautiful.

I do hope to bring a few canvases home with me at the end of the trip, but that's still a long way off. I also haven't quite figured out the exchange rate between Canadian dollars and Tanzanian shillings, at least in relation to bartering a fair price with a skilled negotiator, so shopping isn't part of today's itinerary. But the concept of walking for the sake of exploring, with no specific destination, doesn't always get across clearly in these situations. I give it a try anyway.

"I'm going to walk around for a while."

"By yourself?" Mishi says, incredulously.

I nod, and he stares hard for a moment.

"They will kill you, man." He says this while drawing out the word kill to sound more like keeeeellll. He also drags his thumb slowly across his throat in a menacing fashion, for effect, but I notice he's not specific about who "they" are. Marauding gangs of random murderers at nine in the morning? I doubt it. Instead of getting agitated by the exchange I decide on a different tack and grin broadly, arms outstretched in innocent vulnerability as I give him my best "who, me?" look. I'm 99 per cent sure he's kidding.

Mishi has a huge personality, and after a split-second attempt at stern intimidation he also breaks into his own big grin and there's another round of hand slaps and fist bumps. I will be making my way around the city without a body guard, but it was a nice effort on his part. Confident in the safety assessment – that it's unlikely I'll get mugged or murdered today – I walk down to the corner where the real danger is, crossing the street while still being distracted by the new surroundings.

The danger here is twofold. I'm still a total space case, for one thing. I'm trying to drink in the sights and sounds and smells of the city while they're still novel to my experience and am having a tough time concentrating on trivial details – like not walking the wrong way along what at first seems like a low sidewalk but is in reality the pull-in for a city bus stop, for example.

A gentle honk from behind is enough to get me scurrying to safety.

The thing is, every corner is a challenge. Traffic moves

along the left side of the road, which is opposite to back home, but that's not really the problem. I use visual cues to navigate, and the downtown core is not a strictly laid out grid. There are bends and swerves in the Kisutu district that inevitably lead to me standing on a corner, genuinely surprised by a park or a building that I recognize but didn't expect to come across in that moment. Scratching my head at the wonder of it, the next move is to step out in the street while looking for traffic in the wrong direction.

My inanity aside, the traffic here is something to behold. It does not always move from point A to point B in the orderly fashion no doubt imagined by city planners, but rather flows through time and space like a larger living thing as opposed to a collection of individual vehicles. As I'm standing on a sandy dirt verge in the middle of Lumumba Street near a nondescript intersection with no traffic lights, city buses, tuk tuks, taxis, motorcycles and private cars jockey and weave through the intersection, turning left and right from every direction while carefully avoiding the occasional pedestrian or bicyclist. In one 90-second stretch, 64 vehicles worked their way past. Standing and watching for ten minutes, all I can say is, it's a miracle there were no collisions. Not even a minor fender bender.

Making it to the National Museum and House of Culture after a few wrong turns but without incident, I finally get a break from the hustle and bustle of the city. The main museum building appears to have been retooled from some other kind of use, and after paying the entrance fee I'm pointed toward the sprawling inner courtyard, where a small sign directs visitors upstairs. Passing by the sign in order to explore the larger layout, I notice a number of rooms that look to be classrooms, and dominating the courtyard is an impressive old banyan tree, with close to a hundred individual low concrete stools set in the ample shade cast by the tree. In through another entrance to the building there is a lot of empty space mixed with offices that no longer appear to be in use at all. The occasional random display of ancient jewelry or other cultural artifacts lining the hallways of the little-used wing only reinforces the haphazard nature of the layout.

One of the more interesting oddities is a collection of bones tucked off in a medium-sized room on the second floor. The giant vertebrae and rib bones are clearly from a whale, but they are of unknown provenance because there is no display case or explanatory plaque of any kind. The bones are simply laid out on the floor, waiting to be inserted into a proper exhibit. The fact that the vertebrae extend the length of two walls speaks to the sheer mass of the creature that once was.

Circling back to the staircase leading up to the primary museum area, it would be no understatement that the collection housed here is not entirely well organized. While worldtravelguide.net calls it "limited and somewhat patchy," huyai.com concedes there are some interesting things to see, but also notes, "Despite renovations, however, the museum still has much work to do on appropriate displays and the curation of a coherent narrative."

All this being said, examining the photos and artifacts from the German and British colonial periods, as well as from the Zanzibar slave trade, is at once moving and somewhat disturbing. Some of the sketches trigger a deep empathy for those who suffered untold injustices as the modern world moved in uninvited, and an overwhelming disappointment in the cruelty of man toward man for power and profit hits me deep in my gut. In a separate room, a rock art exhibit restores my faith in the gentler leanings of the human spirit, and in yet another room an exhibit of the work of modern Tanzanian painters and sculptors has something of an art gallery feel to it.

Just when I begin to think that what this place needs more than anything is a major facelift, I find myself at the entrance to the Cradle of Humanity exhibit, which is nothing short of exceptional. It is a walking, almost meandering, tour of human prehistory through a newly renovated section of the museum. The highlight being the large backlit panel paintings from various stages of the development of mankind, complemented nicely with display cases of hominid skulls and bones, animal bones, stone tools and jewelry.

The most recent 125 years have been influential in shaping the modern face of East Africa, but the four million years prior to that laid the groundwork for nothing less than all of humanity's triumphs, failures and foibles. We were born here, in East Africa. Even with prior knowledge of this development it is an amazing concept to wrap your head around as you wander somewhat aimlessly through a rough-and-tumble museum with no prior expectations of what you might find. In these moments my lack of pre-planning actually pays off, because the exhibit is a welcome surprise.

The Great Rift Valley is an interconnected series of rifts and faults that extends from Asia – specifically the Beqaa Valley in Lebanon – all the way down to Mozambique in southern Africa. A distance of 6000 kilometres. Taken as a whole the rift has already created the Red Sea, and is slowly cleaving the African Plate apart, with the Nubian section to the west and the Somalian section to the east. At 1470 metres (nearly 5,000 feet!), Lake Tanganyika is one of the deepest lakes on earth and is so because of the rift.

Looking back in time, it was near the geographical centre of all this slow-moving geological transformation that the future of all living creatures was about to be altered. A dominant species was set to emerge.

In *The Descent of Man,* Charles Darwin wrote:

> In each great region of the world the living mammals are closely related to the extinct species of the same region. It is therefore probable that Africa was formerly inhabited by extinct apes closely allied with the gorilla and the chimpanzee; and as these two species are now man's nearest allies, it is somewhat more probable that our early progenitors lived on the African continent than elsewhere.

Makes sense. The quote from Darwin's book is printed next to a graphic depicting a rough timeline of the hominid species that came and went over the millennia, including *Homo neanderthalensis, Homo erectus* and *Homo habilis,* to name just a few. Most of these relatives come from the Pleistocene Epoch of the Quaternary Period. Some appear in the fossil record and then disappear in the geological blink of an eye, while others survive for hundreds of thousands of years. If not for the visual graphic I'd have a hard time figuring out what the heck was going on, but someone who did have a firm grasp on things was Louis S.B. Leakey. Leakey was a paleoanthropologist and archeologist whose work in Africa – along with that of his paleontologist wife Mary Leakey – helped clarify our modern lineage.

Fortunately for me, a quote from his book *Adam's Ancestors* occupies the same information panel as Darwin's quote, along with a map of Africa indicating the locations of the major dig sites where hominid bones were found. The majority of them in the Rift Valley.

> The study of prehistory is a complicated subject and is not only confined to the search for and interpretation of human fossil remains. This aspect of the subject is in fact only one very small part, although it is the central figure of the picture, so to speak, but the background is made up of studies of the climate, geography, cultures, and associated fauna and flora of the periods of the past history of the earth when man was gradually and slowly evolving into the creature we call *homo sapiens* today.

As it turns out, my favourite of the panel paintings encompasses this idea while depicting a scene from nearly four million years ago. In a generous artist's rendering compressing a broader landscape into a single visual, four upright walking hominids cross a fresh layer of ash deposited by an erupting volcano in the distance. We know someone walked through the ash because the footprints were preserved by subsequent ash deposits and fossilized. We also know they were not made by apes because people *way* smarter than me deduced from the imprints and stride length that the creatures were bipedal, meaning they walked upright and not on all fours.

Conveniently, the ash in the painting has not buried the trees or bushes, and ostriches, elephants and giraffes share the land. There are also no lions present to complicate matters. It's all a little too neat and tidy given the serious geological event going on in the background, but it does give you a rough sense of what the environment was like before modern humans came along.

In the end I walk through the Cradle of Humanity exhibit three times, because it is that good, and because I owe a debt to the past, paid in part with silent reverence now. I'm thankful for the fortitude and resilience of our earliest ancestors in a way I was not even half an hour ago. I may have to navigate the traffic and the touts and the language barrier and the heat in modern Dar es Salaam, but that's nothing compared to the challenging conditions early hominids had to manoeuvre through. They didn't make it in the long run, but *Homo sapiens* did.

And then we took over the world.

3

SATURDAY NIGHT IN STONE TOWN

A new adventure properly engaged, now it's time to start thinking about the bigger picture. As tempting as it would be to just hang around Dar for a little while longer now that I'm getting more comfortable, there is more here in Africa that I want to see. Leafing through my Lonely Planet at breakfast again this morning, in between bouts of staring out at the city of course, my mind spins off on endless tangents as my excitement for this trip grows. The guidebook has a Top 16 list of things to do on this part of the continent. Sixteen seems like a random number to choose, but ten just wouldn't cut it, I guess. Regardless, it is an impressive list.

There are things on there like gorilla tracking in Rwanda, trekking on Mount Kilimanjaro here in Tanzania, white water rafting on the Nile in Uganda, and viewing the big cats of Maasai Mara National Reserve in Kenya. I'm able to sip my way through three cups of milk tea as I shuffle back and forth through the pages, unable to definitively drop any one thing from the original list. Kilimanjaro is a must do, given my weird fascination with mountain landscapes, but everything else looks good too.

Eventually, this raw excitement gives way to a creeping apprehension. The possibilities are actually intimidating in a way. I want to see it all! I want to do it all! I don't want to miss a single thing! That is an impossible goal. One that creates a measurable anxiety, oddly enough. Time constraints and monetary considerations will require making choices, and that chafes. Swinging gently between excited and overwhelmed, it's hard to stay focused, but then I realize that's part of the point. I *don't* have duties to accomplish and responsibilities to stay on top of. This is not a job, it's an adventure, and I don't need to check *everything* off the list. Do I?

Extended travel is the antithesis of modern living, with its organized and structured way of getting things done, but old habits die hard and it's difficult to resist the urge to apply end-game-oriented coping strategies to what should be an exercise in pure, and at times random, discovery. My afternoon at the museum is an example of that theory executed to perfection, but, like I said, old habits die hard.

Jotting down a few notes drifts innocently enough into Nail Down an Itinerary at least, which inevitably comes crashing back to To Do List mode. I should, I should, I should. I should stop sitting here daydreaming and get out there and find something to write about. I should set out a proper itinerary if I hope to see half of what I've read about this morning. I should be practical for an hour at least and go to the High Commission of Canada and register as a foreign visitor in case something goes wrong. *I should, I should, I should.*

As you may have guessed, I don't do well with *I should.* The concept irritates me.

Hoping for distraction, I've opened Facebook for the first time since I got here and find a note in Messenger that I've been anticipating, sort of.

"Yo, mzungu."

The missive is from Kelly Schovanek, a friend from Canmore who also happens to be in East Africa at the moment, working on a project with Photographers Without Borders. The follow-up lines are in typical social-media-ese, not a scrap of punctuation to be found and absolutely in keeping with Kelly's freewheeling style.

"im into dar tomorrow morn. ill be central city crashin. ywca hostel? smack dab in the middle and cheap as chips. gimme shout. i aint climbin kilimanjaro but they got a beer by the same name and thats good enough for me"

While still in Canmore, Kelly and I had been casually discussing grabbing a beer at some point during our travels, but neither of us is what you would call meticulous in our trip planning. We both lean toward the buying a ticket, packing a camera and seeing what happens end of the scale. It doesn't help that we both had to work long hours at our day jobs prior to setting out for Africa. The projects we are working on are also somewhat flexible with regard to schedule. We knew getting together would be a last-minute deal, if we happened to be in the same city at the same time. The trouble is I have not seen the message in a timely fashion. After sending my two-day-delayed response and hoping for company at happy hour this afternoon, I finish up breakfast and go for a walk, because that always settles my nerves when I get into a goals-driven anxiety feedback loop.

When happy hour does roll around, I'm dismayed to find Kelly's already over on Zanzibar. This screws up my plans, such as they are.

The Zanzibar archipelago sits roughly 25 kilometres off the east African coast in the Indian Ocean, a collection of small islands surrounding two bigger chunks of land. The main island of Unguja is informally known as Zanzibar, and the historic old town in Zanzibar City is known as Stone Town. Stone Town is a UNESCO World Heritage

Site and was a significant port for the early seafaring people of the region. Today the archipelago is an eclectic mix of ethnic Swahili, Arabs, Persians and Indians.

I was thinking about paying a visit, but not quite so soon. The logistics are a challenge, and the last of the jet lag is still lingering. I'm only just starting to get my feet under me, to be honest. After finally pulling my thoughts together at breakfast this morning, I decide to spend a week here in Dar and a few days on Zanzibar, walking and biking a little more every day before heading out by bike up the coast. While I am starting to get a feel for the city, I've only been on one short training ride on the bicycle in preparation for taking on the wilds of Africa. That's not nearly enough. While these first few days have been a start, I'm not ready to *go*. Not ready to pack everything up and move on, which is a surprisingly difficult thing to admit in the end. That I'm not ready.

Less than a week ago I was living a completely different kind of life. I was still entangled in the working world with its schedules and responsibilities and goal-oriented focus. Travelling to the far side of the planet is my antidote to that circumstance. It would be nice to ease into the new lifestyle and not just plunge headlong into more go-go-go tied up in every waking breath. So, I'll admit it already. I'm not prepared to uproot from the Chelsea Hotel and get on with the more physical part of this adventure. There, I said it. At the same time, how can you resist going for beers with a buddy on Zanzibar? This is one of those movie moments where the protagonist makes a firm decision in the heat of the moment. The kind of thing at the heart of every *remember that time* story that's ever been told.

As I'm sipping a beer on the patio of the Royal Sports Lounge, the breakfast notes are scrapped, and a new plan is hatched. I'll leave my bike and most of my gear at the hotel, pack an overnight bag and take the ferry to meet Kelly in the morning. Big mountains and wide open grasslands will have to wait. I'm going to the beach. Problem solved. I just needed to sit with it for a little while. See if the idea really takes hold.

Happy hour at the Royal is a relaxed affair. A rough-at-the-edges locals place that still attracts professional types means there are lots of men in slacks and button-down collared shirts sipping beers or soda pop while trying to beat the heat. The ground floor patio is sheltered by a corrugated tin roof that's high enough to let any passing breeze through, and the large ceiling fans also help circulate the humid air. A lone and battered old flat screen TV playing rap videos leads me to wonder where the sports lounge concept comes from, but no matter. Chezo, the manager, recognizes me from yesterday and comes over to make sure I'm doing okay. It's an orgy of hellos and casual hand slap handshakes. Unfortunately, I'm terrible with languages and accents and can't be sure how to pronounce his name properly, and so I have him write it down. He adds his phone number as well, just in case I ever need anything during my stay in the city.

"Thanks, Chezo. But I have no phone."

He is surprised by this admission.

"No phone? Why no phone?"

"A phone is for work. I'm on vacation, my friend."

This is kind of sort of a lie on multiple levels. I actually have two phones, but neither of them is connected to a cellular network. My new iPhone is in airplane mode and will remain that way for the duration. I bought it for the camera, so I can take snapshots and videos without hauling out the heavier gear every time something catches my eye. I also have a cheap cell phone not much bigger than a pager that some friends who were here in Africa last year donated to the cause. I just haven't bothered to connect it. I have resisted because I don't want to be tied to my devices. I certainly don't want to be taking calls. When I can find Wi-Fi, great. I'll exchange texts, but I'm 14,500 kilometres from home. Four p.m. here is six a.m. back home. There aren't a lot of situations where I'll need to talk to anyone in real time.

It's a complicated thing to try and explain to someone you've just met. And, to be fair, I only understand about half of what Chezo says because of his strong accent. But he seems satisfied with my explanation and wanders off to carry on with his work day.

As I sit and contemplate the weekend plan, it's interesting to note the Royal is a bit of a reprieve from the intensity of the city. Apart from the staff, no one tries to strike up a conversation or even ask me where it is I'm from. There are ten four-top orange plastic outdoor patio tables, with orange plastic Tusker Lager branded chairs, and for the most part everyone minds their own business. Even the mobile vendors target the local business men and only offer a vague wave of their wares to see if I'm interested. Most of the shirts and shoes are too small, and what am I going to do with a necktie here anyway? So no, thanks.

Circling back to the situation at hand, I'm still not 100 per cent sure what to do. This must be why people book package tours. You give someone money and they take indecision off your plate. An argument I often make about not planning out every little detail of a trip is that when you do, the spontaneous elements of travel are lost. Zanzibar. On a whim. I can't help but ask, what could be more spontaneous than that?

I simply have to go.

• • •

As I make my way to the ferry terminal at ten the next morning, the sun is beginning to gather momentum, which means – surprise, surprise – I'm sweating. Closer to the harbour a light breeze picks up, but it's going to be another hot one. Thirty-four or 35 degrees Celsius, yet again. I'm not sure I'm ever going to get used to this heat. After walking through the confounding downtown core, I suddenly find myself intersecting Sokoine Drive. Off course, but only a couple of blocks from the terminal. As I pause to confirm my bearings, a man catches my eye and crosses the street to greet me.

"Hello, my name is Daniel."

Before I can even offer up a greeting, he launches into his pitch.

"I was wondering if you could help me. I'm an artist."

"You are?"

"Yes. I'm a painter."

Daniel is tall, handsome and sharply dressed. Not to mention disarmingly charming. I can't help but be drawn into his story.

"I'm a painter but need money for materials."

The idea here is that if I buy a couple of paintings, then Daniel can purchase some canvas and some paint in order to create more art. I'm expecting him to invite me to a local gallery, but instead he drops a small backpack from his shoulder and pulls out half a dozen small canvases. Each roughly 8x10 inches in size. My appreciation for visual art leans toward photography, but as I have mentioned already, many of the works I've seen around town are stunning.

The canvases Daniel shows me are more like light cloth at the edges, with multiple coats of a cream-coloured base layer supplying a more solid platform for the actual painting. To hear Daniel tell it, the oil paint is then mixed with grease to make it pliable. My favourite, three African elephants standing in tight formation – a larger parental figure flanked by two younger animals – appears to have been created with a knife, not a brush. In anticipation of the question *How am I supposed to get this home?* Daniel folds and rolls the elephants, and then flattens them out again with no visible damage to the image, all while explaining the resilient properties of the work throughout the demonstration.

I'm impressed, but have a ferry to catch, and when I try to extricate myself from the conversation Daniel shifts the sales pitch into high gear. It's not that I don't want to help him out, but I am skeptical by nature. There are lots of differing artistic styles out there, but not as many as there are street vendors. They can't all be artists, many of them are undoubtedly middle men. The question is, which is Daniel? A young artist trying to make a go of it? Or just another guy with a pressed shirt and the gift of the gab? I'm not sure.

The thing is, I really like the elephants.

"Okay, Daniel, how much for the elephants?"

"How much do you want to pay?"

I hate this question. I'm still not up to speed on my shilling conversion on the fly, for one thing, and it's human nature to want to avoid being taken advantage of, for another. I have no idea what these things are worth. Worst of all, I'm also an artist of sorts. I write stories for money and occasionally get paid for the photos I print and frame, but any up and coming (insert creative endeavour of your choice here, writer, photographer, painter, whatever) will tell you paydays can be scarce, and they're never quite enough to keep on top of the bills.

All this being said, I really do have a ferry to catch, so I float a number and wait to gauge Daniel's reaction.

"10,000 shillings."

He's not offended, which is good. I don't want to get ripped off, but I'm also not looking to rip him off. Daniel mulls it over and then suggests two paintings for 40,000 shillings, but I'm only interested in the elephants, and 20,000 is more than I'm willing to pay today.

"Okay," Daniel says, "how about 15,000?"

Tanzanian currency comes out of the bank machine in 10,000-shilling notes, and it can be difficult to find someone who can make change. Daniel doesn't have 5,000 shillings on him, but hands me the painting and takes 10,000 shillings and sprints across the street to the Dar Rapid Transit Agency bus stop. When he comes back post-haste with the change, I hand him the outstanding balance and wish him good luck. There are thank-yous and long handshakes and heartfelt goodbyes. Daniel, Chezo and Mishi, my new best friends for life. I still don't know if Daniel is an artist, or just another street salesman, but I like to think I helped him out in the pursuit of his passion. One thing is certain: it'll be a miracle if I leave Africa with less than a hundred different paintings stashed in my luggage. At nine bucks a pop it's going to be hard to resist.

Hustling down the street, I see the pier is, perhaps predictably, a gong show. Zanzibar is a popular weekend destination, it appears – I'm lucky to get a ticket. But the actual crossing is an easy sail on quiet seas. Slipping out of the protected harbour, our giant motorized catamaran chugs slowly past the beachside fish market, and the contrasting views out into the Indian Ocean are striking. In the foreground the small, brightly painted fishing boats are a hard contrast with the massive modern cargo ships anchored offshore, looking like so many grotesque islands on the horizon.

Our vessel, the *Kilimanjaro V*, is exactly like any large passenger ferry I've ever been on. A slightly bigger version of Vancouver's Sea Bus over to North Vancouver, for example. It used to be that for a more authentic experience you could take a dhow (a small sailboat common in the Red Sea and Indian Ocean) for this crossing, but after a number of unfortunate mishaps involving tourists, rough seas and a largely unregulated informal ferry fleet, the practice has been outlawed. Giving Azam Marine and their small fleet of fast ferries a virtual monopoly on the crossing.

After we make the pier in Zanzibar City in well under three hours, the terminal is just as chaotic as on the Dar side of the strait. Five hundred passengers looking to disembark all at once, just as 500 more prepare to return to the mainland. Jostling through the crowd, I am somewhat surprised to have to pass through customs before exiting the terminal. The agent at the desk even goes so far as to put a stamp in my passport: IMMIGRATION OFFICER. 08 DEC 2018. ZANZIBAR SEAPORT. TANZANIA.

It stands to reason that if I'm sailing on a vessel that came directly from Dar es Salaam I would have already cleared customs when I came into the country, but the archipelago and the mainland have not always seen eye to eye. As it happens, Zanzibar is a semi-autonomous region, in the way that Greenland is in relation to Denmark, Puerto Rico to the US, and Tibet to China. These places are not independent countries and at times have fractious relationships with their more powerful "partners."

A separate immigration check is a symbolic measure, I'm guessing, meant to pass on the message *You don't own us* to the central government in Dodoma. There is also still a small independence movement afoot on the archipelago.

Directly outside the ferry terminal there are touts and taxi drivers and tour guides on the make, but I walk purposefully past and quickly find myself on the small beach to the right, which is overlooked by Mercury's Restaurant. There is probably no formal connection to the former lead singer of the iconic British rock band Queen, but Farrokh Bulsara, a.k.a. Freddie Mercury, was born on Zanzibar in 1946. Although his flamboyant lifestyle is unlikely to ever be fully embraced by the powers that be in this morally conservative part of the world, his legacy as a showman and singer of the highest order endures nonetheless. Mercury died of complications from AIDS in 1991.

Down on the beach there are guys working out by doing push-ups and sit-ups and laps of a miniature running track they've worn down into the sand, and a handful of small boats that have not yet been hired for a trip out to some of the surrounding islands wait in anticipation. Beyond the small beach a seawall protects Mizingani Road and the old waterfront from the encroaching ocean. At Forodhani Gardens there is a small park that is peppered with hot cats splayed out in the shade, hoping for a cooling sea breeze. Much as in Dar, there appear to be no stray dogs here. Farther along there are mini soccer games and keepy-uppies on another stretch of narrow beach. There is not nearly enough room for a proper match.

Satisfied with my first tour of the beachfront, I head inland through the narrow alleyways to find a hostel for the night and succumb to the near-irresistible lure of a nap in the blessed air-conditioned comfort of the room. At this point I'm only mildly concerned that I haven't been able to get hold of Kelly. We are both kind of winging it, after all.

Before dozing off I figure it a good time to get caught up on the history of this place, having already seen some of the important landmarks without really knowing what they were all about. I should mention this important detail here: the United Republic of Tanzania would not even exist without Zanzibar. In 1961 the mainland, known at the time as Tanganyika, gained its independence from British colonial rule. Zanzibar followed suit in 1963. In 1964, after the Zanzibar Revolution saw the short-lived constitutional monarchy overthrown, the two merged, and promptly lopped off the first three letters of each name – Tan and Zan – as the base for the moniker to the new republic.

Prominent along the waterfront of Stone Town are Beit el-Ajaib (House of Wonders), Beit el-Sahel (the Palace Museum), and the Old Fort. All three structures speak to different phases of the Sultan's rule over Zanzibar after the Busaidi Omani Arabs laid claim to the island in 1698, having wrested it away from the Portuguese. I have not had time today to explore any of the landmarks beyond their distinctive exteriors, but the buildings do impart a sense of deep history to this part of the city, which in itself is much like a living, breathing museum.

What I will regret from this whirlwind one-day visit, however, is not searching out the Slave Chambers. As someone who has lived in North America my whole life, I have been insulated from the atrocities of the world to some degree, both historical and current. I have not known war, and as a white male have not been subject to persecution or discrimination. I believe it important to be aware of the dark aspects of human history so that I never lose a sense of empathy for my fellow man. My regret will be that I missed the opportunity for a sobering first-hand lesson.

The slave market is now gone, but the chambers remain and are located beneath the Anglican Cathedral and St. Monica's Hostel. Two of the 15 holding cells are open to the public, and my Lonely Planet describes them as offering "a sobering glimpse of the appalling realities of the trade. Dank, dark and cramped, each chamber housed up to 65 slaves awaiting sale. Tiny windows cast weak shafts of sunlight into the gloom and it's hard to breath even when they're empty."

Coming from Canada, I thought the slave trade had always equated to Africans being brought to America to work on farms and plantations. The Atlantic slave trade was how the history I was exposed to in school was written, and most of the 12 million plus souls came from West African countries. Off the East African coast, however, the slave ships weren't bound for America, but rather a trading network developed that inevitably dealt in slaves in addition to ivory, spices and other commodities. The network extended from East Africa to West and Central Asia, India and Europe. Zanzibar was a key hub to much of that trade.

• • •

Refreshed from the nap – if a little heavy hearted at realizing I'm a free man able to explore at my leisure a place where so many were not afforded the same opportunity – it's time for another walk as I wait to hear from Kelly. This time the stroll is from the far beach and then along the seawall and back to Mercury's for fish tacos. Out on the beach a professional film crew has erected a heavy-duty tripod in the sand and is setting up a shot of a young Maasai man holding a small portable radio, to what end I have no idea.

As we get closer to sunset the tide comes up and jumping off the seawall becomes the activity of choice for the athletic-minded set. The junior version in the shallower water on the western side of Forodhani Gardens, while a senior version of some acrobatic intensity draws a big crowd as they launch themselves in a fit of flips and twists into the deeper water to the east.

Walking back along the seawall I find some women gathered around, clapping and singing along to music coming from someone's phone. It strikes me as a fine measure of the beach scenes I've witnessed today. People are happy here, and there's lots of laughter. This is a hard contrast to the darker history of this place.

Settling in to watch the sunset at Mercury's, I'm able to hook in to the Wi-Fi, and finally get a message from Kelly. Something to the effect of "get over here, we're going to a local bar to watch the game." Naturally, he's staying back where I started my post-nap meandering a couple of hours ago, so I finish up my meal and amble back to his hostel, which is a few doors up from Freddy Mercury's childhood home on Kenyatta Road. With no idea what room he might be in, I'm forced to resort to the communication strategy used so often in my youth, before the world was constantly linked in.

"Yo! Kelly!"

This is not very subtle, shouting up from the street, but that's what you do when you don't have an active phone. As it happens, the technique can be effective, because within seconds Kelly's head pops out an upper-story window.

"Hey, welcome to Zanzibar."

I give a little wave and then, with both palms

outstretched and shoulders slightly shrugged, point vaguely toward the front door and the small but well-lit sign to the hostel.

"Seriously?"

"I know, right? I thought you'd like that!"

The name of my first book was *Lost and Found*, and Kelly is staying at the Lost & Found Hostel. This is one of the quirky little details that makes travelling so fun. You couldn't possibly script something like this. I only wish I hadn't already paid for a room somewhere else.

"Hang on!" Kelly shouts. "We'll be right down."

Almost instantly Kelly, Will from the US, and locals Ahmed and Sahid bound out the front door. Will is staying at the hostel, and Ahmed and Sahid have been showing Kelly around the last couple of days. We go through quick introductions before piling into a cab. Clearly, it's time to make some fast friends, but there is a detail that doesn't add up.

"So why are we taking a cab? I thought we were going to a local bar for the game."

Kelly shrugs and gets in, so I follow suit.

Turns out the bar is a locals place, not a local place. A huge open-air compound on the outskirts of Zanzibar City, and we needn't have worried about the ambiance because the place is packed. People have come for the Chelsea versus Manchester City English Premier League game, but it being Saturday, there's also a live band thrown in for good measure. A large, well-lit stage to the right, and a 10x10 foot projection screen to the left make for an interesting entertainment experience because the game and the band are both on simultaneously. There are easily 60 tables, and the smell of barbeque wafting out from grills set up in one of the corners is ever present.

As the beers flow we catch up on Kelly's trip. In addition to working in Kenya with Photographers Without Borders, he has visited Rwanda and Uganda. After a few more days here in Tanzania he will be heading back to Nairobi to catch a flight home. To say it has been an interesting trip would be an understatement. In addition to drinking goat's blood in Kenya with members of the Samburu tribe, he spent time in Uganda talking to a man from Belgium with terminal cancer who was burning through the last of his life savings running an orphanage for at-risk girls. Here on Zanzibar, he attended a championship soccer match at the local stadium with Ahmed and Sahid.

"I think everyone thought I was a scout, because I was the only white guy there."

At this point Kelly is on a roll, and after a few more engaging yarns told rapid-fire style, I can't help but remark, "If you ever wrote this shit down your books would murder mine."

"What can I say, weirdness follows me around," Kelly says, with a huge happy grin.

His retellings of outside-the-box foreign travel are captivating. Kelly has a way of engaging with people that I'm envious of. He's outgoing, fearless and entertaining. Willing to try anything, and dangerous in his ability to encourage you to do the same. Pulling out his cell phone, he shows us a short video from one of the Kenyan villages he visited. The Samburu there had just taught him the *adumu*, the jumping dance used in the coming-of-age ceremony for warriors made famous by their cousins the Maasai. Eager to share a piece of modern western culture in return, Kelly showed them how to slam-dance.

I never would have thought of that in a million years.

The video is hilarious. A handful of tall, sort of gangly Samburu bumping each other gently to imaginary power chords blaring from nonexistent speakers. I suppose without a mosh pit context is lacking, because the energy and violence inherent in that particular style of dance is something they clearly need to work on. One thing is for sure, Kelly has that *thing*. That wild creative spirit that is at the heart of every great traveller's tales. It is part of the drive to engage with, and make sense of, the world. To interact with it in a profound way and bring back stories about the adventures. I can't wait to see some of his photographs, and only hope my time here in East Africa will be half as interesting.

Meanwhile, the band is all over the place. When they play originals and African-inspired beats they're deadly. A smooth, Santana style fused with the world beat influences first brought to international attention on Paul Simon's *Graceland* album in 1986. When they play covers – that necessary evil of the bar band routine – let's just say the experience is not so engaging. A cheesy Lionel Ritchie number is followed up with "Lucille," by Kenny Rogers. It would be a second million years before I would have imagined hearing that track live, in late 2018, anywhere but in a hotel bar in Nashville, or maybe Las Vegas. Fortunately, Bob Marley's "Redemption Song" gets us back on track, and even gets a few people up and dancing.

As for the game, Chelsea are sticking it to Man City. Against the run of play, N'Golo Kanté smashed one into the roof of the net in the 45th minute, and David Luiz has just doubled the lead in the 78th. And yes, in case you were wondering, I did pick the Chelsea Hotel in Dar from the list of options on Trivago largely because of my fondness for the west London club.

The game all but secured, my attention is once again drawn to the band. I've got just the right amount of buzz going, so everything is awesome now, even the bad songs. The group consists of a pretty standard lineup of drums, keyboards, guitar and bass, with the occasional guest singer joining the core group for a song or two throughout the evening. What is not so standard is that the guitarist is blind, and projects a palpable Stevie Wonder cool to the proceedings. Seeing as we're both Canadian, Kelly and I have taken to calling him Jeff Healey 2.0, a reference nobody else here would get, to be sure.

Twice in my life I've been impressed with the pure physicality of a musical act. The first time was Bruce Springsteen and the E Street Band in Calgary in the early 2000s. They played a marathon set of their classic hits, which befits their reputation for giving fans their money's worth, but by the end I was ready to tap out.

Okay gang, enough already! I started to think near the end of the concert. *I can't possibly dance anymore!*

Tonight we're pushing the same envelope. Sure, we're not up and dancing, but as the evening has progressed I can't help but be amazed by the band's stamina. They were playing as we arrived right before kickoff and continued on straight through the entire game. They're still at it now, at least an hour after the final whistle. Three-plus hours up there without a break, with no end in sight. Unfortunately, it's looking less likely that I'll be seeing that end.

Stumbling back from the washroom after my short stint as videographer to this band I don't even know the name of, is when I realize how tired and drunk I am. The buzz is loading up toward a bomb, and I'd better pull the pin myself before it goes off randomly. That tiny, faint voice of reason that often takes *way* too long to make an appearance is voicing an unusually stern appeal: "You're drunk, dude. Go home." I've learned through hard experience to listen to that voice. My body is not offering up much of a counter-argument as I bump a chair at an unoccupied table and nearly trip as I walk by the front of the stage. Back at our table somebody orders up another round of Kilimanjaro Lager, and I take a pass.

It has been a truly epic evening, no question about it, and I'm tempted to carry on until the very end, but it's also been a long, eventful day and I've got to go before things get messy. It's already midnight and people keep joining our table, ensuring the party will continue on into the wee hours. I've clearly had enough to drink, and a few at the table have taken to smoking some weed. If I get involved with that I'll be a stammering, slobbery mess in seconds flat. A development nobody needs to see.

Although I feel it unnecessary, Ahmed walks me out and flags down a reputable cab, negotiating the fare for me in advance. Within minutes, or so it seems, I'm dropped off at Lost & Found, and miraculously do find my own hostel a few blocks away through the maze of alleyways that is Stone Town. Along the way I happen upon a street vendor with a small Hibachi-type grill, which is good news because I'm starving. As I mentioned, it has already been an adventurous evening out, but after examining the late-night menu options in a small deli-style glass case I find I'm only brave enough for the grisly chicken kebabs.

For a moment I'm seriously tempted by one of the large squid on display, which are easily as big as my hand, or maybe the pre-grilled ocean perch with the head still attached, but in the end choose the more familiar option.

I'm sure Kelly would have gone for something more interesting.

• • •

I may be over the worst of the jet lag now, but my sleep cycle is still off. I'm always wide awake before six a.m., no matter what kind of foolishness I've been getting into. A big cup of instant coffee from a station set out in one of the common areas of the hostel makes me feel human again. Almost.

Down in the alley the early morning air has a heavy, sleepy feel to it, and as I stand bleary-eyed trying to get my bearings, two young Arab boys appear on their way to prayers. In the soft morning light, the pair make for an irresistible photo op, two little men dressed in their Sunday best with things to do today. I had the air conditioning cranked in the room overnight, because, you know, it's always freaking hot, and now that I want to take a picture right away my lens and viewfinder are a foggy blur. Still a couple of coffees away from coherent thought, let alone action, I fire blindly, hoping for a usable image, and this catches their attention.

"No photos. No photos," they implore.

I really should have asked for permission first. Dutifully, I give them a wave and delete the handful of images as they carry on chatting amongst themselves and walk past, casting suspicious glances at me as they go.

The rest of the morning is a meandering stroll. First through the back streets of Stone Town, where I come to realize my late-night adventures were not so adventurous after all (Lost & Found is just down a long winding alleyway and around the corner from my guest house, not three or four blocks away as I imagined in my drunken stupor), and then back to the beach for breakfast at one of the swankier hotels overlooking the ocean. There are games on the beach once again, and small boats out in the bay.

Ominously, a huge dark weather system is churning along to the north, the edge of which is blowing leaves around and putting a chop out on the water, but the storm doesn't look to be moving directly this way.

It isn't until lunchtime that I catch up with Kelly again, and we dig into the work he did in Kenya. I've been curious about it because part of the responsibility of a traveller is to bear witness. To go out into the world and take note of what's going on. Any less and you're just a tourist, and there are too many of them out there already. British writer and philosopher G.K. Chesterton said, "The traveler sees what he sees. The tourist sees what he has come to see." I believe it is an important distinction.

Photographers Without Borders (PWB) define themselves on their website as "a community of storytellers (photographers and filmmakers) uniting to support our community partners on volunteer assignments through the PWB Program and inspire new generations of storytellers through PWB School and our other initiatives and resources."

Their mission statement goes on to champion the idea of making "storytelling more accessible for communities around the world who are contributing to the 17 UN Sustainable Development Goals and UNDRIP." The UN Declaration on the Rights of Indigenous Peoples (UNDRIP) was passed in the General Assembly in 2007, and a few of the 17 Sustainable Development goals include Goal 2: Zero Hunger, Goal 3: Good Health and Well-Being and Goal 13: Climate Action.

One of the PWB partnerships is with the Pastoralist Child Foundation, a non-profit that provides sexual and reproductive health education in Kenya, and it was one of five projects for which Kelly threw his hat in the ring.

Within a week PWB contacted him and said, "You're going to Africa." An itinerary was not immediately forthcoming, however, and it was only two weeks before departure that he found out exactly what he was getting into. He was tasked with documenting a community initiative near the town of Archer's Post designed to bring attention to, and create a discussion around, female circumcision.

"One of the women involved, Elizabeth, had female circumcision done to her when she was 13," Kelly says. "It was her choice. She went with her best friend, and her best friend died of complications."

Female circumcision, or female genital mutilation as it is also known, has a long history in this part of the world. It is part of the culture but is not strictly motivated by religious doctrine. A powerful tribal patriarchy remains resistant to change in rural Kenya, and so the barbaric practice persists. Technically illegal in 22 of the 28 African countries where the practice persists, it is now far less common in urban centres, but the evolution of social norms remains slow to come in outlying areas of the country.

"It's done by aunts and grammas and moms. They hold these young girls down and slice them up," Kelly says, and never one to mince words, adds, "It's fucking butchery is basically what it is."

Not to get overly graphic, but there are a number of different procedures performed, depending on traditions of the country or ethnic groups involved, that range from relatively benign ceremonial cutting, to the removal of the clitoral hood, to a full infibulation, which is the removal of the external genitalia and fusion of the wound. The tools used are often unsanitary, and venereal disease is easily spread. Young boys are also expected to participate in the rite of passage, and although infection and death are less of a risk for a male circumcision, gonorrhea and syphilis are among the unintended side effects.

"The guys in the village I was at," Kelly says, "they were telling me at a certain time of year a doctor will come and all the guys will get circumcised. They had an epidemic because everybody got sliced with the same tool and all the blood was everywhere and everybody got gonorrhea."

"And this is recently," is all I can sputter. "This is not the 1950s or 1960s."

"Oh, it's still happening."

Ensuring adequate health services in rural areas is an ongoing challenge throughout the developing world. Dar es Salaam and Nairobi and Kigali and Kampala are now rapidly modernizing cities, and the heavily touristed areas near the major national parks have amenities and emergency services available that didn't exist even 20 years ago. By contrast, the closest ambulance to Archer's Post is two hours away. Performing outdated and unnecessary procedures only increases the risk to individual and community health. Awareness and education are the first steps to curbing dangerous behaviour. To that end a soccer and volleyball tournament was held, soccer for the men and volleyball for the women, with the aim of bringing the surrounding villages together for games, and to deliver informational seminars designed to bring to light issues of women's health. Elizabeth spoke to people who had gathered for the weekend, hoping to bring female circumcision to the front of everyone's minds.

"They had this 17-year-old kid from Seralipi, a neighbouring community," Kelly says, referring to a young man who could very possibly end up being an influential voice in his village one day. "He stood up afterward and said, 'I had no idea there were any negative side effects to this.

My sisters have this done. All the women in my village get this done, and nobody's ever said anything bad about it. As far as everybody in my community is concerned this is just a natural, normal thing, that's totally healthy and totally fine.'"

"A 17-year-old boy said that?" I ask.

"Yeah, he had no idea. He was sitting there, fucking wide-eyed the whole time Elizabeth was talking."

Bringing the issue out in the open is clearly an important step forward.

"We had a lot of women talk about the changes that are happening and how they're teaching the young girls to be stronger and take control of their own sexuality and their own sexual health," Kelly says.

But there's still a long way to go.

Kelly also spoke with a friend of Elizabeth's named Mika, who is a teacher, and mentioned that the oppressive male patriarchy would soon be fizzling out. Awareness and education were changing the complexion of the culture at the base level, and when the older generation was dead a more enlightened population would be emerging.

"As I was talking to Mika," Kelly says, "she agreed, but also said, 'We are teaching our kids and we're doing the best that we can, but we can't even wait another generation. This is something that needs to happen now. Right now, this needs to change.'"

According to Wikipedia, UNICEF estimated that 200 million women had undergone some form of female genital mutilation as of 2016. In November 2018, *The Guardian* reported a sharp decline in the practice across much of Africa in the last two decades. From 71 per cent to 8 per cent in East Africa, from 57 per cent to 14 per cent in North Africa, and 73 per cent to 25 per cent in West Africa. But the article also urged caution in interpreting the new data through the lens of blind optimism. Poverty, poor education and support for the practice among religious leaders were cited as continued threats, and older teenagers and grown women were not included in the study.

Simple demographics also plays a part in the evolving story. It is anticipated that more girls will be living in at-risk communities by 2030, creating a scenario where absolute numbers may increase even as percentages decline.

So, while the newest numbers are encouraging, for too many young women on this continent change still isn't going to come soon enough.

4

BAGAMOYO, A.K.A. FUNKY SQUIDS

Ten days after arriving in Africa, it's finally time to make a move and get out of Dar es Salaam for good. I've enjoyed the city immensely. Far more than I would have expected because I'm not really a city kind of guy. I remember thinking the same thing about Kathmandu. Over breakfast one morning in Thamel I gazed out at the commotion in the street and realized, "Wow, I really like it here." This is odd because even my small town of roughly 16,000 in the Canadian Rockies gets too congested and hectic for my taste in the summer months, when all the tourists show up.

The thing is, when you're just visiting, the hustle and bustle of four million people takes on a different complexion. It's suddenly filled with details that give shape and texture to memory. I love the buses and tuk tuks and the way they move a heaving populace around and around the city, their colourful paint jobs just eclectic enough to remind me I'm far from home. The Kariakoo Market is the central shopping hub, but there are pop-up stalls all over the downtown core, selling fruits and vegetables, clothing, used books, parts for every kind of electronic gadget out there, along with just about anything else you can think of. And I hope I never get used to the kikoi or the kanga or the niqab. Dar es Salaam is a mess of diversity and humanity and energy. I'm not convinced

I would want to live here full time, but it sure is an interesting place to visit.

In addition to being interesting, major foreign cities always have a massive footprint, and the first couple of hours of a bike tour involves escaping that sprawl, which is not exactly inspired riding. Cruising past the Mnazi Mmoja bus stand is easy work because it's Saturday, and there's only a fraction of the buses and tuk tuks competing for customers that I would deal with on a weekday. A left turn on Bibi Titi Mohammed Street is equally low key, as the normally busy boulevard is mostly devoid of traffic. Near the junction where the street veers left and turns into Ali Hassan Mwinyi Road, a convenient bike path–sidewalk set a few metres off the main thoroughfare gets me away from the traffic completely.

It isn't until the junction with Kawawa Road that Ali Hassan turns into Bagamoyo Road, where I'm returned to the traffic flow with a meagre two feet of shoulder dedicated to cyclists and pedestrians. Traffic is heavier here, as city folks make their way to the resort beaches and water parks a little farther north. Even with the increase in traffic the riding doesn't feel dangerous, but I do need to ignore the startling abundance of broken glass from obvious vehicle collisions that is scattered on the ground at most intersections. My tires are a bit splashy and need more air, and I'm not exactly going fast, but overall, it's the start of a good first couple of hours in the saddle.

As the clock ticks closer to noon the heat begins to grow oppressive. As a result, my already slow pace is further interrupted by regular breaks to take on fluids. After the 40-kilometre mark I'm only managing seven or eight kilometres at a time before needing to scurry away into the shade like some kind of desert animal desperate not to fry under a punishing sun.

One of the more memorable stops is at an open-air pub by the side of the road. There are chicken and chips grilling on the barbecue out front, but all I want is a bottle of water and a little time in the shade, so I step into a part of the patio area covered by a tin roof. I've yet to have a situation this trip where I felt uncomfortable wandering around on my own, but the day drinkers here appear intent on messing with me. The waiter, who seems to be a friend of the five guys hanging out drinking beer, stands uncomfortably close as I sit in my chair to order, waiting to see if I'll react to the invasion of my personal space. When I don't, he smiles as if I've passed the test and moves off. Halfway through my 1.5-litre bottle of water one of the five day drinkers (who's at least half drunk by my estimation) gets belligerent and starts to pick a fight with the waiter. They get up in each other's faces and some minor pushing and shoving ensues. It's one of those awkward moments where you're not sure if this is going to get serious or not, and at the height of the tension the drunkard breaks into the "hey, man, I'm just kidding" routine every single person who has worked late nights in a bar dreads. The kidding / not kidding routine is exhausting to be around because you've got to be on your guard from that moment forward. Not kidding is too often the end result after a couple more beers. Better to get fried out in the blazing sun than deal with that, so I quickly pay my tab and wheel my bike out on to the road.

Sometime around two p.m. I just can't hack the heat anymore and pull into the shade of a small takeaway shop to further assess what I've gotten myself into. The heat is amazing now, and I don't know if there's enough sunscreen on the planet to protect me from the sun's punishing rays. The shop is a local general store type of place with a single plastic deck chair out front. After buying some water, cashews and dates, I plonk the chair in the dusty shade and begin to contemplate acclimatization.

Normally that word as it relates to physical activity is associated with adjusting to high altitude, where the available oxygen diminishes the higher up a mountain you go, but I won't have to deal with that part of the equation until Kilimanjaro, two or three weeks from now. The thing is, heat stress is also a thing to be taken seriously when venturing into the tropics from wintery northern environments. Minor symptoms of heat stress include heat rash, cramps and lightheadedness, but heat exhaustion is the progression on the scale where the situation can get serious. Extreme sweating, confusion, nausea and vomiting are among the things to look out for. Should the body temperature reach 103 degrees Fahrenheit, or 39.4 degrees Celsius, then the heatstroke threshold has been crossed, where damage to internal organs and possibly even death can occur.

I'm not exactly sure where I am on the scale at present. I am sweating like a madman, but that's pretty much par for the course. Confusion is the only other symptom I can identify with conviction, and that only relates to the conversion to shillings I haven't gotten a firm grasp on yet. So it is clear I'm acclimatizing to the heat, or at least trying to, but am not in any danger as long as I continue to take short breaks in the shade. In some of the literature I consulted on this issue it has been suggested it can take a couple of months to fully adapt to unfamiliar conditions, but I don't know if that's any help. I'll be flying back to a Canadian winter right about then.

Interestingly, as I stare absently into the dust, it appears I'm also acclimatizing to a different interpretation of time, defined in this case as the African art of just sitting. There's not much traffic on the road at present, and every once in a great while someone wanders past or rides by on a beaten-down old bike, but nobody seems in a hurry to do anything. This is clear counterpoint to the goal-oriented mentality that has crept in today. Now that I've started riding, I feel like I've got to get there, wherever *there* is. I suddenly feel like I need to make up the time I wasted puttering arou… I mean, acclimatizing in Dar. Sitting contentedly in the shade, the urge to push on has diminished somewhat and I'm happy to stick around for a few minutes more at least.

At first the proprietor of the shop was aloof as we executed the simple transaction for food and drink, but as I shift my chair to remain in the small chunk of shade as the sun moves slowly across the sky, he warms up to my presence. A couple of locals come by for supplies, and then some very shy kids come around. They're about 6 or 7 years old and unsure of what to make of me.

"Rafiki," the proprietor says from the comparative gloom of the interior of the shop.

"Sorry?" I say, as I lean in the open doorway to hear him better.

"Tell them you are rafiki. It means friendly."

I give it a try, and to be fair it does elicit some hesitant smiles, but the gesture doesn't completely convince them I'm a really nice guy once you get to know me. Eventually, the boys get some penny candy and wander off. I, for one, am not ready to get moving just yet.

As usual, this language thing is going to be a challenge. I fancy myself a bit of a man of the world, but if the default language of commerce and travel wasn't English I'd be in trouble. I can mime my way through most situations, and for reasons I haven't yet figured out tend to revert to an awkward English/French mashup accent when the going gets tough. As if that would help with Spanish speakers in Tulum, Japanese speakers in Kobe, or Nepali speakers in Kathmandu. Swahili is destined to be another dialect I never manage to get a handle on, but the proprietor does his best to pass on a few helpful words and phrases that I jot down in my notebook.

Back out on the road after a good half hour in the shade, I can't help but notice that despite the challenges today my body is starting to feel like my body again. A physically active thing as opposed to a tired old facsimile of what it once was. I may not be moving quickly just yet, but the minor hip pain I've been struggling with the last couple of months (a lingering by-product of surgery back in 2015) is gone, thanks to walking and biking around Dar and doing some stretching and calisthenics in the hotel room. I've begun to tighten up and have already shed a few pounds. This is a pleasing development.

My skin is also no longer just a bloated red mess; there are shades of brown starting to take hold. These are all slow processes, and I generally don't have much patience with process, but overall it's encouraging.

Out beyond the town of Zinga, the road finally escapes the satellite towns that orbit modern metropolises, the ones that eventually get consumed and become part of the sprawl. I'm not quite out in the bush, but this is my first feel for it. Stopping for one final break while sitting on a log under a tree in the shade, it occurs to me I've been snacking and taking on fluids all day but haven't sat down for a proper meal. I'm not sure if I'm suffering from heat stress or bonking from a dip in blood sugar, but scarfing down the dates tucked into a bike pannier gives me sticky fingers and a little pop for the slow, final kilometres into Bagamoyo.

The worst of the heat has broken now, and the little bump in blood sugar is accompanied by a surge of excitement. It's still a long way to go to Kilimanjaro from here, but I've started the journey, and that's something.

• • •

Bagamoyo was once the capital of German East Africa, but as ships entered the modern age the shallow bay couldn't support the increase in heavy traffic. As a result, the deep-water port at Dar es Salaam became the primary trading hub in Tanzania. Now Bagamoyo is a sleepy little backwater with a relaxed air about it.

Making my way into town from the highway roundabout, I'm thankful for the signs pointing the way to The Funky Squids Beach Bar & Grill, a beachfront hotel recommended in the Lonely Planet guide. After 70 searing kilometres I'm beyond any sort of thoughtful navigating, so the signs are a godsend and lead out past the Bagamoyo College of Arts and down a little side road to a sandy parking lot. After parking my bike, I'm greeted by a cheerful young lady and am quoted 85,000 shillings for a room with attached bath in one of the bungalows. Fifty bucks Canadian is more than I want to pay, but come on, the place is right on the ocean and the name is way too cool to pass up.

Besides, I'm too hot, too tired and too grimy from the road to go traipsing around town looking for a better deal. To tell the truth, it's hard to imagine what price she would have had to quote for me to pass.

The room has a ceramic tile floor that feels almost cool to the touch, a big bed and, most importantly, a large ceiling fan and air conditioner. After getting settled and having a shower I wander down to the beach and am greeted with a steady Indian Ocean breeze. Sitting on a cushioned bench at the edge of the property, I see there's a volleyball game underway on the beach proper, just out over a roughhewn wooden railing. An older gentleman, in his mid-30s to early 40s at a guess, is playing and keeping score with a group of 14- to 20-year-olds.

Physical education is clearly not part of the Tanzanian curriculum, because despite the players being obviously athletic the subtleties of this particular game are lost here. A few good passes and bumps are inevitably followed by wild swipes and complete misses. On the plus side, the enthusiasm is palpable, and the number of times the ball is played with feet leads me to believe football is the chosen sport around here. The two Maasai in traditional dress lend an element of "Sport for All" to the proceedings.

As they bash the ball back and forth I have time to just sit and take stock of the situation. Seventy kilometres is not a huge distance, but in these conditions is a more than fair start and I'm feeling satisfied with the effort. As twilight begins, a few heavy hitters join the volleyball game for the final half hour and it takes on a more serious tone. The beach gets busier with locals out for an early evening stroll, and at one point a dozen cows and an equal number of goats get herded past to a corral somewhere nearer town. After that, I'm not inspired to much except staring out at the ocean until dinner.

Back in my room after dinner it's hot and humid, and the salty breeze isn't strong enough to make it all the way across the compound and through the tight weave of the window screens. Turns out the air conditioning doesn't work, which is probably a good thing because the outer windows don't close tight and much of the cool air would simply escape into the night. The ceiling fan, however, is tip-top, and at full blast moves the air around the room enough to be tolerable. Pleasant even.

It's the mosquito net that puts a crimp in my comfort. After I've pulled it down around the edges of the bed and turning off the light, it doesn't take long for the air inside to grow stagnant. The fan continues to whirl above, but much of its function is diverted by the netting. After only a few minutes I can feel beads of sweat forming on my forehead, but the net serves an important function: it keeps mosquitoes at bay that may be carrying the parasite that causes malaria.

Much like the tropical heat, malaria is not to be taken lightly. Symptoms of the most common form of the disease, *Plasmodium vivax,* include fever, tiredness, vomiting and headaches, but the more serious variant, *Plasmodium falciparum,* adds seizures, coma and death to the list of possibilities. According to the World Health Organization's latest *World Malaria Report*, there were 219 million cases of malaria worldwide in 2017, an increase from 216 million cases in 2016. Approximately 435,000 people died from the disease.

The illness was not of particular worry in Dar, as in the daytime it was too hot for bugs, and in the evenings I would retreat to the sanctuary that was my air-conditioned room. It could be true that I'm not entirely prepared for this trip. I've packed poorly and may not be properly fit for what I've taken on, but before I left home I did make sure to catch up on my immunizations. Lugging around too many t-shirts and feeling slightly out of breath on a flight of stairs is one thing; waking up from dazed fever dreams in a rural clinic somewhere in Tanzania is quite another.

Getting vaccinated for yellow fever is currently a requirement for travel to East Africa, and taking antimalarial medication is strongly recommended. When I checked in with the travel medicine clinic back in November, the nurse on duty, Julie, was kind and funny and we hit it off immediately. She was full of helpful information on my destination and walked me through the proper procedure for applying sunscreen and bug spray in effective layers. It was also recommended I stay away from unpasteurized milk while away. I was hesitant to ask what the repercussions of that particular misstep might be.

After reviewing my records, it was clear a yellow fever shot and prescription for Malarone pills was not going to suffice. A tetanus booster with pertussis upgrade meant another shot. Rubella protection, another shot. Hepatitis A and B booster, another shot. Reports of a meningococcal meningitis outbreak in northern Kenya and northern Uganda led to, you guessed it, another shot. And while we're at it, how about a little influenza protection? Sure. Why not? Since we're already here.

As we were working toward the last act in the play titled *Human Pin Cushion,* Julie said something to the effect of, "Good thing there isn't anything else. We can only give six shots at a time. We would have had to make another appointment."

Good thing. The kicker is this revelation comes less than five minutes after being advised that pumping this much preventative medicine into my body at one time was probably going to make me feel shitty for a couple of days. As she administered the last injection her professionalism slipped, and a deeply compassionate nature came to the surface for brief moment.

"Oh, poor you."

And then I swear to God she giggled. Because we were already fast friends, I let that part slide.

Eventually, I'm forced to pull the netting up from around the bed so the air can circulate more freely. Otherwise I'm just going to toss and turn and sweat all night. Flipping on the lights, I do a quick assessment of my defences. The screens are tight to the window frames and the bathroom door closes tight to the frame and floor. As a makeshift precaution I jam a bath towel up to the big crack under the main door to the room, and then try to get some sleep. Hoping all the while that Malarone is in fact the proper drug for this region, in the event that one of the infectious little bloodsuckers does manage to sneak through.

• • •

This morning is my second in Bagamoyo. The first big riding day was a success, but it took a lot out of me. A little wander into town to have a look around was all I could manage yesterday. The abandoned German Boma is the most obvious historical landmark here. The imposing whitewashed building made of coral stone that was used as an administration office is hard to miss due to its location on a large and otherwise empty lot, but I found the old fort to be more interesting.

I passed on the offer for a guide and explored the aging fortress on my own. It was originally built as a marketplace for trade, The Germans added walls and soldier barracks, and after the First World War the British used it as a prison. After independence it became a police station for a time, and now it's a historical landmark. The compound is big enough to get comfortably lost in as you explore all the nooks and crannies, and I was able to contemplate the lives lived in many of the rooms without distraction, but the hundred or so grade school students visiting on a field trip did make for some loud and rambunctious meetings in narrow hallways and steep stone stairwells.

"Hello." "Habari." "Welcome." "Nice to meet you." The full-volume greetings were both energetic and heartfelt. The local fish market downtown (usually a centre of animation in coastal communities) a half hour later was positively serene by comparison.

These early-day highlights all preceded a long, long nap in the afternoon.

I must say I do feel better today, but it turns out Bagamoyo is pretty cool in a laid-back, the-tourism-circuit-doesn't-stop-here kind of way, and so deserves some additional attention. This is a convenient excuse to lean on when you're too tired and too sore to ride on into the African bush, and convenient again a day later when you probably could, but just don't want to.

Focusing on breakfast, I must say it's fantastic for the second day in a row. Coffee and a generous fruit plate, followed by a Spanish omelet and toast. Dinner last night was similarly enjoyable. I live a thousand kilometres from the nearest ocean, so it's quite a treat to be able to get really fresh seafood. The seafood soup in particular was hearty, a little peppery and nothing short of extraordinary.

The compound here at Funky Squids also does much to help convince me there's no need to rush away to the next town up the road. There are multiple tree varieties, including coconut palms and small banyans that provide ample shade, and a meticulously manicured assortment of beach plants and shrubs and coarse grasses reinforce the tropical ambiance. There is lots of sand, obviously, that the gardener sweeps and cleans of debris every morning. Cicadas trill during the day, and in the afternoon the wind generally comes up enough to keep the mosquitoes at bay.

Earlier, as I was coming out of the bathroom in the room, I spied a troupe of banded mongoose through the window. The half dozen large, housecat-sized animals with grey-brown coats and subtle brown-black vertical stripes were out hunting for millipedes and beetles. I froze immediately, hoping to not spook them, but they spotted me as well, and stopped dead in their tracks as an assessment of the situation was made. I retreated slowly out of view in a comical, exit-stage-left sort of way, and then grabbed my camera and sprinted out the door and down the hall and around the building. A move that could not have taken much more than ten seconds. A banded mongoose might be a social animal compared to their more solitary cousins in the mongoose family tree, but they wanted nothing to do with me. By the time I got there, they were gone.

Despite the relaxed start to the day after that brief moment of excitement, there is some angst brewing in the background. Like a tropical storm offshore, the looming spectre of money troubles is beginning to form. The Chelsea Hotel was the perfect base from which to explore Dar. The room was spotless, the safe was convenient, the staff was friendly, and Nadeem was incredibly helpful while I was getting my bearings. He even agreed to store my cumbersome reinforced bicycle travel bag and a few other items at the hotel at no charge until I return. This beach resort is similarly comfortable and accommodating.

The problem is, I budgeted $25 a day for lodging and I'm spending roughly double that so far. This is not the end of the world if you're gone for a week, but I've still got two months of travel left to go, and the math has me a little rattled.

There is good reason for this worry, I suppose. We are indoctrinated into thinking about money as the measure of things, and so we give it a disproportionate amount of energy and attention as we plan our lives. Even when we consciously make space and time (and stash away savings) to try and *not* think about it for a while, money finds a way to burrow into our thoughts. You can never save enough, it seems. Tim Cahill, in his story called Professor Cahill's Travel 101, addresses the most obvious of travel advice with this simple sentence: "Pack half the clothes you think you'll need, and take twice the money."

Picturing my bike with its panniers stuffed full and the pack and boots that I'll need for Kilimanjaro piled on top, my dilemma is clear. I have too much stuff and not enough money.

I've written about this piece by Cahill before, because it covers a lot of practical travel considerations in seven pages, not the least of which is the importance of having a quest. As it relates to the current situation, however, Rule 8 is what catches my attention. In it, and the corollaries that follow, Cahill says, "It ain't about money," and goes on to say, "Too often money, and the process of saving money, becomes the entire point of traveling. If the nature of your quest is financial, stay home and get into arbitrage."

So, yeah, I'm on board with Cahill's urging to "spend what you need to in order to accomplish your quest," but in an attempt to hedge my bet I applied for a grant from the Alberta Foundation for the Arts. Grant funding is a way for aspiring artists in every discipline to further their chosen careers by providing financial support for projects in all phases of development. Painters and writers and actors and photographers all take advantage of the opportunity in order to create something that wasn't there before. Something that existed previously only in their imaginations.

The German philosopher Friedrich Nietzsche is reported to have said, "We have art in order not to die of the truth." Follow your quest. Don't die of the boring realities of modern living. *These* are ideologies I can get excited about.

With two books already in the can, a few dozen local newspaper articles under my belt, and enough printed and framed photos sold to private collectors to think, "Yeah, maybe I am an artist of sorts," I decided to give public funding a whirl. Lord knows I'm terrible at the financial side of art as a career, but that's what funding is for, no? To help with the failings of the creative personality? To make up for the lack of business acumen? One thing is certain, a grant would go a long way to assuaging the fear that I'm wasting my life with frivolous pursuits, given the weight society places on money as a measure of usefulness and worth. By that metric, I am mostly a failure.

I put a lot of effort into the application. I spent a month on it. Working it, reworking it, and then reworking it again. I consulted a number of people who had successfully applied in the past and included a glowing letter of recommendation from my publisher. One that suggested an interest in not just this book project, but for two or three more after that. I shot for the moon. I asked for the maximum amount of funding available and budgeted for every conceivable contingency. I felt good about what I'd submitted and dreamt about getting my expenses covered like a proper professional would in any other field. Is that too much to ask?

On December 2nd, one day before beginning my African quest, I opened my email only to find this:

"Thank you once again for your application to the Alberta Foundation for the Arts (AFA) Literary Arts Individual Project grant stream. Unfortunately, your application was unsuccessful."

Talk about getting the wind let out of your sails at the worst possible time.

Truth be told, even though I had high hopes I would have accepted anything. Just getting the cost of the flight covered would have been a big help. This is a first-world problem to be sure, one born of remarkable privilege that I fear I don't acknowledge often enough, but there is still no shaking how vulnerable I feel now that I'm on the ground on a foreign continent and there's no going back. It was always a long shot to have "writer" be a proper career, but not getting *any* support at this point in my artistic development still hurts. It hurts a lot. The question has to be asked, am I wasting my time here?

Obviously, I got on a plane anyway, but it has taken almost two weeks to even face up to the depth of my disappointment.

As I lick my wounds I need to find a way to double down on Cahill's advice and stop worrying about money for now. I'm going to be over budget without the grant (with new projections based on the true cost of accommodation adjusted upward to be waaaayyyy over budget), but I have to be here. I had to leap into a new quest or risk falling down the lifestyle hole. The last thing the world needs is another miserable work-a-day drone harbouring dreams of doing something more exciting and more fulfilling that he never acts on. I've had enough experience in that role already, thank you very much.

To that end, I pack up the camera bag, tuck a water bottle in an empty compartment, and head out to the parking lot with the bike. As I spin slowly past the art college (a timely, reaffirming reminder that creativity *is* still important), what looks like a hip-hop number is being rehearsed in the small open-air amphitheater set in this close corner of the grounds. A couple of guys in their late teens or early 20s are working on the dance moves for their performance, and every time I pass by there is something different going on. Musical acts or stage plays, or even the occasional lecture delivered outside of stuffy classrooms. And there is almost always music of some sort coming from somewhere on the grounds, as young musicians and singers try and hone their skills. It's great.

Moving through town is a mix of beat-up old pavements and rough cobblestones, and in the northwestern quadrant is the Catholic Mission and Museum, which sits down a lovely tree-lined dirt road. The museum is small but well kept and chronicles the Spiritans' efforts to evangelize and educate in the late 18th and early 19th centuries. Father Anthony Horner established the Christian Freedom Village here in 1868 for ransomed and liberated slaves, and legendary explorer, missionary and anti-slave crusader David Livingstone was carried here after his death in what is now Zambia, before being transported to Westminster Abbey to be buried.

Six kilometres southeast of town and in the opposite direction lie the ruins of the original foreign settlement in this area. The Kaole ruins date from the 13th century, and in amongst the weathered stone remains of the village is the first mosque built on the mainland. There are also water wells and burial plots, and at the edge of the property, the old harbour, which is now unrecognizable as such, because it is a mangrove swamp. Walking around the site, you can't miss the gigantic baobab, a species of tree that needs to be seen to be believed. It would take five of my outstretched arm widths to make it all the way around the trunk. And the resident colobus monkeys, much like the banded mongooses from this morning, are extremely wary of my interest.

Pedalling along the dirt road back to town, I have to pick my path if I hope to keep up any momentum. There are sandy bits that make it hard to keep a straight line as my wheels sink and swerve in the soft surface, and rough washboard sections that rattle the bike frame right up through to my shoulders. On the hard pack that exists between these two extremes, however, travel is smooth and fast and fun, a reminder that a bicycle unburdened of panniers and a pack and all the gear that goes in them is a beautiful thing.

About halfway back to the resort, a break in the trees and scrub brush in between the fenced-off private oceanfront properties presents itself. I hadn't noticed the view on the ride out due to the angle of the road. From high up on this bluff the bay of Bagamoyo is tranquil and quite becoming. There is rumour of a Chinese effort to transform this sleepy little backwater into a major port, one to compete with Dar es Salaam and Kenya's main port at Mombasa. The project is part of the race to get the vast mineral riches of the interior out to the worldwide market.

That is hard to imagine now from this quiet perch above the bay. The beach runs the length of the bay and has only a scattering of people out walking at the moment, and the town has no proper skyline from this vantage point. Only a handful of roofs poking out from the greenery crowding the shoreline indicate a settlement here. Out in the bay a couple of dozen small fishing boats with small outboard motors wait for the next trip into deeper waters. Farther out, two or three dhows move ever so slowly across the sea, their sails not much more than tiny specks on the horizon.

This was not a view I was expecting to experience today, but it is one of those perfect moments in time that happen when you go out exploring. The whole afternoon has been a collection of scenes that defy logic and planning and any kind of reasoned calculations about value or outcome. It all just happens spontaneously. Happy surprises and informing discoveries that make the effort worth it as the doubt and worry fade away. Out here in the world with the sun on your shoulders and wind in your face is where memories are made.

I need to remember that going forward.

5

SUMMIT FEVER. BAGAMOYO REDUX

Back in 1986, when I was 18 years old, I rode my bicycle through the southern part of the Canadian Rockies and out across a big chunk of the Prairies. The trip was from just outside Hope, British Columbia, to Portage la Prairie, Manitoba, a distance of 2000 kilometres. There were no cell phones back then, and no internet obviously. When you wanted to check in with everyone back home, you cobbled together some coins and found yourself a payphone. When a plan went sideways, you figured it out. On occasion you had no choice but to rely on the kindness and generosity of strangers, to give you a ride to the next town in the event of a mechanical breakdown, or even to put you up for the night as an alternative to your tent as a series of thunderstorms threatened.

Thirty-two years later, there is a big part of me that does not want to let go of that simple and challenging aspect of setting off toward an unknown horizon. Relying on serendipity and my wits has been such a big part of my travel experience that I don't know if I can let go of the approach even if I wanted to. The philosophy is driven by my inquisitive nature. The adrenaline generated by taking a chance and plunging headlong into whatever may come is the only thing that gets my feet moving. The strategy has worked out so far, but that's no guarantee of success going forward. At 18 the possibility of dying out on the road or trail never even crossed my mind. At 50, that potential outcome does drift through my consciousness on occasion. I try not to let that inconvenient detail interfere with getting back out into the world from time to time.

Sylvain thinks the whole idea I've cooked up is nuts.

Sylvain runs Funky Squids with his wife Arlette. He was born in Montreal but has lived in Africa for over ten years. Arlette is from Burundi, and along with their daughter Maya the couple moved to Tanzania in 2011 in search of opportunity. When an offer to run this resort came up a year later, they jumped on it. We've developed an instant rapport, and while sitting at one of the picnic tables near the beach before dinner we've gotten to talking about the plan. They've seen the bike, which is not common transportation for westerners in these parts, and they're naturally curious about why I've brought it with me.

Seeing as it's been a few days now and I'm still in Bagamoyo, I'm wondering the same thing myself.

As we've been getting to know each other better I find I'm trying to massage the conversation away from the coming challenge to avoid getting discouraged. The strategy is to bullshit my way through any interrogations until I better understand what I'm up against, and in the moment I'm hell-bent on going on and on about having travelled in Nepal by bicycle and on foot as a way to convince everyone, including myself, that I'm not out of my depth. Being purposely vague is not just a function of not actually knowing much about what's ahead. It's also a defence mechanism. If I lay a hard plan out clearly – that I'm hoping to bicycle all the way to Mount Kilimanjaro before climbing it – then I'll have to admit I'm nervous about being able to achieve that goal.

From what I can tell, Sylvain is a pretty laid-back dude,

and as a man who left Canada to live in Africa he knows a thing or two about taking chances based on a gut feeling and incomplete understanding of the end result. But, as he gets up to grab a fresh round of beers, a serious tone I've not heard from him before does give me pause.

"I understand your desire to be off grid, but you need to get a local phone number at least. This is not Asia. This is Africa."

Maybe he has a point. He's not trying to discourage the idea of having an adventure, but is encouraging me to be smarter about it, in case something does go wrong.

Thankfully, Niels, a Dane who owns another resort just up the beach, and his Tanzanian wife, Jane, join us, and we get distracted from the details of the bike ride. The conversation is engrossing, and I spend most of the time just listening as the two couples discuss their collective experience in this part of the world. The fact that both unions are interracial speaks to the liberal nature of their characters. I am treated to insights into the challenges of East African business, politics, health care and education, expressed by four thoughtful people from diverse backgrounds who have chosen to spend this part of their lives along a lovely stretch of beach in Bagamoyo.

My takeaway from the discussion is the idea that we are, all of us, simply trying to find our place. Coming together in these moments with like-minded folks highlights a few simple truths about the modern world. In a growingly divisive global environment, the troubles we face are not a regional problem, because we all come from a region. They are not an African problem either. Or European. Or North American. They are a human problem. Thinking that my way, my culture or my language is the best compared to all the rest, is a misguided and self-absorbed way of looking at the world, and completely undermines the possibility of real progress toward social justice and economic equality. We *are* all different, but we are also the same.

There is no spinning the inevitable results of a close-minded, egocentric approach. It's called history. As a worldwide human collective, we've had leaders who've been at the me-first approach for centuries with disappointing results, and yet we default to that position time and time again because we are persuaded to think that unless we take whatever we can get, we will fail. Individually or as a member of any particular group. The thing is, political drama is not an accurate representation of regular people, here or abroad, and the mindless pursuit of wealth and power disguised as patriotism or strength does nothing to address the growing difficulties that hoarding of resources and influence makes for the middle class and the poor.

Shuffling off to bed, I am encouraged by the generous spirit in these people I've met, and how they've inspired me to think about the bigger picture for a few hours, but the scope of my immediate undertaking is also starting to sink in hard. I saw the mileage sign out on the highway by the roundabout before riding into town a couple of days ago. It read, Msata, 64 kilometres. Tanga, 272 kilometres. Moshi, 485 kilometres. Moshi is the jumping-off point for most people who climb Kilimanjaro, and I've been doing a little math. It'll take roughly the equivalent of seven day-ones to get to Moshi, and that's along the main road, which I don't want anything to do with because of its somewhat less than stellar reputation when it comes to bicycles.

The website lonelyplanet.com has this to say on the subject: "Main sealed roads aren't good for cycling, as there's usually no shoulder and traffic moves dangerously fast. We have heard of several tragedies involving cycling travellers." And that is the most generous description I can find. Even if I was motivated to risk it, the heat and the rolling nature of the landscape as you move inland would put seven back-to-back day-ones outside my abilities. Maybe when I was 18 I could have pulled it off. Now, not so much.

The other option is a secondary road, which as far as I can tell is not paved, but I haven't been able to find a decent map to confirm. The road passes through Saadani National Park on the way to the seaside towns of Mkwaja and Pangani. Moving inland, the Usambara Mountains stand between Pangani and Moshi. This is also not a seven day-ones possibility, but the chances of getting hit by a truck are considerably less.

Saadani itself is one of the more obscure parks in Tanzania. Upgraded to national park in 2005 from a game reserve created in 1969, it is the only park that borders the ocean. Technically, it is illegal to bicycle in the national parks of Tanzania, but this one seems to operate outside the accepted norms. Sylvain confirmed that it's a dirt road, and figures you can't get through by bike, but some of the other people at the table earlier tonight are firm maybes. When I brought it up at one of the tourist information offices in town the guy there was adamant it was possible, saying locals walk and ride bikes in the park all the time.

Checking online offers little help. A Google search turns up everything from a definitive *no chance*, to vague references of success in doing so, without any practical advice on accomplishing the feat. After brushing my teeth and setting up the anti-malaria defences – bathroom door shut tight, bath towel covering the crack below the room door – I predict a night of tossing and turning and worry.

Is any of this even doable? What the hell was I thinking? While it's possible I didn't think hard enough about the logistics of this trip beforehand, now I'm thinking about it all way too much.

It should come as no surprise to learn that for the disorganized adventurer, a close companion of the Western Shoulds is the Western What Ifs. The What Ifs are basically a highlight reel of all the things that could go wrong. What if I can't find water is primary among the concerns. On the ride up to Bagamoyo I started the day with 2.5 litres of water and topped up with another 1.5 litres at the first break. Subsequent breaks meant another 2.5 litres, for a total of 6.5 litres by the time I made it to Funky Squids. Amazingly, when I went to the washroom before having a shower, my pee was nothing more than a pathetic bright yellow dribble. Is eight litres going to be necessary to stay hydrated? Or ten?

Even if I can stay hydrated, what if there's no food available on this route? What if I get sick along the way? What if I get eaten by a lion?

These worries go along with, will I have enough money? Something I've already come to the conclusion that I'm not going to have. But this is not big-picture no money, this is a more practical consideration. Are there going to be *any* ATM's along the way? The insidiousness nature of worry is that once you go down the rabbit hole you end up constantly distracted by the future, instead of dealing in the now and working the problems if and when they do arise. You can't be afraid of everything negative that *could* happen or nothing good is ever *going* to happen. So far, there hasn't been a genuinely bad experience on this trip (touch wood), so why am I creating anxiety where there doesn't need to be any?

Fair question, but this is a unique situation with unique details, and that simply ups the anxiety level. Is the road going to be passable? Or am I going to get turned around at the gate, wasting at least a day? Has the lion population in the area rebounded to the point where an encounter is possible, or even probable? And then there's this little nugget that someone mentioned before dinner. Apparently, elephants don't like bicycles, at all, and will charge at the sight of them. By all accounts there are plenty of African bush elephants in Saadani.

Remind me again, why didn't I sort any of this out before leaving North America? Why indeed. Oh well, nothing I can do about it now. I'm here, and it's time to get out there before I chicken out. It's time to jump into the unknown. I only hope I manage to survive the experience again this time. You would think that sooner or later my luck will eventually run out.

• • •

So far, the weather has been co-operative on this trip. Apart from it being incredibly hot, nothing to date has indicated a challenge to travelling in the out-of-doors. It rained a few times while I was in Dar, but the showers were short lived and not terribly intense. In November and December there is a slight uptick in rainfall compared to the long dry period from June through to October, but traditionally the "rainy season" is from mid-March through May. Or so they say.

The meteorological situation has taken an unexpected turn this morning. Ponderous dark clouds are hanging low on the horizon to the north and east and appear to be drifting inland. To the southeast the skies are still largely clear, but things are not looking good in the general direction of Saadani. As I'm riding away from Funky Squids via the sandy back streets that lead to the main road, the heavy clouds begin to loom, but out on the pavement toward the roundabout things open up a bit, and the low morning sun in the east provides hope for a decent day.

Within three kilometres that hope disappears. Abruptly. The big heavy drops common to the tropics smash the pavement with startling force, and within a minute the situation has deteriorated to full downpour. Because I've just started out I'm reluctant to give in to Mother Nature, but my gear is not properly packed for this volume of rain, and soon I'm forced to think about seeking shelter.

At first there is nothing to offer any decent protection. There are some hardscrabble shacks and a couple of more substantial private dwellings made of poured concrete or brick, but nothing I'd feel comfortable just walking up on. There are also lots of small trees and bushes, but nothing you could properly hunker down under. Besides, I'm already wet. All my stuff is already wet. After making so little Point A to Point B progress so far this trip, I remain somewhat determined to keep riding, but it's *really* coming down now.

At the first reasonable opportunity to escape the elements I finally pull over. The one-storey building is poured concrete, with four garage door style openings along the front. This African version of a strip mall is new and does not yet have tenants but does have a four-foot-wide concrete stoop, and most importantly the roof extends out over the stoop. At the far end two women are cooking over a one-burner portable stove, but apart from a wave when I rolled in, my presence can't distract them from their conversation. Soaked and annoyed, I have no choice but to concede that the rain is impressive, and I take the time to repack with the hopes of keeping at least some of my things dry. At one point, an Extra Luxury Coach Line bus bounces over the large speed bump out on the highway, and then rushes away into the distance, the passengers surely unconcerned with the weather. I'm envious.

It is worth noting that in the end, I did take Sylvain's concerns for my health and well-being to heart. I took an extra day and went into town to get the backup local phone connected, just in case, before checking in once again with the tourist office, where a compromise was struck. Now the plan is to bicycle to the Wami Gate at the south end of Saadani, where I'll get picked up by a local guide named Hamisi. He'll take me on safari through the park in search of elephants and giraffes and lions, and then drop me off outside the north end park in the village of Mkwaja. From there, I can ride to my heart's content for a week to ten days en route to Kilimanjaro.

Truth be told, if I didn't have an appointment for later this morning I'd probably turn around and wait for better weather, it's raining that hard, but of course, I can't get any cell reception. Checking in with Hamisi is not possible, and a little bad weather is not good enough reason to be a no-show. Fortunately, after about 20 minutes of waiting it out the weather lets up, at least enough to continue on. At the Saadani turnoff half an hour later it's still raining, but it's a normal rain, not some crazy biblical style tropical deluge. As I'm pulling up to the junction there are a number of scrappy-looking shops, selling all manner of convenience items. The parking lot is muddy and rough, and against what has become the norm the locals are not terribly friendly, but I do need to try and check in with Hamisi to see if we're still on. I figure there's about 30 kilometres of rough track between here and the park gate, so I stock up with some dates and cookies, and find a spot out of the rain to sit down and check my phone.

Cell service established, a text message is received, the plan is still a go.

Slopping through the parking lot, it's obvious that if the Saadani road is in similar condition the day will be over, but the rain has downgraded again into nothing more than a light drizzle, and the dirt road has a sandy component that makes it quite acceptable given the situation. In fact, the dirt here is better to ride on than the paved shoulder out on the highway, which was under an inch of water in a lot of places. There are plenty of puddles, but they are mostly confined to the tire ruts carved into the roadbed by previous vehicles. Overall, it's firm and manageable, if a bit messy.

This is a great relief, and after six or seven kilometres the rain lets up completely, allowing me to relax, get out of my head and have a good look around. The road is miles away from the ocean here – and for the first time it feels like being on the great big continent that is Africa. The surroundings are a green and lush mix of thick bush peppered with stands of low trees, a thirsty landscape quickly revived by today's rain. Along the road there is a wide range of dwellings. Sometimes I can only see a tin rooftop in the distance through the bush, painted green or red, but there are also mud and stick huts, along with a few poured concrete or proper brick dwellings. The surroundings appear fertile, but I'm surprised by the lack of small farm plots.

In his book *Prisoners of Geography: Ten Maps That Explain Everything About the World,* Tim Marshall addresses the historical challenges this continent has faced in the first paragraph of the Africa chapter:

> Africa's coastline? Great beaches – really, really lovely beaches – but terrible natural harbors. Rivers? Amazing rivers, but most of them are worthless for actually transporting anything, given every few miles you go over a waterfall. These are just two in a long list of problems that help explain why Africa isn't technologically or politically as successful as Western Europe or North America.

Modern humans came into existence not too far from here, but the Sahara Desert to the north and two big oceans to the east and west restricted trade and ideas with those who ventured off the continent in the early days of humanity's march toward modern life. Africa has been playing catch-up ever since. In more recent times, colonialism, poor infrastructure, insufficient education and health care – to say nothing of rampant corruption – have continued to hold the resource-rich continent back.

Rolling along at a good clip on this back road, I'm starting to feel like a proper adventurer, and if I do say so myself, kinda cool. I'm here. Riding in the bush in Africa!!! The cool factor is making me cocky. I don't know what I was worried about these last few days, this is just like any other ride in the country I've ever been on, with a few details unique to the area thrown in for good measure. Today I am master of my little part of the universe, where I'm able to take on all challenges and overcome them. A work colleague from back home, where travelling in the backcountry is made safer by keeping a can of bear spray handy, will look at a photo from today that I eventually post on Instagram and comment, rather appropriately, "I hope you brought your lion spray."

It's funny, and lions are possible here theoretically, but

I'm not fussed. The reality is, outside of the national parks the human and animal equation has tipped the way of the humans, just as in most places around the globe. It's a sad fact, but collectively we've managed to push the majority of species to the margins. As I'm pedalling along, it's the sounds of birds and frogs, not hungry lions or hyenas, that accompany me. Eventually, I come up on a solo rider on his one-speed, and we both marvel at the unusual situation as we pedal along together for a few kilometres.

After an hour or two on the dirt, I feel the adrenaline boost begin to die away. My cycling companion has veered off onto a footpath leading into the bush, but conditions are still manageable, and I'm beginning to think the park gate can't be too far away now. Coming up on a huge sugar plantation. I pull over for a rest, and to touch base one last time with Hamisi, but of course, there's no cell service. A few dates and a couple of swigs of water and I'm back at it.

After the plantation the road drops down into a coastal lowland, where "road improvements" have begun. The drop itself is only a few vertical metres, but the roadbed has been built up down the middle to avoid the worst of the flooding during the wet season. There are deep ditches at the sides of the road now, and the land is raw because plant life has yet to grow back where the backhoes have done their work. It's a dark, muddy mess after today's rain, and the entire road and roadbed is now made up of that infamous black cotton soil I've been warned about.

Black cotton soil has a high clay component, with remarkable swelling and shrinkage properties depending on the moisture available. It is also easily compressed. Where the small handful of vehicles that have passed already today have tread, the soil is compacted to a slick black mud. Incredibly slick, as it turns out. Trying to ride in the tracks is a skittery proposition. The alternative, trying to ride on the side of the road or down the middle of the tracks, turns out to be an impossibility for more than a few metres. The mud either grabs at the wheels, stealing away the momentum necessary to remain upright, or gives way under the weight of bike and rider. After about 500 metres in the tracks I go down with shocking suddenness when the tires simply skid out from under the bike.

Picking myself up and throwing my leg over the bike, I make it about 20 metres before almost going down in a heap once again. I ride all winter long back in Canada and have rarely encountered ice or snow as slippery as this. Clearly, it's time to walk.

Walking is safer, but not any easier. It's hard to find footing and keep the tires out of the heavier clinging mud. There is a very fine line between slick track and mucky mess, and as if on cue a light rain returns and changes the dynamic of the surface once again. The slick gets slicker and the mucky gets muckier as the mud begins to accumulate on the tires of my bike, jamming up the brakes while getting all over everything, including the bottoms of my shoes. Any misplaced steps and I'm instantly two inches taller.

The situation is exhausting, and frustrating. Using a stick to clear away the mess brings only temporary relief. Five hundred metres of struggling to keep the bike upright and moving turns into 200 metres before I've got to clear away the accumulated mess to start over. Eventually that turns to 50 metres. Then ten. And still the park gate fails to appear. Every marker or sign by the road ahead looks promising from a distance, only to prove a false hope when I finally get there, and this goes on for who knows how long. Twenty minutes? Half an hour? An hour? It's impossible to tell, but I've got summit fever and can't see that stubbornly pushing onward is turning into a dangerous waste of energy.

Simply put, summit fever is what happens when a mountaineer's obsession with reaching the top of a mountain interferes with the normal decision-making process. Turns out the affliction can apply to horizontal landscapes. *Just one more long straightaway and I'll be there,* I keep thinking. Or, *it's got to be right around the next bend. It's just got to be.* I've lost my perspective, and while I'm taking a break under a huge tree by the roadside my cell phone jingles from inside my now mud-covered handlebar bag. It's an hour-old text from Hamisi that has finally found its way to me. I have to go back. There's too much rain in the river and he can't get across the bridge to meet me. Staring at the tiny screen, I can barely believe it.

Well, fuck! What am I supposed to do now?

Sitting down to gather my thoughts is not an inviting proposition, which doesn't help. The mud here has been ploughed at some point in the not-so-distant past by an industrial grader. There is no deep ditch at this point, and the huge clumps pushed to the roadside provide no easy spot to lean the bike, or even sit comfortably for that matter. The only saving grace is the shelter from the weather provided by a giant tree.

To add to my accumulating troubles, I don't see very well anymore, and the result is almost comical. I'm myopic. The light that enters my eyes doesn't fall on the retina but ends up short of that optimal point. As a result, objects in the distance appear blurry. Today I'm wearing contacts to correct the problem in a way that allows me to wear sunglasses, but the tiny screen of my Tecno local phone is difficult to read in this scenario. The small keypad has the conventional numbers familiar on all phones, but to send a return text that includes the letter L, for instance, you need to press the number 5, three times in quick succession. With the phone held at arms-length it's difficult to see if the correct pressure and timing is applied to get a coherent message across.

It's incredibly frustrating, and before long I give up trying to come to a solution with Hamisi, given that he does not immediately respond to my no-doubt-illegible missives. At this point I'm pretty worked up and need to calm down in order to make sensible choices going forward. After finally getting comfortable enough to sit, drinking some water and snacking on cashews helps me get a handle on the situation, but I am reminded of something Sylvain said as I was getting ready to go: "Expect the unexpected. This is Africa."

Well, sure, but this is next-level stuff, and staring down into the black mud I can't decide if I'm underestimating this place, or overplaying the dangers.

Taking calm stock of the situation, I realize I do have enough food and water on hand for a leisurely afternoon safari spent sitting comfortably in a truck on a game drive, with an evening drop-off in a small village at the far side of the park. What I'm not prepared for is a long return slog over the 40-plus kilometres to Funky Squids. Even the 30-ish kilometres back to the paved road at the T-junction would be a bit of a stretch at this point. If I were a couple of months into this little adventure I've conjured up I might be ready for a night out in the bush, but I'm not there yet. No question about it, it's decision time.

On the one hand, there are probably no services at the park gate, and who knows if the wardens there will be helpful in sorting out a solution to the stranded-on-this-side-of-an-overflowing river problem. It's probably only a kilometre or two to go from here, but I said that three or four kilometres ago and I'm clearly not there yet. In these circumstances, and in my borderline freaked-out condition, who knows what will happen? On the other hand, at least I have an idea about the ground already covered. I hate to retreat, but if I go back to the sugar cane plantation I can probably top up water reserves and figure out a solution to this mess. If I were 18 years old I'd probably just push on and deal with the consequences. At 50, I'm not going to lie, I'm a little bit scared, and so sensible wins out, for possibly the first time in my life.

The only problem is, the conditions are now horrendous. The adobe-style clay is now at its worst. I live in a temperate climate, so none of this is intuitive. I never really understood the chemistry or mechanics or whatever it is that makes building things out of mud possible. Now I get it. With the just the right amount of moisture, this stuff is amazing. Every time I clear away the accumulated mud blocking up the choke point where the wheels pass the seat stay and the forks of my bike, it builds back up almost instantly. Three or four inches accumulates for every three or four metres of travel along the road, then the wheels jam up completely and I simply skid along, the locked wheels dragging a mini-trench in the glistening part of the track. After the inevitable bout of creative cursing, I'm forced to stop and dig the mud out from the wheels for what feels like the hundredth time. It's incredibly hard work that is taking its toll on my back.

After a time, the rain stops once again, and the sun begins to burn through. The temperature spikes almost instantly. Clearly, dragging and carrying my fully loaded bike is an impossible task, and now that the sun has come out it is a perilous one as well. I now have minimal water reserves and vehicle traffic – such as it was – has completely died off. As my lower back begins to cramp up my concern jumps to a new level. Where half an hour ago I was a little bit scared, now it's *panic time*. Let me rephrase: it's high noon in the African bush and definitely PANIC TIME!

Standing still for a moment to assess the situation, I force myself to take a few deep breaths and try and calm down. Clearly, stashing the bike and the gear in the bush and walking is the only hope. If I can find another window of cell reception along the way, I can call in a rescue.

When I'm back up on the firm dirt 30 minutes on from stashing my bike, the skies clear completely and the temperature continues to soar. It's easily over 30 degrees Celsius now and will soon be pushing 35. I'm slathered in sunscreen, so the concern is not so much the harsh sun beating down as my diminishing water reserves and poor memory. The walking is not difficult at this point, but there seem to be far fewer huts and small homes now than the first time I passed by this morning. After about 45 minutes more, I spot a hut set 25 metres off the side of the road. The folks out front had waved as I rode by, and maybe they can help. Some of these huts serve as makeshift convenience stores for the local area, with a small fenced-in general store with snacks and dry goods – and, most importantly, water – available for purchase. Fortunately, this is one of those huts.

The hellos are awkward, and I can tell they're wondering where the hell my bike is, but I'm able to get a bottle of water and a seat on a rickety bench in the shade. There are four people at the hut and only one of them speaks very limited English, so I have to rely on imprecise translations from my guidebook. The situation is made more difficult by the fact that I can't read well because of my contacts. Holding the guidebook away at arm's length, I try to explain that I need to rent a 4×4.

"Nataka kukodi forbaifor."

The nonverbal response is about what you would expect given the situation. If a blank stare could be incredulous, well, this was it, and it came across as something like, *Hey, look around, buddy. Where do you think you are?*

Then the four of them have an animated discussion amongst themselves in Swahili. They are clearly poking fun, and it is deserved. I am on a bit of a fool's errand when you think about it. I didn't really expect to be able to rent a 4×4 here but was hoping they might know where to find one. In my exhaustion the language barrier proves too high a hurdle, but I'm able to thumb down to the option most likely to bring success. According to the guidebook, a motorbike is a pikipiki.

"Nataka kukodi pikipiki."

This brings a ho-hum response, even with a motorcycle parked up on its kickstand less than 15 feet away, helmet slung over the handlebars. But again, I'm too tired to push the issue.

The conversation now at an awkward standstill, I just sit, and try and cool off as the water slowly fills my dehydrated cells. Fear of death in the bush has subsided as I relax and recover and they just kind of carry on with whatever they were talking about before I arrived. After most of the 1.5-litre bottle is consumed, it's time for this surprisingly pleasant break in the shade to end. I have to get out of here. Standing up with renewed purpose, I point to the motorcycle and ask, in English, "Can I get a ride back to the last village? If not, I'll keep walking and find someone else."

Even though the words are probably not fully understood, the intention is, and this gets some action. The owner of the bike comes out from the gloomy interior of the small shop with an extra helmet. Now we're getting somewhere.

"How much?" I ask.

A shrug is the only response, so I offer 5,000 shillings. But no, no. That's not nearly enough.

"Okay then, 10,000."

"20."

"15,000."

Done deal, but I don't need the helmet, thanks. I've packed mine along, just in case.

It is worth noting here that I have not been on a motorcycle in over 30 years, and this might not be the best reintroduction – on the back of a motorbike of unknown provenance or maintenance schedule driven by a complete stranger in rural Africa on a bumpy dirt road at high speed while wearing a bicycle helmet. It's the kind of thing we travel writers reference under the heading *Ill Advised Choices Made in the Heat of the Moment.*

But, after the initial terror subsides, it becomes clear my driver has made this run many times before. He pins the throttle not out of any sense of urgency, but simply because that's how he rides. I expect to be bucked off and hang on for dear life at first, but the physics of the thing soon becomes clear. The balance and core stability needed to stay on a speeding motorcycle are similar to the balance and core stability needed for riding a bicycle. When we accelerate hard, I do feel the need to lean into the shift in momentum in order to avoid falling off the back, but at speed I find I don't actually need to hang on to anything, even over all but the biggest of bumps.

The ground that took a couple of hours to cover this morning is eaten up in under half an hour, and back at the junction I take some ribbing from a few of the locals who are still just hanging around the shops. They laugh and shout out, "Mzungu! Where is your bicycle, mzungu?"

I do not dignify the provocations with a response, and with the cell phone back in service I call Sylvain, who answers after two rings. Thank God.

"Hello."

"Hey, Sylvain. You know anyone with a 4×4 that wants to make a few bucks?"

"Where are you?"

"At the junction where the dirt road to the park starts."

"What happened?"

"It's a long story. I'll tell you when I see you. I need a truck to go get my bike."

"What? Go *get* your bike?"

"Like I said, long story. You know anyone?'

"I'll call you back."

After hanging up, I buy a Fanta Mango (so delicious, why is this not a thing in Canada!?) and sit to reassess the situation. On the plus side, I won't be sleeping out in the open near a mosquito-ridden swamp, but now that I'm physically safe I can't help but worry about my gear. I've hidden it well enough, but one of the features of this area is that people walk everywhere. Through the bush to get to their modest homes, or over to the nearest neighbours. To say nothing of the Maasai herders, moving their cattle and goats and sheep every which way across the landscape. I figure there's about an 80 per cent chance everything will be there once I find transportation, but Sylvain, after hearing the details of the situation, will set his odds at 50 per cent.

As I sit and wait, an older guy, whom I saw at this very spot this morning, comes ambling past with an outstretched palm. He is clearly down on his luck, but strangely doesn't seem to recognize me from earlier. I do give him some coins this time around, because I need all the karma I can get. I'm contemplating the gear recovery odds all over again when the phone rings.

"I'm coming to pick you up. Where are you exactly?"

I'm relieved beyond words. Not leaving my stuff out overnight pushes my assessment of its probable recovery to 90 per cent.

"Sitting in the shade on the left-hand side of the road. Right at the T-junction."

I'm tempted to say, *Big white guy. Red shirt. Hard to miss.* But that seems redundant.

Much like my pikipiki driver-for-hire, Sylvain also drives fast, and after he picks me up we rip along the dirt road with little regard for the uneven surface, hoping to skim over the tops of the potholes instead of pounding down into every single one. It turns out Sylvain is an interesting guy, of the sort that has not followed the well-worn or obvious path in life. In 1999 he went to Burundi to visit his father, who worked for the UN World Food Program. At 24, the experience sparked an interest in East Africa that he has found impossible to shake.

As we drive, he gives me some background on the area, and explains the challenges of doing business here, and what it's like being a white man living in Africa. I tell him the story of my day, and we laugh a lot, because it's funny when you go through something like this and don't die. When we get to the hiding place I tramp off through the mud while Sylvain awkwardly turns the SUV around, and much to my relief everything is still exactly where I left it.

Taking two trips to drag it all back up to the road is the last of what has become an extremely taxing day.

On the way back to Funky Squids we drive fast with the windows open and the music turned up loud. The sun is starting to get low now, and the heat has broken. We are slowed down in some of the muddier sections, but overall, we make good time. Arlette and Maya are going to be wondering where we are by now, and there's cold beer to be had after a tough day. As we get close to the junction with the paved road, we are brought up short by a couple of Maasai herding their cattle. The animals are blocking the dirt track and we are forced to wait them out.

It's an opportunity to reflect on the situation as a whole. A couple of hours ago I was freaking out. Walking along in unfamiliar surroundings with no clear vision of the end-of-day outcome, I'd begun to think maybe this place was conspiring to do me harm. In those nervous moments I was cast adrift in a version of hell on earth, with a fiery end a distinct possibility. Now, with the crisis averted, my perspective has shifted dramatically. The sun has begun its slow descent in the western sky and the light has gotten soft and warm, a welcome change from an afternoon that was harsh and unforgiving. As the cattle jostle for position and meander across the road with little regard for us as we wait to pass, I can't help but think, *Man, this place is so cool.* At times challenging, to be sure, but not cruel. If you know what you're doing, you can survive here.

Maybe, just maybe, I'll have to finally figure out what it is I'm doing before continuing on.

• • •

It's been one hell of a day. Coming up on 12 hours since I pedalled away from Bagamoyo with high expectations of a safari, and with the idea of resting my head farther up the coast firmly in mind, I'm right back where I started.

On the plus side, I like it here, a lot. The gentle ocean breeze is keeping the mosquitoes away, and the soft lighting throughout the well-kept grounds is the very definition of tropical paradise. Extra bonus: the beer is especially cold and refreshing after a hard, hot day. Sure, my journey hasn't exactly progressed, but I'm too tired to care much about that right now. Besides, there's no question today was an adventure at least, even if I didn't manage to get very far.

After a second beer I wander down to the ocean to wash away the mud and sweat and grime of the day. Night falls like an anvil in the tropics and it's already dark, but high above, the moon is three-quarters full and casts a pleasing glow, complete with full moon-dog. The tide is way out and I have to walk 150 metres off the beach to get knee deep. Turning to face the shore, I notice that a clutch of lights dot this edge of the continent, and the rhythmic singing and clapping coming from the arts college next door carries well across the water. Tipping myself over, I wallow in a lukewarm sea that is calm as glass. The water stings the various cuts and scrapes accumulated while wrestling my bike through the mud, but it's incredibly peaceful out here after such a hectic day in the bush.

I have to admit this pleasing tableau is not exactly what I had in mind when I was thinking about this trip. I never put any real consideration into the beach or the ocean. What I did think about a lot was a really big mountain surrounded by the savannahs and exotic animals from the nature documentaries of my youth. But it turns out this is also East Africa. Palm trees and sand beaches and powerful tropical downpours. Apart from the adobe-style mud, most of it has been a pleasant surprise. As I bob gently in the shallows of the ocean I can't help but wonder if the universe is conspiring to keep me here a little while longer, if only to allow a true appreciation of the steaming coast and all of its moods before finally heading inland.

There are worse places in the world to be stranded, that's for sure.

6

THE USAMBARA MOUNTAINS

There's galvanizing appreciation, and then there's beating a dead horse. Itching to get moving, I still find myself in Bagamoyo three days after the Saadani mud debacle. To be fair, it was always unlikely I would've been up for much on the day after returning to Funky Squids. Partly because I was physically beaten up after such a big effort, and partly because my plan to bike to Moshi, which was more like a rough outline anyway, has now blown up completely. My legs and lower back have not gone through that tough a workout in a long time, and psychologically I'm feeling quite fragile.

How do you write a book about adventure travel if you can't physically do the adventuring?

It didn't help that it rained that first day after coming back. Hard. Then it rained again the day after that, and then once again this morning. Sometime between six and nine a.m. a thunderous downpour is now the norm. The Saadani black cotton soil won't be passable by bike anytime soon, at least in the mornings. Page 18 of the Lonely Planet guide to East Africa defines the shoulder season for tourism in the region as September to February, a time when "short rains in October and November rarely interrupt travel." There is no mention of bicycling on dirt roads in Tanzania in December being factored into the equation.

The morning deluge aside, it is always hot and dry by one in the afternoon. As I walked away from my gear stashed in the bush a few days ago the sun came out and the heat quickly dried all but the muddiest sections of road. If I had hunkered down under that tree for an hour or two the slick, sticky mud would have firmed up and I could have ridden the final couple of kilometres to the park gate without much trouble. I mentioned this to Sylvain yesterday while he was working on his boat down near the water's edge.

"Sure," he said, with a measure of reason befitting a man who has lived in Africa for years, and has subsequently seen a few things, "but how could you know that at the time?"

True enough, but I know now, and it still doesn't help much. There's no accommodation near enough to the park gate to wait out the aftermath of the morning showers. Besides, doing any kind of exercise at all – let alone riding a fully loaded touring bike on a dirt road – between two and five p.m. would be punishingly hot work. That said, I'm starting to go stir crazy. I've got to get moving. But I don't want to ride the main inland road because of its reputation for reckless truck drivers and a minimal shoulder. With the original plan in tatters, it's time for a reboot. And fast, because I'm starting to freak out. My trip is getting away from me.

The Eastern Arc Mountains are the oldest range in East Africa, and after looking them up on Wikipedia I realize I've misunderstood them. On just about any map there is an obvious arc of mountains that runs from Mount Meru and Mount Kilimanjaro in the northwest, over to the East Usambaras near the coastal town of Tanga. The thing is, Meru and Kili are volcanic in origin, and not part of the chain. The proper orientation is from the Taita Hills over the border in Kenya, and down to the Udzungwa and Mahenge Mountains in south-central Tanzania.

Regardless of this technicality, the Usambaras are where I want to be. I need to get away from the coast, and if I can't ride there the best option is to take the bus. That's why I find myself standing in the rain at the roundabout just outside of town, hoping I can catch the correct bus to Lushoto, a small town in the heart of the Usambaras.

Here at the roundabout there isn't a proper bus station, just a collection of ramshackle wood and corrugated tin shacks selling tickets or tea and coffee and light snacks. There are a few tarps strung up to protect against the weather, but they are wholly inadequate for the number of people waiting to travel north. The morning downpour came early today and has settled into an intermittent drizzle, so I opt to stand out in the rain instead of cramming uncomfortably under a tarp and getting wet anyway because of the gusty breeze blowing raindrops every which way.

The bus route that links Dar es Salaam with the mountains to the north travels along the road I cycled up last week, before turning inland here at Bagamoyo to Msata. From there it heads north again through Korogwe and Mombo to the tourist towns of Moshi and Arusha. Most of the buses that come past have Arusha, and sometimes Moshi, posted in the front window, but I'm not entirely sure my bus will have Lushoto properly marked. The town is off the main road, 32 kilometres up in the mountains.

Standing in rainy uncertainty, I find the ticket seller on duty is not much help. I bought my ticket yesterday at the tourist information centre in town and was dropped off by tuk tuk this morning at seven, with an assurance I'd be notified when my bus comes past. But this guy is way too busy making deals and hustling seats on each bus that stops to pay me any mind. It's coming up to the busy Christmas season, and every bus that pulls up is chased down before it even comes to a complete halt by street vendors looking to sell pop or fruit or candy bars through the passenger windows, hopeful folks trying to secure a seat, and the ticket seller and his assistant trying to cram one more person aboard.

Adding to the chaos, private vehicles are also slowing down before entering the roundabout to pick up passengers if the right deal can be struck. The highway is narrow, and the gravel shoulder is a rough drop-off the edge of the pavement, so it's a miracle someone doesn't get run over. After stepping eagerly forward for a couple of buses that clearly aren't mine, I finally get a handle on what's going on and stand by my bags and watch. And wait.

In time the right bus comes along (with a Lushoto sign clearly visible in the window) and the ticket man gives me a nod through the crowd to confirm. I grab my backpack and step to the back of the bus where one of the driver's assistants has opened the rear luggage compartment. As I'm about to put the bag in, the bus lurches forward as two parked vehicles up ahead pull away. I'm momentarily startled by this and instinctively run along behind before throwing the heavy pack in and slamming the door shut, just as the bus comes to a complete stop for loading. I'm the only mzungu waiting for a ride today, and this little piece of theatre draws a laugh from the assembled crowd waiting for future buses. I can't help but wave and give a small bow. This brings another laugh.

Boarding the bus, I see there is not a seat to be had except the one right at the front to the left of the driver, seat

1A. In fact, there are even a couple of people standing in the aisle. Seeing as I only booked yesterday, I can't help but wonder who has been bumped to make the space available. I'm not entirely comfortable with this privileged tourist status, even though being at the front affords a view out the windshield of the road ahead, which is of great interest to me because I want to see first-hand what the conditions are like, and if I could have cycled this route or not.

The first 30 kilometres don't reveal much. We pass by the unoccupied storefronts where I waited out the worst of the rain a few days ago, and then the T-junction where the Saadani road veers off to the north. Beyond that, huge pineapple stands pop up at every little village along the route, and there are lots of random vehicle and motorbike inspections by local police. Sometimes we get stopped, and sometimes not, but the continuation of a wide shoulder and abundance of bicycles and pedestrians indicate this stretch would be doable at least.

Reaching the first junction will be telling. The thing is, I don't know if I could have faced cycling 65 kilometres to Msata, only to get turned around a second time.

Shifting my focus to the inside of the bus, I notice the onboard entertainment is decidedly youth oriented. Ray Vanny and Chumbo music videos get a lot of airtime on the small flat screen awkwardly mounted above the driver, but I've never heard of them before. The only recording artist on the playlist I do recognize is Nicki Minaj. The rest are all African pop stars as far as I can tell. At most villages a couple of vendors selling cashews and chocolate bars will jump on to ply their wares for a stop or two, before jumping off again to make a return trip on a different bus. And directly above the windshield is a large digital clock, with a dual thermometer. Right now, it's 27 degrees Celsius outside, and 29 degrees inside.

Turning north at Msata, the road does get sketchy for anything smaller than a motor coach. The shoulder is much narrower here, maybe a touch over two feet wide, and in places the drop away to the ditch is steep and unforgiving. In other spots, the roadside greenery encroaches onto the pavement, making the shoulder even narrower. To make matters worse, the width of the lanes appears designed for cars and minivans. The luxury buses and the transport trucks using this route are big, and I have to say, are driven with a somewhat cavalier approach. Staying in line on a hilly highway with heavy traffic in both directions is clearly an affront to the wannabe race car driver in each of these guys, judging by the way everyone drives.

I can see the speedometer from my seat, and sometimes while rolling along behind the big heavy transport trucks we are reduced to 20 kilometres an hour if we're climbing even the most minor of hills, but it's hard to pass because of the oncoming traffic. Other times it's a crazy free-for-all of oversized vehicles racing on the downslope of every rise. It's an insane bus and truck slalom replayed over and over again. Out on the flats a lack of real power keeps anyone from passing and tearing off into the distance. The irony is that every time we break 85 km/h, a loud alarm sounds inside the cab and the driver is forced to slow down. It's the recklessness of the driving that makes it feel like we're going way faster than we are.

While this needless jockeying is going on, brave locals walking the shoulder get blasted by the air being pushed forward by the bus. In addition to offering a clear view of the speedometer, clock/thermometer and road ahead, my seat location is in prime position to witness this terrifying show. Perched high, I can see directly down out the side window onto the narrow shoulder. Tailgating tight to a truck or bus, a tiny human form will suddenly flash into view. Sometimes we only miss them by a foot or two, and I cringe at the idea of what kind of sound it would make if there was a miscalculation. Once, a woman jumped rather acrobatically into the ditch to avoid being hit.

So for the first half of today's journey I have a *damn, I should have tried/no fucking way* argument going on in my head, one that flips back and forth between the two after every couple of kilometres. Where it's flat and open, no problem, I could have made it. On curves or in the narrow chutes where the roadbed is cut down through a section of rolling hill, well, that's another matter.

Spying the prominent sign for a lodge while passing through the town of Kabuku is yet another *well, maybe* moment. I saw a lodge advertised on a sign back in Msata as well. This is relevant because accommodation is a worry. Whether there will be appropriate places to stay along this route plays almost as heavily on my mind as the road's bad reputation. There have been no bicycles for long stretches, but some local cyclists do appear around the bigger towns, swaying my emotions even further. To the point where I actually begin to feel *guilty* about being so lazy. As if riding 400-plus kilometres through the hot Tanzanian interior was an easy thing to take on.

Just when I am beginning to think *this really would have been doable*, we pass the absolutely mangled remains of a large truck that got the worst of a head-on collision. The wreckage is a day or two old at most, and in between Msata and Korogwe we end up passing a total of four serious recent accidents. At one vehicle collision a crowd is gathered, offering assistance to occupants of the cars who are still inside. Witnessing that sends a chill down my spine. After finally settling down to the reality that this stretch of highway would have been extremely dangerous to ride on, or maybe even suicidal, the novelty of the overall experience begins to wear off. Now I'm just on a long bus ride. Fortunately, I kind of like long bus rides, and have used them before to help me settle down after a planned bike tour has gone astray. I've done it before in western Canada, and in Australia too.

Aristotle once said, "The man who is truly good and wise will bear with dignity whatever fortune sends, and will always make the best of his circumstances."

Worth a shot. And so, after a few hours in transit, I finally drift off into the pleasing, spacey hum of long-distance travel. This is a time for a wandering mind, and who am I to resist the opportunity to let go? It's a guilty pleasure and is one of my favourite states of being. Parking the ever-present battle between my id and my ego, I'm just out here in the world, observing without opinion or judgment. It allows my innate curiosity to come to the surface, unhindered by expectations or thoughts of right or wrong. I'm simply witnessing.

For example, as we motor along, the two driver's assistants randomly chuck their Red Bull cans and plastic water bottles out the window. It's discouraging, because litter is a big problem here, and this is a perfect example of why it is so. It seems strange to me because of my background, and the fact that for most of my lifetime anti-litter awareness programs have been the norm. The thing is, I'm not at home, so being somewhere where the idea has not taken hold is jarring.

Another curiosity is that the driver religiously obeys the 50 km/h speed limit at every small village and tiny settlement we come to, and yet drives like a bat out of hell the rest of the time. Sure, not-so-subtle speed bumps make racing through a village a challenging task, but still. Once, he answered his cell phone while passing a transport truck on a long bend with no clear view up the road ahead. Putting the memory of that mangled truck aside, I find it interesting that road safety is so randomly considered.

Turning my attention out the window, I see the low rolling hills spread out as far as the eye can see whenever we come to the top of any rise. Tanzania is a big country. Thirteenth biggest in Africa, and 30th largest in the world at 945,000 square kilometres. By comparison Germany is 62nd in the world at 357,000 square kilometres. The island nation of Barbados is 182nd at a miniscule 430 square kilometres. What is amazing about Tanzania is that 38 per cent of the land is protected, either as a national park, conservation area or game reserve.

As we roll along I am able to daydream about the animals that live in one of those protected areas. To the northwest of the Usambaras is Mount Kilimanjaro, and to the west of that is Serengeti National Park. The Serengeti is world-renowned and is home to 500 bird species and roughly 70 different large mammal species, including a healthy lion population. Eventually, I will make my way there, and the thought of it makes me happy as I daydream the miles away. I am suddenly quite pleased to be continuing with my adventure, even if it is by bus. Things may not be going exactly to plan, but I do still feel blessed. I do still have the opportunity to visit a part of the world not everyone will get the chance to see in their lifetime. I've gotten over myself, for now. I've forgiven myself for stashing my bike in Sylvain and Arlette's garage to try this quest in a different way, for now.

A step in that forgiveness is realizing that this is not the Nepal trip of two years ago. As I stare out the window at the Tanzanian countryside, that is obvious on the face of it. The red-tinted dust and termite mounds that are beginning to feature the farther north we get remind me of riding a Greyhound bus through the Australian outback three decades ago, not cycling up and down through the forests and past the small terraced farms of Nepal's Middle Hills. But there are more subtle differences too, which have been prowling around at the back of my mind trying to get out.

In the year and half prior to setting out for Kathmandu, I had two major surgical procedures that meant I couldn't walk properly for months at a time afterward as I struggled through recovery. One on my right hip, and then one on my left knee a year later. Part of my quest in Asia was to see if I could still get out there and travel across the landscape under my own power. The itinerary was loose, I could take all the time I wanted, but the route was deliberate. Kathmandu to Jiri by bicycle through the towns of Dhulikhel, Lamosangu and Charikot. Then on foot from there up into the Khumbu Valley, and eventually to Everest Base Camp.

When it came time to go again this year, I thought I wanted to replicate that deliberate, if admittedly unhurried, intent without realizing I'm different now. My motivation is different. What I want from this adventure is proving different. I'm not recovering from a series of debilitating injuries anymore. Apart from being middle-aged and out of shape, I'm physically fine. As it turns out, I'm more curious and restless, not so much driven. Replicating a straight-line journey from Point A – the Indian Ocean at Dar es Salaam – to Point B – the summit of Mount

Kilimanjaro (one of the Seven Summits and the highest point in Africa) – is not resonating in the way I had hoped it would. I have not been able to rally the motivation to battle the black cotton soil a second time, endure the stifling heat, or brave the dangers of this main road. I wonder, will that be okay with me in the end?

Beyond Korogwe, the landscape levels out to a degree, and the road suddenly looks much more accommodating. An extra foot of shoulder, and somehow, less traffic. The transformation gets me to thinking about my choices all over again. Mapping it out in my mind, I figure day one to Msata would have been long and boring. Days two, three and four would have been insanely dangerous, but day five would have been *awesome*. The Usambaras are now coming into view to the right as the road veers to the northwest to avoid the massive natural impediment they represent. The range is roughly 90 kilometres long and about half as wide, and is cleaved into an east and a west by a four kilometre wide valley dividing the two.

As the surrounding landscape slowly dried up and transformed into open savannah, these highlands continued to receive enough rainfall to keep their tropical forests intact. With no widespread glaciation this close to the equator at any point in the earth's recent history, the local flora and fauna has had an uninterrupted run of evolution. There's an unusual number of endemic species here, and the area is considered to be ecologically significant because of its biodiversity by those whose job it is to determine such things.

From below the scruffy hills rise tentatively above the surrounding plains, but after a while the hills begin to become more abrupt, and then a few cliff faces emerge, giving the range an air of significance. At Mombo, as our bus leaves the main highway and turns up into the mountains, the temperature peaks. It's *only* 33 degrees Celsius outside but is a positively suffocating 36 degrees inside. Remember what I said about loving long bus rides? Well, I can safely say I'm over it for today. I'm soooo over it.

Suddenly, Lushoto cannot come soon enough.

• • •

The bus park in Lushoto is in the heart of town, right across from the central market, and after a solid six hours in transit it's nice to finally get off the coach. Unfortunately, it's raining again. It's not a hard rain, but after being cooped up for most of the day I'm hungry and am beginning to get cranky as a result. Getting wet is not helping the situation much.

Lushoto is a town of about 30,000 people tucked high in the Usambaras, and much to my surprise the bus park is a madhouse. There are regional buses coming in and going out to and from Dar, Moshi and Arusha, as well as local buses that service the surrounding mountain villages, all vying for space that simply doesn't exist. There's barely room to unload the luggage, and I have to be careful not to get clipped by a local bus trying to navigate through the largely unmoving mass of glass and metal that has clogged up this central square. After executing the pointless yet satisfying act of slapping the side of the vehicle, I don't get ten feet before a young man approaches me and asks if I have a place to stay.

Probably not the best time to be bothering me.

I brush him off by telling him I just need to get out of the rain, but he follows me to a takeaway shop overlooking the bus park. After buying a Coke, I sit down on my backpack to survey the scene, and my new friend tries once again to launch into his pitch.

"Please," I say with a mixture of agitation and exasperation, "I just need to relax for a minute and get my bearings."

He nods and joins me in simply looking out over the mayhem playing out in the square. I expect him to walk away at this point, but he doesn't, and after finishing my Coke I turn to him and say, "Okay, let's hear it."

Ngoda works for TAYODEA, the Tanga Youth Development Association. The group offers half day, full day and multi-day walking tours to points of interest in the area, including the Magamba rainforest and Mkuzi Waterfall hikes. Ngoda speaks fluent English and has a ready smile, but it's his full-on Rastafarian personal stylings that lead me to believe he'd be an interesting guy to walk with if it comes to that. I am looking for something more than a day trip, and have read about Mtae as a must see destination in the Usambaras, but I'm not inclined to agree to a multi-day outing with a complete stranger based on first impressions alone. A recommendation for a decent guest house is much appreciated, though.

Walking through a space between the shop and an adjacent building, we get onto a small footpath and come quickly to an open field bordered by a small, stagnant creek, where buses that are off duty until tomorrow's schedules are parked. There are a couple of maintenance bays, and a rough at the edges roadhouse type bar that looks more like a barn than anything else. Out front, some upcoming English Premier League games to be shown on TV are advertised on a chalkboard nailed to a power pole. Brighton vs. Arsenal, Liverpool vs. Newcastle and Man United vs. Heddesfild. I'm assuming that last club is actually Huddersfield Town, but if some crazy upheaval has gone on in the league since I've been off grid then I'm sure Heddesfild is thrilled to have been promoted to the high-profile top flight. I only hope they are ready to field a team.

After a five-minute walk from "downtown" we come to Cast Away Lodge, a single-storey guest house with a handful of rooms. The setup is fairly basic, a common room with a TV and a couple of couches, with a lone dining room table in the middle where the complimentary breakfast is served. The rooms are at the back, and by the look of things the enterprise is a new addition to the local accommodation selections. A big bonus is that the price is right. Twenty-five thousand shillings (about 15 bucks Canadian) a night might even help me get back on some kind of budget.

Making my way downtown the next morning after breakfast, I bump into Ngoda outside the TAYODEA office and we easily fall into a casual conversation. He is the only person I know in town, after all, and it couldn't hurt to listen in on a brief presentation about things to do in the Usambaras. The bike ride foiled by circumstance and a lack of preparation, I still have hopes of climbing Kilimanjaro. If I don't get some hard walking in first I won't stand a chance on the mountain.

I follow Ngoda up to the small office, and he launches into a relaxed description of various tours and outings on offer, while pointing out highlights on a hand-painted map with a bamboo stick. Ngoda's demeanour puts me at ease. There's no high-pressure sales tactics being used here, which I appreciate. I've already decided on a walk out to Irente Viewpoint later today, but decline the offer of guiding services, thank you. The thing is, walking to Mtae is a bigger commitment. What Ngoda is suggesting in that case is for US$60 a day I would get a guide, park fees, accommodation and food all included. Route finding would be removed from the equation, and places to stay are predetermined. It all sounds reasonable, but my first thought is it's December 23, and the Christmas season can be disruptive to day-to-day schedules in most places where the holiday is observed. Christianity is the dominant religion in the region.

"When would we be able to go? Boxing Day?"

"We can leave tomorrow," Ngoda says without hesitation.

"Tomorrow?"

"Yes. I will take you."

"You'll be my guide?"

"Yes."

Well, that would remove the awkward getting to know you phase at least. Ngoda seems legit. The office seems legit. After a moment's contemplation, I book it and we hash out the finer details.

After leaving the TAYODEA office I'm riding a new high. There's a new plan and a new purpose. The disappointment of the failed bike ride can quickly be put behind as I begin preparing for this new challenge. Irente Viewpoint is the beginning of that preparation. Walking purposefully along a dirt alleyway 50 metres up from the office, I quickly come to a paved road that leads over a ridge above town. At the first junction the pavement ends and I'm able to stop and catch my breath, under the guise of not being sure what fork in the road to take. There are a large number of open-air motorcycle repair shops doing brisk business, and small shacks selling pop and bottled water, but no clear signage pointing the way.

Sensing my indecision, a man of about 50 catches my eye from across the road and points down one of the five available options. I give a wave of thanks, and he shoots me an enthusiastic thumbs-up.

As it happens, these highlands are a collection of forested valleys cut with big swaths of farmland divided into small and medium-sized plots. Dropping down from the ridge, the well-maintained dirt road descends to a wetlands area inside the Irente Biodiversity Reserve. Along the way I pass a few farms and a couple of schools before reaching a small village near the viewpoint. Taking the locals route to avoid passing through the grounds of the Irente View Cliff Lodge, I happen upon an old man in a pinstripe suit jacket herding his four goats along the narrow trail. As I step aside to let the five of them pass, the view takes over my attention. From here, as I look roughly northwest along the edge of the range, the Tsavo Plains stretch out in the hazy mid-distance, and in the foreground the mountains I'm standing on rise up from the lowlands below. The grade is steep, and in places the land breaks out of the cover of scrub grasses and small trees to expose bare rock and towering cliff faces. It's a beautiful vista.

A couple of hundred metres farther up the trail the view is even more dramatic. Out over the edge of the bare rock perched at the top of a cliff, the plains below spread out from the northwest all the way around to the southeast. The hard stone is covered with the names of previous visitors painted in yellow and red and blue, and the main highway leading to Moshi is a clear ribbon across the landscape, with a cluster of homes and businesses interrupting its path every five to ten kilometres.

Farther out, the horizon is dotted with random hillocks and small mountains poking out against the sweeping flatlands as they desperately vie for attention against a smothering haze. Only one of these minor eminences comes anywhere close to being as high as this viewpoint, and all across the plains high puffy clouds cast dark blotchy shadows on the ground below. I am disappointed by the haze, as it mutes the hard edges of what is already a pretty dramatic scene. One that would only be more so if the skies were clear, but I am in the wrong season for that opportunity. Late June to October brings drier, clearer air.

I'll have to put that in the mental Rolodex in the event I return to this part of the world at some point in the future.

Another thing that comes to mind, as I relax in the shade near the edge of the cliff before returning to town, is how positively unfussed the day has been. It's the weekend, Sunday to be exact, and two days before Christmas, yet I've had this walk all to myself. In the Activities section for the Usambaras, my guidebook offers a warning that did give me pause this morning. While the walking is generally easy going according to reports, "a spate of robberies of solo hikers, mostly en route to Irente Viewpoint, means that for all routes hiking with a guide is recommended."

I've interacted with a couple of locals along the way, and there is one other westerner here now with his guide, but apart from that, nothing. No tour groups, no solo hikers, no bandits. Nothing.

Returning from the viewpoint is as simple as retracing my steps, but it's also an important fitness exercise in preparation for whatever comes next, and so I approach it with a certain enthusiasm instead of begrudging the slog. Breathlessly regaining the ridge above town, I find I already like Lushoto, even though I've only been here for a day. The surroundings are lush and green, and the town itself is a little bit scrappy without having the sensation of being intimidating or dangerous. I believe you would call it character. This place has an underlying character I connect with. It's rough and tumble with a little can-do pluckiness, and one of my favourite details is that the temperature only ever tops out at about 27 or 28 degrees Celsius, which is far more pleasant than the 32 to 35 degrees I've been dealing with since arriving in Tanzania. I cannot adequately express how much more pleasant that is for someone who does not enjoy the heat. I also do get a laugh out of the wandering Maasai vendors selling attractive handcrafted sandals skewered on long sticks for easy carrying, who themselves are wearing the standard issue chopped-up-motorcycle-tire-tied-on-with-string version of the casual footwear.

And the kids up here are eager in their smiles, as if they are more accustomed to foreign visitors than the village kids between Dar and Bagamoyo, who only see white people pass by in buses or cars. As I was leaving the guest house this morning, a young boy of maybe 4 was walking with his father. When I caught his eye, he shot me a mischievous grin and quietly said "mzungu," as if he was only letting me in on this little secret if I promised not to tell.

Back at Cast Away after 18 kilometres of wandering around downtown and then out to Irente and back, lying down for a late afternoon nap to the sounds of the neighbourhood kids playing outside is glorious, and I wonder if my little friend is out there among them.

7

CHRISTMAS AT THE CONVENT

Africafe instant coffee is turning into my guilty pleasure. After oil, coffee is the most heavily traded commodity in the world, and the top five exporting countries in Africa moved a staggering 877,980 metric tons of Arabica and Robusta beans in 2018, according to Wikipedia. There are also an amazing number of options available locally for the discerning palate, as each region boasts a unique flavour profile. Ethiopian coffee in particular is world renowned, and Africa.com lists Tanzanian Peaberry Coffee as its Number 1 brand on a recent Top 10 list.

Despite all of this, Africafe instant is still my favourite, go figure. I'm also quite fond of Zesta brand red plum jam, which comes in an old-fashioned tin, not a glass jar. I'm especially fond of it when I get to slather it on fresh, thick cut brown bread like I've been served this morning with my Spanish omelet. Sometimes in life, it's the little things.

Going down to meet Ngoda at the TOYODEA office before setting out, I'm a bit nervous, but also cautiously excited. I'm finding this to be a common reaction to having no bloody idea what to expect over the coming days. The village of Mtae sits on a cliff top at the far western edge of the Usambara mountains and is 55 kilometres from Lushoto. In the TOYODEA brochure it says this hike can be done in three to six days. I've paid for three, so it looks like we'll be hoofing it.

As it happens, the Magamba Nature Forest Reserve is on the outskirts of Lushoto and is our first stop en route. After working our way uphill along a mix of paved roads, dirt roads and single-track shortcuts bisecting small farm plots and homesteads, we enter the forest. This protected land is virgin rainforest, and I've been amazed at how lush the town itself is. Banana trees, with their enormous arching leaves, share space with all manner of tree, great and small, and flat spots on the valley bottom inevitably support healthy-looking garden plots that almost without fail look ready for harvest.

By comparison this reserve is real jungle. A tangled mess of greenery complete with thick underbrush, hanging vines and giant soaring trees reaching up 100 feet at least. While the developed area around town is impressively fecund, this is next level. Unfortunately, there's not a lot of this pristine forest left. The overall Usambara environmental degradation follows a pattern that has been repeated over and over again all over the globe in one form or another during the century and a half since the end of the First Industrial Revolution.

Seventy per cent of the virgin timber in these mountains is gone. A small percentage has been used up by a rapidly growing local population to build homes, cook and keep warm in the cool of the highland evenings, which is understandable. Habitat pressure and population growth go hand in hand, but more damaging to the greater health of the landscape is the extraction of resources by outside interests. Most of the big trees here have not been logged by locals for community benefit. They have been removed by companies, with profit in mind. The majority of the raw materials and financial benefit has been shipped away to markets with little interest or understanding of the impact these activities have on the people of the Usambaras.

On April 17, 2013, grist.org published an article titled "None of the world's top industries would be profitable if they paid for the natural capital they use."

The gist of the Grist piece is that externalities are "the costs imposed by businesses that are not paid for by those businesses." The author, David Roberts, goes on to explain that "industrial processes can put pollutants in the air that increase public health costs, but the public, not the polluting businesses, picks up the tab. In this way, businesses privatize profits and publicize costs."

A link in the article references a report done by the environmental consultancy Trucost, focusing on the top 100 externalities in business. The 81-page report is far too detailed to examine in depth here, but this concept is easy enough to extract from the article and report: "Unpriced natural capital" refers to the process of using up the "ecological materials and services" without adequate compensation. These resources are consumed by the "top industrial sectors" in a way that is disproportionally beneficial. The current accepted process overlooks the fact that the individual businesses involved are not required to pay a commensurate fee for the opportunity to plunder the land.

Clean water and a stable atmosphere are naturally occurring, but it appears that if you are in the right avenues of commerce in the 21st century you can still take advantage of available loopholes and ignore any responsibility for the true costs of using the land, effectively exploiting the resources without repercussion. Abandoned oil well sites awaiting reclamation that is unlikely to happen anytime soon in my home province of Alberta come immediately to mind.

Broadly speaking, Roberts lays it out this way: "The majority of unpriced natural capital costs are from greenhouse gas emissions (38%), followed by water use (25%), land use (24%), air pollution (7%), land and water pollution (5%), and waste (1%)."

This regional landscape is not nearly vast enough to warrant the attention on a global scale that deforestation in the Amazon gets in the land use category, but the effects *are* palpable locally. When lumber is looked at as a commodity, the responsible management of it, as with any other natural resource, takes a back seat to the intoxicating allure of making money. Cash crops, like tea, are also increasing land use pressures in the area, and the way the equation goes in most cases is that shareholder value outweighs local interest and environmental concerns every time.

But things are not all doom and gloom here in these mountains. Growing conditions are favourable, so new forest can spring up comparatively quickly, and the untrained eye would have a difficult time identifying the scope of degradation of the original habitat here. At first glance, it is very, very green everywhere. Restoration efforts are also in full swing, as 8billiontrees.com reports a newly established and favourable partnership with the Lushoto-based Friends of Usambara Society, whose nurseries just off the main road through town prepare seedlings for their final planting destination somewhere in the range. This is good news.

Turning my attention back from the trees to the walk itself, I find it is not overly difficult, but is not exactly easy going either. The trail through the woods is exceedingly narrow at times and a bit muddy in places, but Ngoda is adept at setting a reasonable pace for my fitness and ambition levels, which he easily reads and adjusts to. Since I was hoping to avoid overheating today, I've chosen to wear shorts, which might have been a tactical error given the number of times I've been scratched by the encroaching underbrush. I can only hope none of these plants are poisonous.

As we walk, Ngoda and I have also gotten to know each other a little bit more. This situation is bound to be awkward, as we've only just met and now we're going to spend three days together, but we've been working on some of the nomenclature necessary for people from vastly diverse backgrounds to bond. *Poa, poa* means good, good in Swahili, and Ngoda often frames it as a question to see how I'm doing, while *polepole* means slowly, which is a wise approach to take when embarking on a long walk through the mountains, especially on the uphill bits.

Coming after a time to Kigulu Hakwewa Peak, we step out of the forest cover into a natural clearing that leads to the top. There are sparse grasses and low bushes and the trail here is a distinctive red-coloured gravel. We've gone from roughly 1300 metres to 1840 metres in a couple of hours. Seventeen hundred vertical feet (540 metres) is a decent enough start to our journey, and, make no mistake, I'm ready to drop my pack and take a rest before continuing on.

I move over to a simple bench by the trail, and the view is impressive. To the northeast the small valley just below is part of the reserve and is jam-packed with towering tree tops. One valley over, the second and third generation of growth is somewhat patchier but is still more forest than field. Almost directly south, in the direction of Irente Viewpoint, the edge of this range appears especially dramatic. We are above the ever-present haze of the plains and many of the puffy cumulus clouds as well. The contrast of the green foreground against the background of white below accentuates the precipitous drop just beyond the edge. The widest view from here is directly down into Lushoto. The valley is broad with a couple of minor ridges running through and is dotted with homes and businesses and small farms. There is minimal haze in this direction, and after two hours of solid work I swear I can still pick out the roof of my guest house, which is not exactly encouraging if the plan is to get to Mtae in three days.

After escaping the narrow trails of the eastern portion of the reserve, walking down an old dirt road on the far side of the mountain is much easier going, and we begin to make good time. After our nine a.m. start this morning, we break for lunch at the 12-kilometre mark somewhere around 12:45 p.m. Because we booked this outing on the fly I wasn't entirely sure what we would be doing for lunch, but assumed we would pop into a local restaurant along the way. Instead it's a picnic lunch in a field just to the far side of a small village. The surrounding hills are now high above us, and we will spend much of the rest of the walk passing through sections of forest that are separated by small farms and traditional villages.

Looking around, I know one thing is certain, I would have had a hard time finding the route. There is no signage, and most of the intersecting trails look essentially the same. Without a GPS, it would be difficult to choose one over another. A nice touch to the morning is that Ngoda has been good at pointing out different plant and tree species in what to the uninitiated is simply a huge swath of green. At one point on the way up to Kigulu Peak, we stopped at the base of a huge tree set at the side of the trail for a water break. He knocked a small piece of bark off the trunk with a rock and handed it to me. The scent of camphor was pleasant and powerful. I had no idea camphor came from a tree, and I've tucked a small piece of the bark into my pocket, where it will hold its scent for days.

Lunch today is fresh vegetables chopped into guacamole that Ngoda mashes up on the spot from incredible, oversized avocados. The mixture is tucked into soft chapatis, and a boiled egg and a samosa round out the main course. Dessert is fruit, of course. The oranges are, "eh, whatever," but the mangos!!! Oh, my goodness, the mangos positively explode with flavour in a way I never knew fruit could do. They're so tasty I'm now ruined. Mangos and avocados are two foods I will never be able to eat back home again because it just won't be the same.

As we first sat down, I wasn't sure a picnic lunch would be enough to refuel after the morning's effort, but it has turned out to be a basic yet satisfying midday meal. Sometimes I forget that simple food is simply soooo good after a long walk.

After lunch I want to help clean up, but Ngoda insists I relax before we set out again. I'm feeling energized after a rigorous morning but can't find the will to argue. As he finishes up the dishes and repacks his bag, I lie back in the grass for a moment to stare up at the fluffy white clouds drifting slowly across the sky. In this moment all I can think is that life is good. Life is beautiful and good.

As if on cue, Ngoda asks, "poa, poa?"

"Everything is poa, my friend," is my contented reply. "Everything is poa."

• • •

Christmas day dawns with a morning fog, which should come as no surprise. This is an equatorial mountain ecosystem after all. While it's not technically a cloud forest, some of the same principles apply. Significantly more rain falls here than in the nearby lowlands, for instance, and it is not unusual for damp clouds to sweep over these hills, as is happening at this very moment. Standing over by a new building going up at this homestay with my coffee, I've found the only spot where a break in the trees and the clouds offers a view down into the valley. Native birdsong is accompanied by the sounds of roosters and cows coming from the farms below. It is all very soothing, and there's not a whisper of mechanical intrusion of any kind. No bus horns, no train whistles, no car engines revving. It's all quite lovely.

There is also no denying the homestay itself has a certain homey charm. It feels a bit like being at the cottage as a kid. This place is basic and rustic, but the simple allure did push my limits upon arrival. After another six or seven kilometres on foot yesterday afternoon – broken up in the middle by ten kilometres of bouncing along a dirt road in an overcrowded local bus – the shower that amounted to splashing water on myself from a bucket, and the hard, cold cement floor of my room all left something to be desired.

After a good night's sleep, however, the minor deficiencies in the experience are easily forgotten. The owner, Emanuel, is gracious and friendly, and there's always tea or coffee on offer, which I take him up on often. Sharing that tea and coffee this morning is a family group out trekking with their guide Ali, whom Ngoda is friendly with. Nelson is from the American Midwest and works in Dar es Salaam with an international aid organization. Along with his wife Judith, he is on an adventurous Christmas vacation with sons Max, Avery and Zayk. Dani, Avery's girlfriend, has also joined them. We had not bumped into them on the trail because they have chosen the four-day walk to Mtae, and they covered the ground we skipped over yesterday afternoon by bus on foot.

Much like Ngoda, Ali is easygoing and friendly without coming off as too eager to please, which helps me get a bit more comfortable with the whole guiding concept. My reluctance to rely on a guide is twofold. My preferred style of travel plays a part, as does my suspicious nature.

Having covered a lot of miles across parts of five continents over the years, I have figured out how I best interact with the world. I'm slow, both physically across the landscape and in the way I process and interpret new information, and so signing up with a guiding outfit makes it difficult to set my own itinerary as the journey develops. I have never been a fan of the forced march approach to exploring an unknown landscape, and do enjoy stumbling across a new favourite location, like Bagamoyo, or Namche Bazaar in Nepal, for instance, where a combination of circumstance and deliberate "un-planning" allows enough time to get a real sense of a place.

This causes no small amount of anxiety, of course, because I inevitably feel I should be doing more, trying harder and covering more ground, but the reality is I never enjoy the experience as much that way. Professor Cahill's Travel 101's Rule 5 does help explain my preference in approach: "Boredom greases the cogs in the machinery of marvels." So true, and yet I constantly need to be reminded of this. Thanks, Tim.

The other reason I hesitate is that I'm naturally wary of people's motivations. Don't get me wrong, I celebrate the resplendent majesty of the human spirit every chance I get. That's where good art and music and writing comes from. But we humans are also venal and selfish and opportunistic, and I am reminded of a detail from the conversation with Sylvain, Arlette, Niels and June at Funky Squids a week or so ago. We were talking broadly about traditional African belief systems and attitudes about family and community, and it was brought up that if a local African from a small town does become affluent through hard work, good fortune or any combination of factors that befall individuals entering the workforce, then they immediately begin thinking like westerners, with money never far from mind.

I don't have enough experience here in Africa to speak to that directly, but do have a cautionary tale from Nepal about the pursuit of wealth, and what it can do to you. On August 21, 2018, the UK's *Daily Mail* published an article about a helicopter rescue scam being run in the Himalaya. The gist of the story is that trekkers are coming under increasing pressure from guides to agree to helicopter evacuations for comparatively minor ailments. The "rescues" are then charged to the insurance companies and everybody involved takes a cut – the guides, the guiding company, the helicopter company and the health care professionals who sign off on the diagnosis.

Make no mistake, acute mountain sickness is serious, and sometimes even fatal for hikers in search of nothing more than a challenging walk. Even those with no intention of scaling the high peaks in Nepal can get themselves into trouble. Insurance is a good idea on the face of it, but the key sentence in the story that relates to my distrust of humans in general, and guides in this particular circumstance, is this. An investigation into the scam "found evidence of guides putting baking soda, which acts as a laxative, in food to give tourists diarrhea and then pressuring them to be airlifted."

Not cool.

On the other hand, Paul Theroux, in *Ghost Train to the Eastern Star,* wrote, "Most travel, and certainly the rewarding kind, involves depending on the kindness of strangers, putting yourself into the hands of people you don't know and trusting them with your life."

To travel is to risk, it seems, no matter how you go about it.

Setting out from the homestay before the Americans, Ngoda and I quickly drop down into the valley before beginning the long, slow climb toward a break in the ridge on the far side. Ngoda is 32 years old and is one of nine guides who work out of the TOYODEA office, and I do admit I'm not worried about the decision to hire him anymore. He strikes me as a genuinely nice person. He also appears to have a good sense of humour, but never does quite catch on to my Canadian sarcasm.

"Steep is finished," he says whenever we reach the end of a stretch of uphill walking.

"Sure it is," is always my reply, with an emphasis on the word *sure.* I remain keenly aware that when walking through the mountains steep is never a distant prospect.

"It's not far now," is a common early afternoon Ngoda lie.

"Sure it's not."

Ngoda laughs a lot, but never at my dry and curt quips. It could be I'm just not that funny.

We stop in a dusty village for water, and 14 local kids gather around as we sit on a mound of dirt at the side of the trail near an important junction. The kids are curious, but also shy and skittish. Despite this being a major hike in the region, I get the impression not a huge number of westerners have caught on to this route, and there are no tourist facilities in this village. There are a variety of languages spoken in these small mountain communities, and Ngoda speaks to them in their native dialect, but that doesn't immediately allay their suspicions.

Eventually, though, their curiosity does get the better of them as I scribble away in my notebook. As they get used to the big white guy with the pen, a few of them shuffle in quite close. The game becomes *I dare you to sit right next to him*, and a couple of the brave ones do, only to scooch away nervously if I turn toward them. If I stay eyes forward, no problem. If I make any move at all, it's *danger, danger!* The game is good for nervous laughs all around. As it happens, this village is largely Muslim, and in the local language Ngoda's name means stick, which is also endlessly hilarious to the kids.

As we get ready to continue, the Americans catch us up, and I have to mention one member of the party that I've neglected. Uncle is a big chocolate lab type dog, and although he's friendly enough, I would not describe him as calm. A stray leaf blowing on the wind or stone kicked down the trail and Uncle kind of loses his mind in a fit of spastic activity. This is disconcerting for the children. Much like in Dar, dogs do not feature here, and Uncle's sudden appearance sends the kids scattering even though he is essentially harmless, and on leash.

•••

Taking the last tired steps of the day before I'm able to forget about carrying my pack again until morning, I make my way up the driveway past a couple of vehicles parked under an open air carport that protects them from the sun. One of the vehicles has a magnetic decal on the door, that I will promptly forget the exact wording to because I'm trail weary and unmotivated to stop and make a note of it. My focus is on dumping the pack as fast as humanly possible and maybe having a shower. Rangwi Sisters Guesthouse, or maybe its Rangwi Sisters Convent. Wait, Rangwi Sisters Convent and Guesthouse. Whatever the choice of words on the decal, the Rangwi Sisters are an order of approximately 55 nuns who also happen to put up tired hikers for the night. With me identifying as agnostic with a lean toward Buddhism, a convent is perhaps the last place on earth I ever expected to be on Christmas day, but there you have it.

Even though I did not grow up in a religious household, Christmas was a *big* deal. It wasn't the presents or the tree or the carols or the feast that I remember most. It wasn't any one thing, it was everything. Looking back, it was all about family, and we would often do more than one big celebration. One at our house, and one at an aunt and uncle's or grandparent's place. No matter how the logistics worked out, there were always lots of people around, and anything less than a dozen for dinner was a low turnout.

After I moved out west and away from most of my family, I was always working in the restaurant business over the busy holiday season and enjoyed – no, check that, desperately looked forward to – the peace and quiet of a full day off, away from people. Christmas day was spent revelling in doing not much of anything. Once, while living in Calgary, my brother Jesse and I had spaghetti and watched old movies on TV, and it was great. Today I'm just happy to have a place to sleep and the chance of a simple meal.

Back in Canmore there is not much open on Christmas day, so I am mildly concerned about the dinner prospects.

My room at the convent is spartan, but clean and spacious, and the shower room down the hall is something I would imagine from a prison block in the 1960s. However, one of the nuns does bring me a bucket of piping hot water to offset the cold shower. After drying off and squaring away my gear, I head back up to the main building, where Ngoda is sitting on the steps waiting for me. Before I can inquire about dinner, he asks if I'd be interested in a Christmas drink.

Would I? That sounds like a fantastic idea. In the absence of television and internet, happy hour is a welcome distraction in the long hours of late afternoon, and Ngoda, Ali and I wander over to the village with hopes of tipping a glass in honour of the baby Jesus on his big day.

I've been in some interesting bars in my time, and I can safely say the local pub in Rangwi is an experience not to be missed. Located down a narrow footpath between buildings off the dusty main street, it's dark and gloomy with music playing at excessive volume from oversized speakers. The pub appears to be men only apart from the waitress, and I must admit, I wouldn't feel quite as comfortable without my travelling companions. It hasn't happened often on this trip, but I'm ever so slightly uneasy. The dozen or so fellow drinkers present are not menacing, exactly, but are also not as friendly to the foreign intruder as so many have been before.

The décor, however, more than makes up for the less than warm reception. It is an eclectic mix of dive bar posters plastered on every wall and is punctuated by a colony of wasps who have built tiny nests on the ceiling. Popular beer and gin brands share space with Kate and Leo from Titanic and the Tanzanian National Football Team and, curiously, a surprisingly detailed account of the rise and fall of Saddam Hussein. What that has to do with Tanzania, I'll never know.

Hovering above it all the resident wasps don't seem to concern anyone but me. Remarking on this unusual detail, Ngoda explains that one day the wasps moved in, built their cluster of small nests, and because they don't bother anyone they have become a fixture. A collection of tiny mascots thought to bring luck. Fair enough. They never do fly lower than a foot from the ceiling, and come in and out of the room through a huge crack in the ill-fitting door to the pub.

As I watch the wasps, the three of us engage in some idle chit-chat, and Ngoda surreptitiously checks his phone under the table. He checks his phone often while we're on breaks out on the trail, and especially at the end of the day when the walking is done. At first, I thought he was simply part of that younger generation who are constantly attached to their devices, but over our Christmas drink it comes to light that Ngoda has a young son at home and is checking in with his partner to see how things are going. This revelation brings with it a tinge of guilt for keeping him from his family today.

Back at the convent I take up a spot on the steps outside the guest dining room to enjoy the coming twilight. Whereas the bar patrons were aloof, the nuns are intent on taking hospitality to the next level, although it does take some time to figure out what the heck is going on. All I was hoping for was something – anything – to eat, but this is the Lord's Day, and kindness toward strangers is a concept the Rangwi Sisters take seriously. Ngoda is unsure when exactly dinner will be, but I'm assured something special is being prepared.

After the sun sets, a clear starry sky emerges above, and frogs come alive with song in the pond next to the chapel. Ngoda checks once again on the prospects of dinner, and comes back with a surprising update: we've been invited to eat with the nuns. I try to be nonchalant about it, as if breaking bread with a group of nuns on Christmas is an everyday occurrence.

"Okay, that's cool, but when *is* dinner?"

He shrugs.

"But you can get a beer if you want," Ngoda mentions as consolation.

"What?"

"Yes."

"The nuns sell beer?"

"Modern nuns," Ali points out helpfully.

Moving inside to avoid the mosquitoes, beer and notebook in hand, I am now perfectly comfortable waiting a bit longer for dinner. The guest dining room is a simple affair, a large communal table, lots of windows, and crosses and pictures of past Popes up on every wall. The Americans are playing cards and invite me to join, but I'm content in the worn old armchair by the door, thanks.

Toward the kitchen, hustling junior nuns are coming and going every few minutes, collecting pots and pans and plates and cutlery and serving dishes from the cupboards in the wide hallway. It all seems impossibly industrious. Then finally, it's dinnertime, and we're all led up the exterior stone stairway to a separate building. Entering the large but simply appointed banquet room, I could never have imagined what was awaiting us, but the scene does help clarify the hustling and bustling in search of plates and serving bowls from earlier.

The long rectangular room is positively buzzing with energy. The senior nuns in light blue habits are gathered on a collection of chairs along the back and left-hand walls, and my highly trained eye spots the contents of a box of red wine being poured into plastic cups. On the right, five rows of folding chairs five chairs wide are set up and are filled with junior nuns in white habits, who are facing the front of the room. The central area is clear, but at the very front of the room an elaborate banquet table has been set up, where the monsignor, the mother superior and a pastor from another nearby church are sitting waiting for us. Turns out we haven't simply been invited to dinner; we are among the guests of honour.

How on earth did this happen?

I'm a writer, and thus lean on the enhancement of details in order to create a compelling scene designed to elicit an emotional response, and thereby generate an interest in the reader strong enough to compel them to continue on with the story. If I can get you to turn the page, I've done my job. Occasionally, while in search of experiences worth writing about, a set of circumstances comes up that needs no embellishment. We're there. The head table is set for 12, a common number from the Christmas dinners of my youth. In addition to the aforementioned clergy, there is space for myself, Ngoda and Ali, and the six members of the American party. Already laid out are ten silver restaurant-quality insulated serving dishes with ladles balanced on the lids, in addition to half a dozen large bowls with plates taking on the role of covers. Evenly spaced on the L-shaped table are two clusters of Safari and Kilimanjaro beer bottles, flanked by an assortment of soft drinks. The table itself is trimmed with white bunting across the top and light blue bunting along the bottom. A bright yellow latticework of shiny polyester fabric separates the two. At each corner large bows and garlands of colourful flowers complete an impossibly festive scene.

After prayers, we are encouraged to dig into the feast, and as a bonus to what I thought was going to be a simple repast and is anything but, we are treated to an East African interpretation of the story of the baby Jesus, done in full costume by the older junior nuns. The extravagant play, complete with stage direction and music from a small boom box set up in the corner, is intricate and obviously well rehearsed, and I only wish I had a sharper grasp of what's going on.

I've never even been to Sunday School, so my most pertinent frame of reference for the dramatization of this story is Monty Python's *Life of Brian*, and parts of tonight's production do seem like an urban drama put on by an off-off-off-Broadway stage company in a church basement, except we're not in the basement. In one scene one of the young women has a teal dress on that I would describe as *70s urban businesswoman*, while one scene partner is wearing a maroon golf shirt and white baseball cap, and the other a powder blue Adidas soccer jersey, sunglasses and a black and red Rasta cap. It's all very confusing.

It probably isn't helping matters that everything is in Swahili.

But the performance is still compelling, and judging by the laughs elicited by the actors from the audience of assembled junior nuns, the legendary comedy troupe of Chapman, Idle, Gilliam, Jones, Cleese and Palin would no doubt approve.

After the show is over, the night is capped off with the time-honoured tradition of gift-giving. Plucking a present from under the tree to pass to a family member is *way* too subdued for this group, and besides, there's no tree. In this rendition of the tradition, the junior nuns in white habits dance and sing for the monsignor before presenting him with a present wrapped in pink paper. Unfortunately, trouble with the boom box does put a damper on the performance. Technical issues remedied moments later, a second presentation is organized. The junior nuns come dancing and singing from the back of the room this time, in two single-file rows of six. The music is rhythmic and joyful, and the young women shuffle, bob and weave their way to the head table in something that approaches a rehearsed unity.

Trailing behind, the senior nuns in their light blue habits are more restrained with their dancing but do have a dignified swing in their collective step. Making their way to the front through the junior nun honour guard, they also have a present for the monsignor, this one wrapped in purple paper. Part of the tradition is to feign handing over the gift, and they do fake him out two or three times before finally making the exchange. Taken as a whole, the entire evening is amazing; the food, the dancing, the play. Everything. I must say, and I say this with all due respect, but who knew the Catholics were so much fun?!

Skirting the edge of the chapel and making my way up the path to my room with a decent buzz on, I hope everyone I know back home had a Merry Christmas this year, because I certainly did.

8

A NEW QUEST

Every new quest starts in doubt. It would be nice to report that after a lifetime of striking out on adventures both great and small this trip would be easy going by now. That would be a lie. I have woken up this morning in a state of anxiety. It is mild, but present nonetheless. I am tickled by uncertainty. Bedeviled by doubt. To be honest, these are often my companions as I pack up after making a temporary home in some guest house or hotel somewhere, unsure of what the next town will bring. The unknown is an exciting concept. It is also intimidating in its unpredictability. Coffee helps.

I'm back in Lushoto after successfully completing the trek to Mtae with Ngoda, and now it's time to move on from the Usambaras, which means it's time to go to *the* mountain, Kilimanjaro. After slogging through the jungle on the way up to Kigulu Peak, I gave myself about a 25 per cent chance of eventually climbing Kili. A couple of days later, after roughly 65 kilometres on foot including the Irente Viewpoint walk, the odds of success in the new quest have improved. The self-assessment has climbed to roughly 75 per cent.

Fortunately, there isn't much time to dwell on that nagging 25 per cent this morning. My omelet is late, and as a result thoughts shift away from the theoretical to the practical, namely, *Will I miss my bus?* Coffee and fruit was delivered promptly when I sat down at 6:50 a.m., but my omelet and toast didn't arrive until 7:09, putting my 7:30 departure at risk. Hustling down to the village with my bags after scarfing down breakfast is not exactly a relaxing way to start the day, but the booking agent I bought the ticket from yesterday is great. He's picked me out of the crowd at the perpetually packed bus park, helped me stow my backpack down below, and has made sure I get my designated seat on the oversold holiday departure. Taking the time to walk me right up onto the bus is a nice touch.

Amazingly, the 7:30 departure actually leaves at 7:32, destroying the "Africa time, things happen when they happen" narrative that was becoming the norm, but true to form we've only managed to travel ten feet in the first five minutes. That's how busy the morning bus schedule from Lushoto is, and how chaotic the small bus park always seems to be. After clearing the congestion, we only travel about a kilometre before stopping for gas, which brings up the obvious question, *Why didn't you top up before loading*?

After finally getting out on the road for real, we sweep on down to the sleepy hamlet of Soni in the blink of an eye, or so it seems, and the 32 kilometres from Lushoto to Mombo disappears before I've even gotten completely comfortable in my seat. My placement on this regional route is not so privileged as on the express bus from Bagamoyo. A window seat four rows back means I can only see 20 metres up ahead, which is probably a good thing on an exceedingly narrow mountain road that technically supports two lanes of traffic but only barely manages the feat on the tight switchback turns. The upper parts of the front and side windows are also painted with colourful slogans, so not only is my forward view obstructed, but I have to crane my neck into an uncomfortable position to see farther out the left side than the ditch. There's no chance of seeing anything out the right side.

Down on the baking plain, the landscape is dotted with waist-high termite mounds and is cut periodically by dried-out creek beds. Acacia trees – famous for the thorns that help protect them from grazers – come in many different forms, and bush-sized versions dominate here. Small herds of goats and diminutive, heat-resistant cattle pop up occasionally to add a bit of variety to the scene, and dusty footpaths snake off into the bush at irregular intervals. The red earth and termite mounds are reminiscent of the Australian outback, and the horizon is studded with remnants of a once-mighty mountain chain that has not yet succumbed to erosion completely. Some hefty masses are interspersed with small nubs rising two and three hundred metres above the plains, and it occurs to me this is the view from ground level that Irente Viewpoint afforded from up high about a week ago.

All of this hard, hot beauty is diminished somewhat by the unfortunate – bordering on appalling – litter situation. The countryside is drier here than it is closer to the coast, and the thinner roadside brush exposes a depressing number of bottles and cans and random plastic waste by the roadside. The rubbish aside, it is still an interesting landscape, and as I settle into another long bus ride I begin to relax into it. Before long the absent-minded daydreaming begins. As acacias and goats flash past the window, I realize it is imperative that I learn to ride out my moods more effectively, since they are so often fleeting, and ultimately unworthy of my concentrated attention. This morning it wouldn't have taken much to move from anxious about going to the mountain, to panic-stricken about the prospects of climbing it. Hustling down to catch the bus broke the spell with a measure of concentrated attention to that task, and a leisurely and pleasing ride down the highway has replaced the angst.

With no responsibilities beyond staring out the window, I have time to idly reflect on the rest of the walk to Mtae, which after a challenging start, really could not have gone much better. I find that breaking the trip up into distinct parts, made up of moments, helps to define a bigger picture, which in turn calms any lingering anxiety that tries to resurface. Collectively these moments are not goals to achieve, but experiences to be had, and together they present an image of this part of Tanzania that I wasn't privy to before. It by no means adds up to a complete appraisal – that would take years – but these moments all contribute a little something to the enhancement of my being, and deepen an understanding of both myself and the world.

For instance, when I woke up at the convent on Boxing Day my body felt more in tune with this adventure than at any other point on the trip. After thanking the monsignor, who happened to be having breakfast as we were leaving, I donned my small pack and strapped on my camera bag and my body all but said, *Oh, we're doing this again, eh? Fine.* As the day progressed I found I was recovering on the fly as we passed through villages and climbed up ridges. After every steep section my breathing and heart rate came back to normal quickly, and a sure marker to feeling up to the task was that I kept catching myself singing Bruce Cockburn, Sheryl Crow, Midnight Oil and Blues Traveler tunes in my head as I walked, instead of fretting about how out of shape I am.

Another standout moment came just after lunch on the first day. As we walked along the valley bottom we skirted a number of farmer's fields before coming upon a group of villagers in the process of pressing sugar cane. Not for use as a sweetening agent in food and drink, mind you, but to make a form of beer. We paused for a moment as Ngoda explained how it all worked, and not wanting to repeat the reluctant Muslim boys incident on Zanzibar, I asked Ngoda about a photograph before pulling out my camera.

He translated, and the request was accepted provided we proffer something in return. Being a typical westerner, all I could think of was my wallet and moved into position for the best possible photo, expecting to pass over some cash once the image was captured. After struggling up a low berm so the angle of light was optimal, I realized Ngoda had taken a different approach. He'd moved into position at one end of the long bamboo pole used to turn the wheels of the press and was already leaning into the effort.

It was but one instructive moment in a string of subtle insights into daily life in the Usambaras.

Returning to the current bus ride, I am again amazed at the discipline shown by our driver as the hours slip past, at least as it relates to travel through the villages. Much like the driver from the Bagamoyo bus, he takes the 50 km/h speed limit extremely seriously, and as we get closer to Moshi the villages increase in frequency. Combined with the frequent drop-offs and pickups of passengers on this regional bus, the last 50 kilometres take forever and a day, or so it seems. Passing through Same and Mwanga I begin to get a sense of the Pare Mountains to the right, but still can't get a decent view no matter how much I contort in my narrow seat.

As we approach the major road junction near the town of Himo, a bank of heavy weather up ahead also begins to stir the imagination. There are more than just clouds out there in the distance. The sightline in that direction is narrow from my seat, maybe 30 degrees from the front left edge of the bus to the indistinct spot where clouds and haze merge on the horizon further left, but pressing my face to the glass of the window I can feel it. It's out there, obscured by a weather system created by its own impressive bulk.

Kilimanjaro.

If there was any doubt about the mountain having the ability to inspire, it's now gone. I have goosebumps springing up on my arms and adrenaline coursing through my veins. Much like Mount Everest, Kili has an undeniable power. A unique gravity that draws dreamers and adventurers and storytellers to her slopes to gaze upon her with their own eyes. There is a pull that extends across these surrounding plains, and well beyond that even to the magical place where imagination and inspiration meet.

In his short story "The Snows of Kilimanjaro," Ernest Hemingway wrote, "There, ahead, all he could see, as wide as all the world, great, high, and unbelievably white in the sun, was the square top of Kilimanjaro. And then he knew that there was where he was going."

I may not be able to see the mountain just yet, but like so many who have gone before, I'm being pulled helplessly in that direction, and I'm almost there.

• • •

Constantino is a no-show.

You can't enter Kilimanjaro National Park, let alone climb the mountain, without a guide. Having overcome my resistance to the whole guide idea while hiking with Ngoda, I asked him if there was anybody he might recommend. Yes, he said. My friend Constantino, he said. He'll even pick you up at the bus station and take you to the hotel, he said.

Sure he will.

There are no snows of Kilimanjaro here in the centre of town. Just a hot, crowded and noisy bus depot, and no Constantino either.

Moshi is a big town. With roughly 200,000 residents, it's making the transition toward being a small city, and the energy at the bus depot reflects that. Instead of a congested mess of vehicles like in Lushoto, each bus has a designated stall to pull through for loading and unloading, but there are far more people milling about here. As I step up on the curb in front of the terminal building to wait for my ride, the bus I just got off is a hive of activity as people try and secure the recently vacated seats for the trip on to Arusha. To the right of the mostly orderly queue, an impressive amount of cargo is being stuffed into the luggage compartments, and scattered all around there are vendors intent on selling trinkets and drinks and snacks to the passengers through the open windows.

Interestingly, nobody pays much attention to me as I wait, but everyone who does walk in my general direction triggers hopeful anticipation because I have no idea what Constantino even looks like. Giving up after 15 minutes, I flag a cab and get absolutely hosed on the fare to The Secret Garden by a driver who is clearly *not* dazed and confused after five or six hours on a crowded bus. Normally I like to wing it with regard to accommodation, mostly because I'm often not sure where I'll be until a day or two before, and sometimes not even until the actual day. Cast Away Lodge at the last minute turned out great, and Funky Squids was a suggestion taken from a guidebook that was over five years old. It was also great. Some friends were here last year around this same time and recommended The Secret Garden. I'm glad they did.

I know I'm in the right place because as I'm led to my single room behind the main building a pair of friendly resident dogs make their introductions, and the small private cabin is named Wonder Lust. Doing a double take, I wonder if it's meant to say Wanderlust, but either one works just fine. The cabin is circular, with a tiny attached bathroom, and the standard-shaped rectangular bed makes the space ergonomically unsound, but it is still one of the coolest hotel rooms I've ever stayed in.

After squaring away my gear and freshening up, I find the open-air dining room on the second floor of the main building is also delightful. The rough-hewn wood furniture suits the casual nature of the hotel perfectly, and although the roof does leak in multiple places when it rains hard, the view is largely unobstructed to the north toward the mountain through a convenient gap in the trees and out over the front yard of the neighbours. The air feels heavy and humid after a week in the highlands, but before long a pleasant breeze moves in to break up the heat. Kili is out there, still shrouded in cloud and reluctant to reveal itself, but today's travels are over with and I've got a small pot of tea coming. I can wait.

After the tea, a short walk to stretch my legs is in order. Secret Garden is located along a rough dirt road a couple of kilometres from the downtown core, and directly across the road is an open field. The land is part of the Moshi Airport, but the only runway is way down to the south of the huge property; this field is fallow. According to the hotel information sheet on the nightstand in my room it is illegal to venture into the field at risk of a fine, but there is no fence and no guard on patrol, and I have already seen half a dozen locals using it as a shortcut to get downtown. Besides, the open space affords an amazing sightline toward the mountain. Illegal or not, how can I resist?

As soon as I step to the edge of the driveway of the hotel compound, the dogs are onto what I'm up to and leap up from the front entrance to join me, tails wagging all the way. Out in the field the view is indeed splendid, or at least would be if it weren't still cloudy to the north. Even so, the reality of the actual size of the mountain is beginning to sink in. The left flank is not even visible from here, obscured by the trees lining the road, but the right flank seems to slope away for miles as it slips beneath the clouds and behind the handful of tall buildings of downtown that are visible through the trees rising up on the far side of the airport.

High up on that right flank, Mawenzi Peak, an extinct volcanic cone and one of three distinct high points on the mountain, does drift in and out of view as the clouds shift in space but don't ever really move out of the way. It isn't until 20 minutes later that the white crown does begin to break apart. A sliver of dark rock and evening blue opens up on the right edge of the Kibo summit cone, and in languid fashion slowly but surely expands to reveal the entirety of the main peak.

The Kibo cone is 24 kilometres wide at the base, according to Wikipedia, and while it is technically dormant but not extinct, the last eruption here was approximately 150,000 years ago. Uhuru Peak is the highest point on the Kibo crater rim, and that makes it the highest point in Africa at 5895 metres (or 19,341 feet) above sea level. Kilimanjaro is also the largest free-standing mountain on earth, rising nearly 5000 metres (or 16,000 feet) above the surrounding plains. The summit is blocky and broad, and for the moment is now perfectly framed by cloud as it catches the last of the late day sun. My goosebumps return with a vengeance, and it's 15 minutes before I can turn my gaze away from the mountain.

Heading back inside for happy hour, I discover that Constantino has managed to track me down. After brief introductions, he asks what I might be interested in doing while here in Moshi, and seems pleased when I mention climbing the mountain and then maybe going on safari after that. The cursory planning complete after only a few minutes, Constantino explains that he'll be back at eight a.m. sharp tomorrow, in order to drive me to the office to make proper arrangements.

Sure he will.

As I wait for dinner, the top of the mountain continues to sit in the cloud window as night falls and the light drains from the sky. After a long day I'm of two minds. On the one hand I am inspired and energized by this first encounter with such an iconic peak, one that is no longer part of my imagination but actually exists out there in the growing gloom. This fact spurs on a surge of pure, unadulterated excitement. Goosebumps, round three, and the small glaciers visible from here don't belong in the tropics, and yet there they are. The mountain, in this early unveiling, isn't how I imagined it exactly, but at the same time is exactly how I imagined it. I am reminded of Dr. Seuss's last book, *Oh, the Places You'll Go!*

Yes, indeed I will. And am amazed once again by how cool the places end up being when I eventually get there.

The thing is, I'm also kind of looking forward to the down time between adventures. It'll take a few days to organize the climb, and in the interim I hope to enjoy exploring this growing town set at the foot of the mountain. If the simplicity of watching the clouds swirl around all afternoon is any indication of the relaxed vibe I'll be experiencing over the coming days, I'm going to like it here.

• • •

True to his word, Constantino does pull into the driveway at 7:58 a.m. and chauffeurs me downtown to the Amazing Usambara Adventures travel office. His boss, Ronaldo, is waiting there, and I am once again relieved. That the office seems legit, that Ronaldo and Constantino seem legit, and a cursory Google search last night revealed a website that seems legit, if a little thin on content.

This renewed concern about who I'm getting involved with is the result of a startling morning revelation. Dawn broke mostly clear today. Not an obscuring cloud in the sky, just the usual haze and some high wispy cirrostratus that had no chance of blocking the view. As you can imagine, Kilimanjaro was appropriately impressive in the soft slanting light, and more than a little intimidating.

It's the snow that freaked me out.

At this time of year, which is technically high summer in the southern hemisphere, it's amazing to see snow at all, even from a distance. It will be 32 degrees Celsius in town today, and yet a noticeable, and somewhat remarkable new snow level has crept down the mountain overnight. It boggles a mind accustomed to distinct seasons of warm and cold, where the appropriate precipitation falls in the appropriate season. Sure, we get snow dusting the local peaks around Canmore in fall when it's still pleasant enough in the valley bottom for nothing more than a light jacket. In late winter and early spring, when warm chinook winds blow over the mountains from British Columbia, a t-shirt is possible even as the last of the slushy snow melts away around your sneakers. But brand-new snow and t-shirts, this is not a regular thing.

Have I mentioned Kilimanjaro is not just in the tropics, but only three degrees of latitude from the equator? Well, there's that too. The geographical midpoint of the earth that separates north and south is roughly 300 kilometres to the north. It doesn't make sense. You can read up on the technical details of what makes this whole scenario possible all you want, but until you stand in the heat at the foot of such a behemoth as it busts up the horizon in front of you, and then try and reconcile not only the revelation of fresh snow, but the idea that there are also permanent glaciers up there, then you can never fully appreciate the magnitude and scope of this mountain.

Standing in stunned awe, I was able to snap off a couple of pictures before thinking, *What have I gotten myself into here?* So, along with the amazed wonder comes the requisite slap of reality. Kilimanjaro is a serious mountain. A very, *very* big mountain, capable of bringing bad weather at a moment's notice, even in summer. To say nothing of the deadly potential of altitude sickness, which should never be underestimated.

Generally speaking, the minor effects of Acute Mountain Sickness (AMS) begin at about 3000 metres and get progressively more serious the higher you go. Kilimanjaro is nearly twice as high as that base measure. The key to minimizing the chance of getting sick or dead is acclimatization, which takes time. Most commercial treks last between six and nine, days, start to finish, and safe ascending at altitude is considered to be 300 vertical metres a day. If you do the math, night two on our trek will be at Shira Cave Camp on the increasingly popular Machame

Route. The camp sits at 3750 metres, a full 2800 metres above Moshi. That's a big jump to start. From Shira Cave Camp to the planned six a.m. arrival at Uhuru Peak it's 2145 metres taken on in about 72 hours. An average of 715 vertical metres a day. That's a *really* big jump at altitude.

The tour operators don't like to talk about it, and certainly don't advertise it, but people die on Kilimanjaro because they don't understand or don't pay heed to these simple equations. The website climbmountkilimanjaro.com, in an examination of the underreported reality of climbing high on the mountain published on August 14, 2017, estimates that an average of six or seven people a year don't make it back down after setting out for the peak. Official stats on casualties for porters and guides are hard to find, but it is believed a similar number of people working on the mountain succumb to falls, altitude sickness, or other ailments every year.

Turning my attention to the details of this briefing as Ronaldo explains some of the logistics doesn't help my feelings of vulnerability and inadequacy, but it's not the climbing part that's got me rattled now. I've been to altitude before in Nepal, I understand the math and will turn around if it comes to that. It's the cost of making the attempt that has jumped to the forefront. Looking at the mountain this morning may have made me feel small and exposed, but coming to terms with the financial realities of taking on this challenge makes me feel reckless.

After taking a couple of days to accept the disappointment of not getting the AFA grant while in Bagamoyo, I haven't spent much time thinking about finances since. Long-distance buses in East Africa are cheap. Cast Away Lodge was right on budget, and three days with a guide, food and accommodation included for 60 bucks American a day while walking through the Usambaras is more than reasonable. Coming to the Tourism Capital of Tanzania that is Mount Kilimanjaro and the Serengeti Plain means I'm entering the Big Leagues on the adventure travel circuit, and I will pay accordingly.

As Ronaldo runs through his recommendations for trekking and going on safari afterward, all I think is, *What am I doing here, spending money I don't have?*

The problem is, my motivation is intrinsic, and I wrestle with this contradiction all of the time. This is what I'm supposed to be doing. I know it because I feel it. Getting out and learning something about this landscape and the people who live here gives me first-hand knowledge that has value that goes way beyond what money can measure. In these moments of doubt, referencing the reflections of some of my travel heroes does much to fire up the necessary motivation to push past all of modern life's tiresome rules, ridiculous schedules and budgetary concerns to do the real work of living, which as far as I can tell is to engage in experiences worth remembering.

On June 25, 2019, dailyhive.com published an article by Kellie Paxian titled "11 Anthony Bourdain quotes that will inspire you to travel with your whole heart."

On what would have been Bourdain's 63rd birthday, Paxian wrote, "It's time to honour his legacy by living life to the fullest, just like he did." Before going on to say, "Bourdain was the epitome of eating well, living large, and travelling like you're supposed to – with an open mind, open heart, and thirst for adventure."

Okay. Yes. Absolutely. Budget be damned. The first two Bourdain quotes are also especially poignant at the moment.

1 – "If you're twenty-two, physically fit, hungry to learn

and be better, I urge you to travel – as far and as widely as possible. Sleep on floors if you have to. Find out how other people live and eat and cook. Learn from them – wherever you go."

I contend you don't have to be 22, or physically fit, for this to be imperative in supporting a balanced and open-minded outlook on life. I'm 50, and not all that fit, but still need to take on these outward journeys in order to keep being amazed by creation. It's how I stay sane in a world explicitly designed to bore you to death with routine.

Quote number two is no less impactful.

2 – "Travel changes you. As you move through this life and this world you change things slightly, you leave marks behind, however small. And in return, life – and travel – leaves marks on you."

I've always loved Bourdain. His book *Kitchen Confidential* was the one that set a lightbulb off in my head: "Hey dummy, you can write whatever the hell you want." His views on travel are as enlightening and entertaining as his thoughts about food, and the business of cooking it as a job. I am inspired anew.

After settling on the Machame Route – a six-night, seven-day expedition that at least attempts to mitigate the altitude issues by traversing the mountain for a couple of days before attempting the final summit bid – and agreeing on five days in the wildlife-rich national parks to the west afterward – it's time to stop waxing poetic about doing this and face the music. How much?

Even with Bourdain's words bucking me up, the gritty details are still a shock to the system. US$1,685 for seven days includes four porters, one cook and one guide, as well as food and park fees. The quoted total is not budget basement, but is about as affordable as you can get while still keeping safety in mind. Without Ngoda's recommendation I would probably shop around to get a feel for how other operations present their product, but to be fair I was expecting to spend two grand American at least. I've seen this same route advertised by one of the bigger outfitters for three thousand American.

Still, three million, nine hundred and fifty-nine thousand, seven hundred and fifty is a number no one would want to lay out for anything, no matter the denomination. That Tanzanian shilling total translates to 2,329 Canadian dollars! Ouch. But I can hear Bourdain whispering from beyond the grave, "Necessary travel writer business expense." He does have a point. No – cough, cough – problem, I tell myself, before reaching into my camera bag for my small card wallet.

"Put it on my Visa, please."

"I'm sorry," Ronaldo says, "it has to be cash."

Pardon?

And herein lies the problem with going with a smaller outfitter. Park fees need to be paid immediately if we want to go in the next few days. Visa has a window of time where transactions are "pending" until the money actually gets transferred. The two time frames don't match in this case, and this is not a complication I saw coming. But I don't have much choice at this point.

After I've agreed to the terms and price, Constantino offers me a ride back to Secret Garden, but the Amazing Usambara office is only a couple of blocks from downtown, and I want to have a look around. Besides, I'm going to have to start the ATM shuffle as soon as possible. I've got a couple of days to come up with nearly four million shillings, procured 400,000 shillings at a time because that's all the ATMs will distribute in a single transaction – with an 8,000 shilling (and at some banks 11,000 shilling) fee attached to each transaction – fuck you very much.

With a C$700 limit on my debit card, and empty or non-functional ATMs the norm not the exception, the process proves to be – and how do I say this diplomatically? – Oh yes, it's: So – Much – Fun. After getting a million shillings from my bank card, it takes three ATMs at two different banks to withdraw an additional one million, six hundred thousand shillings before my Visa card gets blocked. Apparently, multiple withdrawals at more than one bank in East Africa is a red flag for the folks at Visa. Strange, that.

These are the annoying details that don't belong on an adventure; money, schedule and any of the other trifling minutia of travel have no place in the discovery of wonders, but there you have it. This is modern reality. Taking a few deep breaths, I realize that smashing up an ATM isn't going to accomplish much beyond introducing me to the local authorities, so I tuck away the thick wad of cash I've managed to extract into the depths of my camera bag and head back out into the city, hoping that Moshi has a charming character to offset what has been a trying hour and a half.

Sadly, I'm going to be disappointed, in oh-so-many ways.

Moshi is much bigger, obviously, than Lushoto, with more tourist services and amenities, but it's also more annoying as well. It's not rougher, exactly, but it is harder somehow. More callous perhaps, or more calculating maybe. I'm not sure how to describe it, but there's lots of money that passes through this town now, especially since recent upgrades to the Kilimanjaro International Airport were completed. The airport is midway between Moshi and Arusha and delivers approximately one million visitors a year to the area. The desire to get a piece of that visitor cash is decidedly more palpable than what I experienced in Lushoto, Bagamoyo and, strangely, Dar es Salaam.

Here's the thing that makes it complicated, however: sometimes people are just curious and friendly, not predatory or opportunistic. Walking along the backstreets of downtown, or in the less-explored neighbourhoods near the edges, I notice the nods or waves or simple greetings are cordial gestures, not attempts at introductions designed to lure me into a purchase. It can be hard to screen for the touts and scammers and bullshit artists when you travel, but I like to think that, deep down, honest curiosity and generosity of spirit is an important part of the human condition, and is more prevalent than the less endearing alternative. Moshi is testing that theory.

James is the first to get under my skin. Over the next couple of days, he will implore me to come and visit his shop that sells paintings and sculptures and t-shirts every time he sees me walk past. Never mind that I'm not in the market for any of these items at the moment; he is insistent that the deals on offer will convince me otherwise. Stopping for coffee at the venerable institution that is Union Café is an opportunity to give him the slip, but I'm disheartened to discover they are still charging for Wi-Fi. This is a practice that has fallen out of fashion in most tourist towns. Free Wi-Fi in coffee shops is like TV in bars, sort of expected as part of the experience unless you're in the middle of absolutely nowhere.

Moving on from Union Café, I remain determined to not be disappointed by Moshi. Just south of the downtown core I enter a leafy neighbourhood with lots of restaurants that eventually turns into a couple of square blocks that doubles as the local market. I am headed in the vague direction of Secret Garden, but don't remember any of these buildings or roads specifically. As I wander along, a middle-aged man matches my pace and launches into the I-can-get-you-the-best-price-on-anything pitch. We don't even exchange names because the vibe he's giving off is unrepentant con artist, but it does take three blocks to shake him.

As I'm trying to get my bearings, the idea of fresh fruit and maybe a big bag of cashews to snack on strikes me as a fabulous idea, since the market is overflowing with these items. The plan is to inquire on a price with a couple of vendors to gauge the going rate and go from there. As I approach an old woman with bananas and red plums for sale, my conman appears like magic from out of nowhere to facilitate the transaction. I explain politely that I don't need his help, but he is undeterred. As I try and talk past him to the old lady, he quickly interrupts and begins yammering at her in Swahili, saying something to the effect of, "I'll take care of this, we're going to fleece this mzungu."

Stopping just short of an outright "fuck off," I can't manage to negotiate a fair price past my conman, and I abruptly walk away before getting too angry about it.

Slipping out of the market district a block farther south, I come to a set of railway tracks, and it dawns on me – I'm lost. My visual cues are out of whack, and I don't remember ever crossing any railway tracks on the way to Secret Garden. Unfortunately, the most obvious of those visual cues, Mount Kilimanjaro, is lost again in cloud, although the long right-hand flank does look familiar from this angle, sort of. As I'm contemplating the situation my conman appears once again out of nowhere, this time carrying some bananas and a bag of red plums. "No, thanks" doesn't seem to be a phrase he's familiar with, and a couple of other local conmen have gravitated toward the commotion of our exchange. There's a pickup soccer game going on in a dusty field just over the tracks, and I pretend to pay attention to that with hopes they'll all just go away. They don't.

The experience is not threatening, but these guys are aggressive, and it is exhausting. Eventually, I pull out a few thousand shillings just to be done with them.

Circling back through the market with my bag of fruit, I'm now hot and dangerously frustrated. I don't know which way is which and find myself almost right back downtown before tapping out and flagging down a tuk tuk for the ride back to the hotel. Along the way I see the obvious turn that I missed, the one that sent me off course, and when we arrive at Secret Garden I find the fare to be less than half what I paid the cab driver yesterday. Tipping the tuk tuk driver 1500 shillings is a pleasure, because he's the first guy in town who *didn't* try and hustle me.

Sipping a beer on the patio and processing the events of the day before ordering a late lunch, I am intrigued by what sticks in memory, and what symbolism feels important upon reflection. On one of my meandering walks through central Dar, I stumbled onto a beaten-up old four-sided clock tower standing tall in one of the roundabouts, with holes worn clear through parts of the reinforced concrete. The inscription near the base read: ERECTED BY THE CITIZENS OF DAR ES SALAAM TO COMMEMORATE CITY STATUS – 11 DEC. 1961.

Here in Moshi there's a clock tower in one of the roundabouts as well. It's new by comparison and looks to have been recently whitewashed. In my agitated state, what caught my attention about it was the shameless branding. There was no message to pay tribute to an important moment in time, but each of the four faces on the clocks was emblazoned with a logo recognized the world over, written in the distinctive flowing script that I can't replicate here for fear of copyright infringement – Coca-Cola. Clearly, walking around Moshi didn't turn out as I had hoped. It's not a sleepy small town like Bagamoyo or Lushoto. It is also not a big city like Dar. Moshi is sort of an awkward in-between, sporting an unpalatable underlying vibe. As the day progressed all I could think was, *This, this is where mass tourism takes you.*

By contrast, Secret Garden is everything I was hoping for, and more. One of the waiters is named Goodluck, which I think is fabulous, and Rosie, one of the waitresses, has taken it upon herself to teach me at least a little Swahili. I've already nailed down *maji* for water and *bia* for beer, but she's determined to get me to the conversational level. *Maji makubwa* is "large water," and *namba bia mojo* is "one more beer, please," but when I try more complicated phrases people just look at me funny, so this is going to take some work.

At any rate, my cramped but charming circular single room is very close to that "cabin in the woods" overworked and overstressed North Americans dream about escaping to, and every time I step outside the two resident dogs are ecstatic to see me, unless it's the middle of the day when the heat is at its worst; then it's a languid wag of the tail that says, "Hey, we'll play later, okay?" Gazing out at the mountain, hoping for a glimpse that is not going to come today, I am nonetheless content with the stunning rainbow that's materialized after a brief yet powerful downpour. As I wait for the mountain, anticipate the mountain and worry about the mountain, all of today's Moshi aggravations and disappointments are easily washed away.

Clearly, I am under Kilimanjaro's spell.

9

POLEPOLE

Happy New Year, everyone! Bring on 2019, it's going to be great!

That's what you're supposed to say on January 1st, isn't it? It's the optimistic way of thinking about a new year, anyway, and who am I to buck tradition? The thing is, January 1st didn't have much in the way of inspiration or energy. Day three of the ATM shuffle continued, and in the evening we had a final briefing on our climb, after the last of the instalment payments were made. It isn't until day two of my new year that things really get started, and even then, it's taking a good long while to gain any momentum.

When you're a control freak – as I am once a plan goes from vague idea to real thing – it's always a little terrifying to put your experience in the hands of others, but the final briefing at the hotel last night was positive. Yet even with Ngoda's recommendation, and the time spent over the last few days with Ronaldo and Constantino, the reality is that I don't know these guys at all. I have no idea what spending a week on the mountain with complete strangers will be like. Or how organized and professional the operation actually is. Sitting with Ronaldo and Constantino and Cornel, the lead guide for our climb, to talk about altitude and water and clothing helped put my mind at ease. They've quite obviously done this a few times before, and I don't need to be babysat up there, I just need access to the mountain, a tent and some food. The rest is just walking.

Our less than alpine start to the morning, however, is making me nervous. The pickup from the hotel into town is pretty much on time, but the driver is not someone I've met before, and he's brought me to a coffee shop to wait for the crew. After about 20 minutes of watching every vehicle come and go without stopping, I'm beginning to wonder if I've been had for a couple of grand, and I'm glad I made sure to sit between my new driver and the door, just in case he tries to make a break for it.

It isn't until somewhere around ten a.m. that our expedition team finally turns up, and after hasty introductions are made we make it away. And by make it away, I mean halfway across town to pick up the gear, which hasn't yet been sorted out for some reason. This is actually our second stop for rental equipment, after a brief layover near the coffee shop, and now I'm getting really nervous. The third stop is at a convenience-style shop at the edge of town for final groceries and snacks, and the fourth is at a roadside butcher in a small village off the main highway.

It isn't until 11:45 a.m. that we finally reach Machame Gate and the trailhead for our route up Kilimanjaro. Upon arrival there's a lot of people hanging around. Doing what, you ask? You guessed it: waiting. The other groups starting their treks today look just about as disorganized as we do, which does make me feel a little bit better. The parking lot is a mass of minibuses unloading passengers and gear, and all the free space on the pavement is taken up by porters and guides filling up backpacks and duffle bags with food and equipment. The loads are distributed equally and must be weighed by the wardens before a group is allowed on the mountain.

As this is going on, the clients retreat to a large gazebo as the skies open up and the rain begins to pour down. It's an interesting mix of mzungus in their 30s and 40s, with a few older folks sprinkled in, all of them hoping to knock a big peak off the bucket list. Almost everyone is decked out in high-tech rain gear and boots, much of it looking quite obviously new, and there's one blonde Barbie type in a tight white running top and short shorts who appears more intent on showing off her body than being comfortable, but one thing is for sure, this is not going to be an isolated commune with nature. There are way too many people for that.

Fortunately, I am prepared for this reality. On November 15, 2016, *The Guardian* published a travel piece by Morgan Trimble that led with the following:

"Many trekkers arrive at Mount Kilimanjaro dreaming of a grand wilderness adventure on the world's tallest freestanding mountain. At the very least, they expect some peace and quiet to contemplate the toughest physical challenge they might ever face. Finding a circus instead of solitude can be mighty disappointing."

While it's true Kilimanjaro is a big mountain – one of the famed Seven Summits that attracts serious mountaineers – it is also just a walk up. No technical climbing skills are required. As a result, it does draw a crowd. Fifty thousand people a year make the attempt, and for every paying customer there are an average of four to six support staff. With Constantino tagging along as an assistant to Cornel, I've got seven people assigned to my climb.

But, as the minutes tick away, none of the groups actually begin to walk. The assembled crowd remains in the parking lot and under the gazebo. For all the aspiring trekkers, our first meal on the mountain is a fixed boxed lunch at the gate, which has been the design all along. Everyone gets an identical lunch regardless of which company they've signed up with. The problem is that all this waiting around isn't doing my head any good, I'm starting to psyche myself out. A phantom headache has suddenly appeared, way below where any altitude problems can be expected, and the achy hip that was bothering me during the first days in Dar has flared up again. These are psychosomatic ailments that need to be walked off, but we're not going anywhere anytime soon, and so I pace.

Sitting just outside the gazebo, the Machame Gate trail marker is not much comfort, no matter how many times I read it. On it there are distances and times laid out as a guide for what's to come. From here it's 11 kilometres in five hours to Machame Camp. Shira Cave Camp is 16 kilometres away and will take 11 hours to get to. Baranco Camp, 26 kilometres in 17 hours. There are two additional camps after that, and Uhuru Peak is 40 kilometres away. It will take roughly 32 hours of walking to get there. When the altitude math from the other day is taken into account, it all adds up to a big effort, and I just want to get going already before I completely lose my nerve.

Eventually the rain stops, and we make our way from under the protection of the gazebo to the far end of the parking lot where the trail begins. Groups that got here early are in the final stages of checking in. Their paperwork being complete, porter bags are now being weighed in at three stations manned by wardens that don't appear close enough together to be coordinated in any reasonable sense. Accepting that my group will be among the last to be processed, I sit back to watch the show. There are animated discussions and lots of moving bags around from one place to another but no real sense of order, and there are no checked bag tags to confirm a load has been weighed. It's hard to gauge what has been cleared and what hasn't, and an outfitter who's adept at three-card monte could easily skirt all the regulations, as far as I can tell.

As the chaos unfolds, it becomes apparent there's a problem with one of our porters and the load he is carrying. At first I don't recognize him as one of our porters, but once Constantino gets involved in the conversation I take a renewed interest in the proceedings. Obviously, I don't understand the details because they're all arguing in Swahili, but the situation takes a turn for the worse when the porter makes an ill-advised attempt at a bribe. This sets off the park official and an old-fashioned brouhaha ensues. At one point, the agitated warden even takes a swing at the porter, which seems an over-the-top reaction to the 10,000-shilling note the porter was flashing around.

I'm not sure if the warden has high moral standards, or if 10,000 is an insult, but once cooler heads prevail the end result is we're down a porter, and we're pretty much the last group to get going. As Constantino scrambles to make new arrangements, Cornel and I start out, and it's more than a little disconcerting to be leaving the gear and the porters behind as they repack the bags once again. Did I mention that it's now almost one o'clock? Well, there's that too. With a five-plus-hour hike ahead of us I have growing concerns about my choice of operator, needless to say. *Polepole* – slowly – is something I learned in the Usambaras from Ngoda. It's not only a relaxed mantra for how to approach life but is also the safest way to go about walking a big mountain.

I just didn't anticipate that the idea would extend to simply getting away from the trailhead.

• • •

Walking makes everything better. Starting up an at-times-muddy-but-otherwise-well-maintained dirt road, that eventually turns into an at-times-muddy-but-otherwise-well-maintained trail allows me to put my worries aside for a while. I have to admit, it's an exceedingly pleasant walk to start. This is a montane rainforest with vines and mosses clinging to everything, and a highlight early on is a troupe of colobus monkeys high up in the canopy, the largest of which looks not unlike an oversized long-haired skunk that can climb trees.

As we walk, our porters catch up at various times as each travels at his own pace along the trail. Cornel is the only one who stays with me all afternoon, and while all the guys seem friendly and cheerful, even with the heavy packs they're carrying, Cornel is closer to my age and comes off as more reserved. This makes sense, of course, because he's not just responsible for my success and well-being on the mountain but is also in charge of everyone in the party. It's a lot of responsibility, and I must admit, it's nice to have nothing much to worry about except walking and looking at the forest as it slowly passes by.

It's also interesting to note that we are on a surprisingly mellow grade for the first half of today's hike. We're travelling up, no question about that, but it's not as steep as I imagined it in my mind's eye, and I don't feel completely breathless in the effort. There isn't much in common between a five-hour bus ride across the lowland plains and five hours out on the trail, with one key exception: there's an awful lot of time to think, and since I'm not struggling to keep the pace it's easy to let my mind wander.

For a couple of weeks now I've been playing around with a title for the book that will eventually come from this journey to East Africa. I consciously put the idea in the back of my mind at the airport in Calgary but have yet to come up with anything that feels right. Usually, I would have figured this part out already. A couple of days of idle musing out on the trail, or an hour or two sitting with it in some atmospheric pub over a beer, and a snappy summation of the broader concept has always bubbled to the surface.

My first book, *Lost and Found: Adrift in the Canadian Rockies*, was an amble through the national and provincial parks that make up the stunning backdrop to my hometown of Canmore, Alberta. Getting a little lost in the wonder of nature in order to find a piece of oneself is a pillar of adventure storytelling. Simple enough.

For effort number two, *A Few Feet Short: An Uncommon Journey to Everest*, there was exactly zero chance I was going to climb the tallest mountain in the world, but I was inspired to walk in amongst the high mountains of the Himalaya. Sixteen, seventeen and eighteen thousand foot peaks and passes require no small effort, proving that in a land of true giants like Cho Oyu, Lhotse and Everest you can still find a measure of adventure, well, you know, a few feet short of the summits to those imposing peaks.

As I was walking through the Usambaras I thought for sure something good would reveal itself for book number three. The bike ride didn't live up to expectations, so "hopelessly inspirational" is now out of the question. *Sea to Sky: A Journey to the Roof of Africa* is off the table, but I have been working different options for the last couple of hours. *My African Adventures: Tanzania, Kenya, Uganda and Rwanda.* Too generic. And given the relaxed pace I've adopted here in Tanzania, who knows how many countries I'll eventually make it to from here? *Polepole. Poa,*

Poa: Slowly, Slowly. Good, Good. Too eclectic. *I'm Cool: Travelling Around East Africa Alone by Bicycle and on Foot.* Waaaay too pretentious, not to mention a bit wordy. *Beaches and Mountains and Plains: A Mzungu Survives East Africa.* Hmmm. Maybe.

Bashing the possibilities around in my head is a welcome distraction even without coming to a final decision, especially now that the grade has gotten steeper and it has started to pour rain again. This is a cold, hard, driving type of rain that is decidedly less pleasant than the warm tropical downpours experienced on the coast and is way more intense than the cloudburst down at the trailhead earlier today.

Eventually Constantino catches up after hiring on an emergency porter, and a dynamic begins to develop among the three of us as we walk. Cornel is the stoic leader, setting the pace, while Constantino is much more chatty, and ends up being the comic relief as well. As we near the end of the day he says, "Don't worry, we're almost there. Five more minutes."

I am immediately reminded of Ngoda and his favourite saying, "Don't worry. Steep is finished."

Half an hour later I turn back to Constantino. "Five minutes, eh?"

See. Hilarious. Lucky I already understand that an African five minutes can end up being anything between two minutes and two hours. But what we do agree on is a mantra for our now laboured walking: "polepole kinyanga," which translates roughly to "slowly, slowly, like a chameleon." Back in the Usambaras, Ngoda had the uncanny ability to spot chameleons despite their ability to blend in with the surrounding foliage. We'd be walking along and suddenly Ngoda would point into the trailside bushes and say, "There, there." Inevitably, I would stare directly at the animal for a few seconds before recognizing it as *not* bushes, and a chameleon's talent for changing colour to mimic the background was only half the challenge. They also move very slowly, and with a halting gait, so that they look like a leaf or a tree branch being rustled on the breeze.

That's what I am, or at least what I aspire to be: the world's largest chameleon lurching my way up the mountainside.

Rolling into Machame Camp as dusk begins to take hold, I quickly change into the dry clothes from my daypack in order to stay warm, but Cornel informs me our tent site is not quite ready yet. It's 6:15 p.m., which means we made good time after a morning that seemed determined to sabotage our first day. Standing and making small talk with Cornel is awkward, and to kill a bit of time we wander over to the camp office to sign in. By the time we get back our site is ready and it's almost dark, but my tent has been set up for me and my gear is already inside. Accommodations have not been talked about specifically, but it looks like I'll have a four-person bright yellow Eureka! tent all to myself. I'm encouraged to get in, and I have to admit, it's remarkably spacious inside. I can even sit upright. After laying out my insulate pad and sleeping bag and taking off my boots, I can't help but wonder about dinner.

Stepping back outside and over to the cook tent, I peek in to find one of the guys already working away on the one-burner stove attached to a small gas canister, while one of the other guys cuts vegetables. The tent is no bigger than the one I've been given, but it's packed with gear and food. After asking a couple of questions about the evening itinerary, I get shooed away to my tent and am instructed to relax before dinner, which will be soon.

Let me guess – five minutes.

As I go, I try not to think too much about the dead chickens and slabs of meat of unknown provenance tucked in with all the vegetables in wicker baskets by the cook tent entrance. It's not like someone is hauling a refrigerator along to keep things fresh, and we're going to be up here for a week. At any rate, I'm not used to relaxing at camp until dinner is cooked and cleanup is done, but before long Omari, my porter-cum-waiter, approaches my tent with a tentative "Hello."

"Yes, yes. Hello."

There is a fussing of zippers that will be a function of mealtime for the remainder of the journey, but then what Omari lays out takes me completely by surprise. It all starts with a small red tablecloth and a large thermos of boiling hot water. That done, he unloads a 25-pack of Kilimanjaro brand tea bags, a tin of Africafe instant coffee (Yes!), a plastic jar of hot chocolate and a large tin of powdered milk, in addition to a personal cup and spoon and some sugar. As I'm trying to figure out what I want to drink (one cup of hot chocolate to start, followed by a cup of milk tea), Omari returns from the cook tent with a big bowl of popcorn. Brilliant!

It's sort of weird settling into my own personal tent for tea service and dinner, but kind of cozy as well. Now that the sun is down it's getting chilly out, but my body heat and the warm tea make the small space more than comfortable. As I sip the tea I also have time to process the fact that I'm the only client on this trip, which I was not expecting when I signed up. I figured I'd be one of two or three other clients who would be getting to know each other real quick in the close confines of this tent, but it hasn't worked out that way. I feel like a sultan, or an 18th-century explorer setting out on a months-long expedition. It's sort of crazy and weird – not to mention uncomfortable in the realization that the seven other guys will be sharing two tents – but I'm way too tired to make any sense of it.

After tea is done and cleared, dinner is served, which is soup to start, followed by a huge main dish. Tonight's offering is batter-fried fish and fried potatoes, topped with avocado, tomato, green pepper and red onion. All of it finished off with fruit for dessert. Once this hike is done, it will prove not too much of a stretch to say I've never eaten so well in a seven-day period, regardless of circumstance, let alone on the side of a mountain. The food tonight is way better than I ever could have imagined based on the way the first half of the day went, and a shout-out to my chef, Jomo – a culinary genius on a one-burner camp stove – is warranted.

Another shout-out goes to the crew in general. These guys are tough, no doubt about it. They do the same hike while carrying way more gear, and then set up and cook and serve and clean before settling down to eat and take a rest themselves. Some of these guys have been on the mountain dozens of times – Cornel has been up here hundreds of times – and not once will I hear any of them complain about anything. They are truly amazing.

By 9:15 p.m. I can't keep my eyes open any longer, and as I head to the washroom before bed, night has fallen hard. There is no moon, and a riot of African stars fills the sky. Taking a moment to appreciate the circumstances, I am grateful for a solid uphill effort to start my climb, a truly spectacular meal to refuel after a big day, and a beautiful evening to see me off to sleep.

All the early hiccups aside, 2019 is proving to be pretty awesome so far.

•••

The land at my feet is mesmerizing this morning, there is simply no other way to describe it. Mount Meru stands in the predawn light like a sentinel some 70 kilometres away. I have heard Meru described as Kili's sister mountain, but also as Kili's younger brother as well. Whichever your preference, it does give the impression of a younger sibling stuck in the shadows of the first child. This is undeserved, as Meru is impressive all on its own. Another dormant volcano, Meru last erupted in 1910 and stands at 4562 metres, 1333 metres lower than Kilimanjaro's summit. It is nevertheless Tanzania's second-highest peak, and Africa's fifth highest, and this morning it is putting on a show.

Here at Shira Cave Camp – our second camp on the route up Kili – we've reached 3750 metres, so from a distance we look roughly on par with Meru's summit. A prominent ridge to the west here on Kili obstructs the view ever so slightly, but beyond that Meru is cutting a classic strato-volcanic pose, the near-perfect conical shape the only feature on the otherwise blank canvas of a horizon. As dawn approaches, the pale pink high in the atmosphere slowly creeps down the sky, pushing the bluish-purple shadow cast by the earth closer to the ground with every passing minute. Then, as the sun's first rays brush the peak, a subtle shade of orange overwhelms the pink until the same time tomorrow morning. Weather permitting.

This subtle and somehow sensual light show – earth and sky caressing each other with a tenderness only seen at dawn and dusk – has taken me completely by surprise. Arriving in camp yesterday to a smothering overcast belied any idea of the long view earned after climbing this high. I was simply getting up for a pee this morning and was stunned by this clear view. Here in the shadow on Kilimanjaro's west side my hands are freezing and it's time for breakfast, but you couldn't possibly pull me away just yet. It's simply too beautiful to miss out on.

By the time breakfast is done and the camp is packed, the moment has gone, and for 45 minutes the sky has been growing ever brighter, as you would expect. As I take a long last look before starting today's walk, Meru hardly even seems like the same mountain. The morning light is high now and the shadows are gone. With white, fluffy clouds lapping the north flank and a low haze obscuring the plains, a subtle blue tinge now dominates. Roughly 8,000 years ago the caldera on Meru collapsed, and that depressed physical feature has emerged from the early gloom and is now clearly visible.

The light may have changed, and the magic has evaporated, but this evolving memory of Meru will endure.

Returning to the task at hand, we continue to walk on a relentless uphill vector. Climbing toward an acclimatization stop at Lava Cone Camp, our route quickly joins up with the Shira and Lemosho routes, and strangely the increase in human traffic does not bother me much. In the months leading up to this trip I revisited Trimble's *Guardian* story often, and this line in particular: "Finding a circus instead of solitude can be mighty disappointing."

Up to now there have been plenty of people around – I counted roughly 75 tents in camp last night – but vegetation cover and the nature of the route so far meant you could never see more than five to ten people out on the trail at any one time. That number jumped to 20 at one picturesque spot for a water break early on day two, but that's still not overwhelming. Often it was just me and my trusty guides making our own space on the mountain. As we transition from moorland to alpine desert that dynamic is bound to change, but so far the human presence hasn't felt oppressive. A key point is that we are not bumping into people coming the other way. There are seven main routes up the mountain, and the intrepid hiker with a little more time can combine trails to find the least busy options as Trimble has, but everyone descends via the most direct Mweka Route, and that keeps the ascending trails comparatively clear. Stretching a few hundred people along a five-kilometre length of trail is much different than sidestepping someone coming in the opposite direction every few minutes.

Another factor is that the blind guy has shifted my focus somewhat.

While taking a break for snacks and water I am still contemplating the crowding issue when a blind hiker walks past cautiously. He's part of a bigger group (maybe a half dozen westerners in all), and one of his friends is leading a foot or two ahead. The blind guy has his hand on the lead's elbow, and every time they come to a rock on the trail or a change in footing is required, simple instructions are given to navigate the impediment. The system works well, and the group travels at a rate comparable to any other group on the mountain. Watching them pass certainly puts things in perspective. *Overcrowding?* Not the end of the world. *Wind and rain?* What exactly did you expect? *This is too hard and too far and too steep.* Well, there is a blind guy doing it, and I don't hear him complaining.

Sometimes it's possible to pick the people out of the crowd who are going to be instrumental in inspiring your own success in an endeavour. I only hope I manage to remember this impressive display of determination when things do get tougher higher up.

10

MOUNT KILIMANJARO

I'm having an emotional reaction, and not in a good way.

It's somewhere around three a.m. and a fine, almost imperceptible snow has begun to fall sideways, driven on a heavy wind. These are not soft, fluffy flakes drifting casually to the ground, but they are also not hard pellets being pushed by a new weather system brushing across the top of the mountain. This snow is ephemeral, almost like a hoarfrost that has been pitched airborne. Not 45 minutes ago, or so it seems, we had the opportunity at each short break to look back down at the lights of Moshi and Arusha and the surrounding towns and villages on the Sanya Plain. Once again, there had been no early moonrise and a riot of stars littered the sky. At one point, once we climbed above the col between Kibo and Mawenzi peak over in the near distance, we could even see the lights from several villages burning brightly over in Kenya. Now we can't see much of anything at all except the hard trail at our feet and the snow whipping past in the beams of our headlamps.

We're firmly on the main summit cone of Mount Kilimanjaro now and the full weight of this endeavour is apparent. Although we do not have to put our hands to the rock in order to ascend – it's still just walking – it's amazingly steep. Shockingly steep. Breathlessly steep. So steep, in fact, that before the clouds rolled in it was possible to catch glimpses of the headlamps of fitter and more motivated individuals up above as they struggled through their own battle with the mountain. And I mean waaaay up above. When someone is a mile ahead of you on an open plain and you can still see them, that's one thing, but when they're a mile above you that's something else altogether. It plays tricks with your mind. I would argue it's sometimes better to be oblivious to certain realities. This is one of those times.

The thing is, now that we've lost the sightline it feels like the mountain will never end, and that we will just climb forever in this cold and hostile landscape until we drop from exhaustion. In light of this unpleasant possibility I've called for another break, not 15 minutes since our last stop. I'm suddenly very tired, probably hypoxic, and am completely losing my shit as a result. After making our way up into the clouds I've turned into a big whiny baby, and I can't help myself. I'm completely drained, my hands and feet are freezing, and I want to go home.

The guys are having none of it. I've been looking for a proper excuse to quit for half an hour, and none is forthcoming. Being tired and having cold hands are inconveniences, not reasons. After saying something to the effect of "I don't think I can do it" for the third or maybe fourth time, I'm not so much ignored as presented a window of escape that I must take on my own. Until I physically point my boots downslope we're going up. If I turn, Cornel and Constantino will follow, but they're not going to lead me that way no matter how much I complain. Scarfing down a Snickers bar I bought down in Moshi six days ago for just such an eventuality, I hope the sugar bump will set me right, because clearly, we're going to continue. It's still possible I may simply lie down and quit, but I can't bring myself to retreat.

It's no surprise that I'm tired, of course. It has been a challenging three days. After leaving Shira Cave Camp we walked up to Lava Tower Camp for lunch, and then ambled down through a hard charging fog to Baranco Camp, but that short bump to the Lava Tower at 4600 metres triggered the beginnings of my slow dance with Acute Mountain Sickness. By dinnertime I had lost my appetite and developed a low, humming headache that made me nervous about the challenges to come.

Altitude sickness is a finicky thing. I've suffered from it – and written about it – before. Pulling some information from my last book, *A Few Feet Short,* we see that the numbers are the same in Africa as they are in Asia. High altitude pulmonary edema (HAPE) and high altitude cerebral edema (HACE) represent a reality of mountain travel that has serious and potentially fatal consequences no matter what continent you're on. Avoiding trouble requires a sensible approach to acclimatizing.

As the human body ascends into the atmosphere the amount of oxygen available to feed the muscles and organs decreases. Optimal conditions for humans occur at sea level, where the air is a positively thick 21 per cent oxygen, with an average barometric pressure of 760 mmHg. At 3658 metres (12,000 feet), roughly the height of Shira Cave Camp, oxygen remains at 21 per cent, but the barometric pressure is only about 480 mmHg, which translates into 40 per cent fewer oxygen molecules available for consumption. The result is an increased breathing rate, even at rest, and it takes 24 to 72 hours for the body to get used to this oxygen deprivation. While you're busy breathing hard, your body is also making subtle changes to how the internal equipment works. Pressure in pulmonary arteries goes up to force blood into portions of the lungs not used in normal breathing, and the body starts creating more red blood cells to carry oxygen. Production of a type of enzyme that helps the release of oxygen from hemoglobin is also increased.

So my body has been working very hard biologically in its attempt to acclimatize, and instead of allowing the process to play out naturally, we continued to walk, putting more pressure on my internal workings. The next two days to Barafu Camp were pretty and scenic in that alpine desert kind of way and, admittedly, not overly difficult. After scrambling the Barranco Wall in the persistent fog – the only point on the whole trek where we had to put hands to stone in order to navigate the route – we emerged at a smooth rocky outcrop to a rapidly clearing sky and stunning view of the Kibo summit cone, which suddenly appeared very close indeed. The rest of the walk was up and down through gullies and across huge rocky plateaus as we traversed to the eastern side of the mountain.

Ten kilometres in eight hours from Barranco to Barafu might not seem like much in two days, but at an average altitude above 4000 metres it is still plenty. After an 11-hour break that focused on food as fuel and trying to nap, our scheduled midnight departure for the summit bid did get away at 12:03 a.m. this morning. Now here I am, staring absently at the hard-packed earth at my feet in the beam of my headlamp, a half-eaten Snickers bar hanging limply in hand, wondering what the fuck it is I'm doing up here. Hoping beyond hope that Cornel or Constantino will have mercy on my tired soul, put their arm around me, and say, "It's okay, big guy, you're done."

Come to Tanzania, the travel brochures say. You'll have the experience of a lifetime, they say.

Yeah, right. I'm having just the best time ever.

Top: Mnazi Mmoja bus stand and Dar es Salaam city centre.

Bottom: A bustling seafood market at the edge of the port of Dar es Salaam.

Top: Stepping to the edge at the Irente Viewpoint.

Bottom: The author's bicycle before the "battle of the black cotton soil."

Top: Pressing sugar cane in the Usambara Mountains.

Bottom: The busy bus station in Moshi.

Top: Slogging mindlessly toward the summit after Stella Point.

Bottom: Celebrating a successful climb with beers and Cokes down in Moshi.

Top: A lioness with her cubs in Tarangire National Park.

Bottom: Red-billed oxpeckers hunt for ticks in Tarangire National Park.

Top: Hippos debating the concept of "personal space" in Serengeti National Park.

Bottom: A group of zebras stops for a drink in the Ngorongoro Crater.

Top: The violence of Camp Kigali, Rwanda.

Bottom: Mount Sabyinyo and the Volcanoes National Park's office.

Top: Contemplating the meaning of life, or just resting between mouthfuls. It's hard to tell.

Bottom: Security personnel strike a pose before the hike up to Karisoke.

• • •

Through the miracle of persistence, we have made it to Stella Point. It's 5:30 a.m., still dark out, and bitterly cold. Stella Point marks the crux of the climb. It is here that the massive lava cone that makes up Kibo Peak levels out toward the top of the mountain. There's a huge boulder next to the trail that is a common spot to take a break and maybe recharge with a cup of hot tea brought up from camp, but the wind and the snow are conspiring against such a plan. Instead of sheltering us from the elements, the boulder focuses the tempest coming out of the east. This should be a celebration of accomplishment, as there's only 30 to 40 minutes across comparatively level ground left to go, but it's just too cold and unpleasant to linger.

Before shouldering my daypack after abandoning the idea of tea, I wonder if Matt and Elizabeth have made it as well.

"Matt. Liz. You here?"

"Yes, we're here," Matt replies from behind one of the headlamps gathered in the dark.

Matt and Elizabeth are from the US and are on their honeymoon. We've been chatting intermittently out on the trail since Barranco Camp, including once or twice already this morning, and I'm glad they've also made it this far. I like them. Anyone who does something like this instead of an all-inclusive at some beach resort for their honeymoon gets mad props in my book.

"Hey, great. Congratulations."

They return the good wishes, and then my inability to moderate my feelings in the moment gets the better of me.

"Thanks, but I'm not going to lie to you, I could not have hated that more."

The comment was supposed to have a sarcastic, or

maybe ironic undertone, but as the words were ripped from my mouth by the wind to be smashed against the giant boulder at our backs, they just fall flat. At this point, more whining is apparently all I can manage, but at least I'm telling the truth. Or my truth, anyway.

After Stella Point I turn the Zombie Walk on full blast. The Zombie Walk is something I perfected on cold, windy days above 4000 metres in Nepal. The technique is simple: head down, mind turned off. The goal is to keep your feet moving as you struggle through the tougher moments. With the biting wind at my back this time at least I'm still coherent enough to appreciate the surroundings, but only just, and maybe by appreciate, I mean vaguely acknowledge. After all this effort, the experience of being so high up a mountain should be awe inspiring. The whole of Africa spread out below is a romantic vision, after all. Kilimanjaro's unusual designation as the biggest free-standing mountain in the world only encourages that foolish fairy-tale, Hollywood-movie-ending-style fantasy.

Reality is less inspired; 20 or 30 metres of flying frost in any direction is the best it's going to get. The one good photo I do manage is of the frost-covered boulders over at the edge of what I can only assume is the gapping Kibo crater. I plan to call the photo *Walking on the Moon*. Someone has stepped tentatively over toward the edge and has left subtle boot prints in their wake. The temperature is well below zero, and the lively wind creates a chill factor approaching minus 20 degrees Celsius. This is a rough guess, as I have no way of actually figuring it out, but I can confirm its buggeringly cold out.

I am absently reminded of Jon Krakauer's opening paragraph from 1997's *Into Thin Air*. In it he describes standing at the top of the world, with one foot in Tibet and one foot in Nepal, and how difficult it was to properly appreciate the surrounding landscape or celebrate the culmination of months of effort it took to get there. The key line: "But now that I was finally here, actually standing on the summit of Mount Everest, I just couldn't summon the energy to care."

In no way do I mean to imply climbing Kilimanjaro is as difficult as climbing Everest. It's not. Not even close. But fatigue and altitude have a funny way of transcending circumstance to render any one of us compromised in both mind and body. Struggling on, I find the grade does indeed get much easier at this point, but I don't have the legs or the lungs for it. I have to stop often, but don't want to quit anymore, and that's something. As the sun comes up behind us the diffused light is disorienting. The light filters through the flying frost and reflects off the rocks and boulders to create an otherworldly glow. On more than one occasion I find myself stepping off the trail to let another hiker pass, only to turn and find no one behind me. I'm walking ahead of a giant solar headlamp through a foggy cloud of hypoxia, and it isn't until the third time I turn around that I realize the glow is actually the sun rising behind us.

At one point during this comically slow shuffle upward, Matt and Elizabeth come past in the opposite direction on their way down from the top (when, exactly, did they get so far ahead?) and offer congratulations once again.

"It's not too far now," one of them says in passing.

I'm so relieved I want to cry, and can't resist the overwhelming urge to hug them. In my addled state the sudden burst of emotion almost sends the three of us tumbling to the ground.

At the top there is an iconic summit sign, with some key details about the mountain proudly displayed for those with the perseverance to make it this far. Two sturdy wooden posts support five slats with pertinent information carved into their faces.

MOUNT KILIMANJARO
CONGRATULATIONS
YOU ARE NOW AT
UHURU PEAK TANZANIA 5895M/19341FT AMSL
AFRICA'S HIGHEST POINT
WORLD'S HIGHEST FREESTANDING MOUNTAIN
ONE OF THE WORLD'S LARGEST VOLCANOES
WORLD HERITAGE AND WONDER OF AFRICA

This is the gist of it, anyway. The hoarfrost sticking to everything does make some of the script difficult to read. I think AMSL means *above mean sea level*, and at the bottom I think it is meant to read WORLD HERITAGE *SITE* AND WONDER OF AFRICA, but who am I to be a stickler for details at this point? Fifteen minutes ago I thought the sun was a giant headlamp.

It's bright enough now that my hallucinations have dissipated with the stronger frame of reference provided by the sign, and my motor skills are also returning to something approaching normal. The minor charge of adrenaline associated with getting this far probably doesn't hurt in this regard, but it turns out the top is a massive disappointment. Twenty-five people hanging around in the most unlikely of places, jockeying for position with hopes of an unobstructed selfie with the signage, reveals a shit show of human unpleasantness.

All the way up the mountain I have been pleasantly surprised by my fellow man. Everyone I've talked to has been friendly, polite and humble in their efforts. Not a single prima donna in the bunch. Respect for the mountain has also been high, and litter has not been nearly as big an issue here as along the highways or around some of the small towns I've been to in Tanzania so far. But at Stella Point all routes up Kilimanjaro converge. Although there are only 25 of us here at the summit at this exact moment, there are probably 200 of us on the upper part of the mountain today, and the mob mentality has won out. Coming to the back of the group waiting for photos, there isn't any rhyme or reason to the gathering. Order is lacking, and decorum has been abandoned. I'm sure everyone is suffering from some level of hypoxia, but people in groups don't generally know how to act at sea level, so I suppose this development should come as no surprise.

At first, I try to be the moderator to the disorganized mass, because it is in my nature. A pair of Brits who have clearly been waiting their turn have begun to argue with a man from the Middle East who has jumped the queue and is now sitting on the rocks at the base of the sign with a flag from his country. He's not in the way of standing with the sign, but if you want a photo, then you're sharing it with a stranger. This has worked up the Brits, and quite a few others are slowly trying to crowd in for their own photos. Still others continue to hang back in a spaced-out stupor that only confuses the situation. Who's going next? Who has gone? What is happening here?

Suddenly agitated, I yell at the dawdler and give him a little shove to get him up and moving – he's already got his summit photos, his camera has been returned, and his climbing partners have vacated the prime spot around the sign – but he's having none of it. Part of me just wants to punch him in the head. After another minute or two he begins to fold up his flag, but the Brits are now in a heated discussion about queues and common courtesy, and who knows what else, with someone trying to push up from the back.

"Guys, let's go. Your turn" doesn't get the desired response.

Hypoxic and distracted are not a recipe for action, and in the absence of anyone at all stepping forward I succumb to my baser instincts and jump up on the stones supporting the sign when no one else seizes the opportunity. I get a series of photos with Constantino, and then quickly with Cornel, well ahead of my actual turn at the top. Many of them featuring the dawdler, and some with a random woman standing off to the side, looking completely out to lunch and blissfully unaware that she's photobombing everyone's summit shots. Stepping down from the rocks, I find I want nothing more than to get out of here as quickly as possible. The sign suddenly seems not so much iconic as obscene. A blight on an otherwise pristine landscape that attracts, horror upon horrors, *people.* I'm embarrassed by my opportunistic actions, not to mention exasperated by the lot of us in general. I came. I saw. And I acted like an obnoxious tourist, just like everyone else.

So proud.

It doesn't take long to be distracted from my indignation, however. As we trudge downward it becomes clear that while I'm not 100 per cent in body or mind, I'm doing far better than some. Passing a young woman being propped up by her guide and one of her porters, I am shocked by her incoherence. She cannot comfortably stand on her own, but continues to be led forward, with encouragement that "it's not far now." Which is true enough, it's only 50 metres to the summit, but I doubt she'll remember any of this tomorrow. If she lives that long. This is the dark side of guiding at altitude. Operator websites advertise summit success rates but downplay or ignore the negative experiences that are inevitable in this hostile environment. So what if she doesn't remember anything; there will be a photo of her at the top and the company reputation will be maintained.

I'm grateful that I still have my feet under me and my faculties relatively intact, when we eventually come upon a group of Koreans near Stella Point who are also in trouble. They're heading down, and the four men in the group of six are a disaster. Two of them swerve noticeably as they walk, and the other two need to be held upright by their guides. The worst of them is being hustled down the quickest for obvious reasons, and after Stella Point everyone takes the scree slope instead of clomping down the hard trail. This guy is absolutely legless and it's scary to watch. Every time his guide has to let go of him in order to navigate a high step or section of firm rock interrupting the scree, the Korean crumples to the ground like a man with no bones and has to be dragged over the impediment. I can't pass for fear of getting knocked over, and I'm in no condition to help. It's taking everything I've got to stay upright myself.

Back in camp by 9:40 a.m. the skies have cleared, and the temperature has risen above freezing. After I collapse into my tent Omari brings me an early lunch, that I force myself to eat even though all I want to do is sleep. Trying to make sense of the past ten hours while it is still fresh in my mind is difficult, but I don't want the details to slip. It occurs to me I was not lying to Matt and Elizabeth up on Stella Point – I really did hate that, and I'm glad it's over. But so much of this week has been amazing, and I'm thinking of that too.

This tent spot is just one example. Barafu Camp is one of the busiest on the mountain, but the guys have pitched my tent at the far western edge of the rocky site, right next to the steep drop and sheer rock faces that lead down onto the neighbouring plateau. With the tent door and fly unzipped, I've got a spectacular view of the plateau and a hulking ridge a couple of kilometres distant from between a pair of boulders just outside my door. The orientation of my tent and the persistent wind effectively blocks out the surrounding humanity, and there's the illusion that I've got the mountain all to myself.

It is inevitable that after I return home people will ask, "How was it?" I want to be prepared, but it's not an easy question to answer when referring to such an involved undertaking on such a diverse peak. "Big. Beautiful. Brutal." That's one way to go, I guess, but it does seem a bit abrupt. I suppose, "Loved the mountain, hated summit day" is both fair and succinct, because the truth is most people don't have time to get into the gritty details, they just want the Coles Notes.

"Loved the mountain, hated summit day on that big, brutal beauty." Yeah, maybe something like that works.

Pushing my fruit aside to finish when I wake up, I have to say I would definitely come back and circumambulate the summit cone, given the chance. The Northern Circuit looks intriguing on the maps, and walking over to the Mawenzi Tarn Camp would offer a great sunrise view of the main peak, but it's extremely unlikely I would bother with the top again. Unless it was a clear day; then maybe that wonderful view of all four corners of Africa from way, way up high – along with a closer look at the glaciers that remain in such an improbable place – would be worth the effort. A clear day with a noon summit time. Yes, maybe then.

These idle daydreams are how you get in trouble, of course, and I can almost feel a plan coming together in my mind. Fortunately, I pass out cold before I can think about it anymore.

• • •

I don't actually dream of climbing mountains. I don't acclimatize well, for one thing, obviously, and I'm also afraid of heights. Put a little bit of exposure on this route, and there's no chance I would have slogged to the top. But put a bump in an otherwise flat landscape and sooner or later I'm going to go over and have a look. I'll even travel halfway across the world to do it. It's an addiction, a compulsion and a gift. I simply can't help myself, and I am grateful for it. I may not do these things in fine form, but I get there eventually, and I'm never sorry I went.

In a book he wrote about travelling through Australia, Bill Bryson laments that "an awfully large part of travel these days is to see things while you still can."

He was referring to the unfortunate displacement of many native species of plant in a particularly unique and fragile ecosystem he happened to be visiting at the time, but 20 years later the same idea can be extrapolated to include cultures, and increasingly, whole landscapes. The relentless habitat loss that has been accelerating over the last two or three decades has translated into the death of billions, if not trillions, of individual plants and animals. Entire species have also gone extinct at an alarming rate. There are some who believe this rapid decline in everything wild is actually the early stages of planet Earth's sixth mass extinction.

A complete ecological collapse is next level compared to despoiling a small corner of the landscape or losing a few local species, but Bryson's concern from 2000 was nothing if not astute, and is certainly a step or two beyond merely cautionary today.

The cold conditions we experienced this morning, so close to the equator, belie a planet that's heating up. When the wind chill begins to push minus 20 you can easily be fooled into thinking the climate threat is overblown, but the glaciers here are melting back, and are expected to be gone completely within 25 years. Sadly, what is happening locally is happening everywhere in one form or another. At all corners of the globe extreme heat, drought, storms and floods are the new normal. Biosphere earth is interconnected, and Kilimanjaro's glaciers are simply one canary in the coal mine to the ever-growing climate crisis.

While disappearing ice and snow are an obvious and measurable warning of trouble to come, in the immediate future I worry not so much about the conditions up high, but out on the baking plains where it is already 33 and 34 degrees regularly. A degree or two more warming and just a little less rain and the surrounding savannah might turn into desert, but not before fires burn uncontrollably and important habitat is decimated. What happens then? Will the landscape bounce back? Or will it be forever diminished?

For example, devastating bush fires consumed a shocking amount of Australia's wild lands in late 2019 and early 2020. All told, the fire season stretched on for three months and burned an area the size of Bulgaria. Much of Tanzania's low-lying landscape in this region is of similar makeup in temperature and rainfall patterns and distribution of plant life. The balance is tenuous, and it's frightening to think about what an errant spark would do here if conditions were just a little bit drier.

Leaving Barafu camp after a long nap full of hypoxic fever dreams about the end of the world, I'm happy to be going down. Some people opt to hike all the way to Mweka Camp after summiting, but it's been an eventful day and we decide Millennium Camp will be far enough. This allows us a leisurely pace and a chance to rest often. The quiet and relative solitude after all the wind and people of the past 24 hours is welcome, and as we take our first break after descending from the high ridge, Cornel takes the opportunity to explain a peculiar and unnatural feature that has popped up on the landscape. Scattered in amongst the volcanic boulders along the trail are what look like the strangest unicycles I've ever seen.

Some handy welder has attached a motorcycle tire to a sturdy metal stretcher with heavy-duty handles added to both ends. If a climber succumbs to altitude sickness or has an accident, then this is the evacuation vehicle, apparently. There are about a dozen of these custom litters left randomly near the trail, and they're down here and not up at Barafu Camp because the tourists end up playing with them if given the chance.

"Seriously?" I ask, somewhat incredulously. It seems like such a drunken frat boy thing to do.

"Yes," Cornel says.

Apparently, people from certain parts of Asia think this is especially great fun.

Then, completely unprompted, Cornel launches into a story about the Koreans from earlier, who in hindsight, could have used one of these contraptions during their limp-legged descent. Having overheard them as they stumbled along, Cornel reports that one of the guys who was worse off kept muttering, "Fucking Kilimanjaro, why closed? Why closed?" A Korean speaking in English as interpreted by a Tanzanian whose first language is Swahili about the weather disrupting the view *is* hilarious. It's a mashup of accents that plays through my mind like no other, and we have a good chuckle about it before continuing on.

As we walk, I notice there seems to be a lightness in Cornel's demeanour that has been coming out over the last couple of days. He is less the stern, professional guide and more like one of the guys out here on the mountain. Maybe it helps that I proved to be not completely incompetent as time went by, a bit whiny near the end maybe, but I didn't have to be carried up the final section at least. Or back down to camp, for that matter. Now that we're back below 4000 metres the chances I'll die on him are slim. No wonder he's so relaxed.

As we continue to clomp along down the trail in the absence of other hikers, I wonder, can we be friends? Money changes the dynamic of everything. His job is to guide me across the landscape. Pick the right route and oversee the crew so that I get what I paid for, and with a little luck, summit the mountain. That objective satisfied, and the crowds now way out ahead, this feels more like a walk in the wilderness with a new friend than a guided trek. It took a little while for us to gel, but after six days we seem to be settling into the beginning of a relationship that extends beyond the business of tourism.

This is a pleasing development.

• • •

From Millennium Camp to the trailhead at Mweka Gate it's 13 kilometres of downhill walking. After a good night's sleep, I'm feeling surprisingly strong. There are plenty of big rocky steps to be wary of along the way, but also a lot of easy grade on smooth trail where gravity is finally my ally instead of my foe. As we descend through the moorlands, vegetation steadily increases and the view down the trail and out onto the low cloud cover we're walking toward is beautiful. It may not be the whole of Africa laid out in every direction, and it is a bit hazy, but it's still pretty cool.

Eventually, we make it back into the thick canopy of trees skirting the lower third of Kilimanjaro and the sky closes in and lets loose, dumping buckets of rain down upon us. Offering one last challenge to our comfort while confirming that this montane forest is in fact a tropical rainforest, connected yet independent of the other climatic and vegetation zones that make up the greater mountain ecosystem. The rain has come just in case there was any doubt about what this particular zone is all about. The last couple of kilometres of the trek are along a rough dirt access road, and the sun comes out once again as we approach Mweka Gate. It's as if the mountain is letting us know it holds no ill will and was simply testing our fortitude and worthiness one last time before we go.

Even Moshi is softening in my eyes. Rumbling back down into town through the coffee plantations and roadside villages, the van is a mass of happy souls who don't have to walk anymore today. After navigating the Coca-Cola clock tower roundabout – and remarking on the unusual sight of a Maasai on a mountain bike pedalling furiously in the traffic – we turn onto a crowded dirt side street and pull up in front of one of the many locals restaurants. It's hot as Hades down here, at least compared to what we've grown used to over the last few days. I'm guessing a 50-degree Celsius difference from what we experienced at the windswept summit of Kilimanjaro in the early hours of yesterday morning.

Upon our arrival at the restaurant a white plastic table and an assortment of chairs are produced and set up in the dust under a tree. Immediately the beers flow and stories from the week are told with ever-increasing animation and volume. Eventually, Cornel and I are brought river fish steaks with rice and vegetables, followed by grisly chunks of barbecued meat served "en famille" style for all to share. Luca, one of the porters, has his big personality on full display now, and everyone is feeling the giddy effects of the beers except Omari, who has opted for a couple of Cokes instead. Just as I begin seriously contemplating why there is a white plastic stool lodged high in the tree we are under, Constantino leans over and says, "There's something you should see."

We step away from the table and move a metre or two down the exceedingly narrow alley behind us where there's a nondescript, well-built iron tower roughly five metres high. The perpendicular beam that extends outward at the top is less than a metre long. The setup looks sturdy and serious and it takes a second to figure out, but then it dawns on me – this is the hanging pole.

"That building across the street," Constantino nods in direction of our table, but slightly farther afield, "in Colonial times it was the courthouse. If the Germans didn't like what the Africans were doing..."

"They would string them up here."

"Yes."

In moments like these – and at places like the Catholic Museum in Bagamoyo, or the Natural History Museum in Dar es Salaam – I cannot help but be astounded that

Africans of this generation even allow white people onto the continent anymore, given our brutal history. More than that even, our little group is all here together this afternoon, sharing a rip-roaring good time just steps away from a spot where countless injustices no doubt occurred in the name of "Law and Order," and yet I am accepted without question. Staring up at the hanging pole, I experience a surge of collective guilt. A vague yet powerful sense of remorse has washed over me. I didn't have anything to do with what went on here, obviously. Nor, to the best of my knowledge, did any of my ancestors. But, as a thinking and feeling person, it is impossible to deny the human capacity for cruelty. What do you say in this kind of situation? *Sorry* doesn't even begin to cut it.

As if he was getting a sense of what I was thinking, Constantino puts his arm around my shoulder to lead me back to the party, which is still in full swing. Having just spent a week with him on the mountain, I'm familiar with his dry sense of humour. His statement strikes me as part absolution and part tongue-in-cheek reassurance that there will be no impending retribution.

"Don't worry," he says, "you're not German."

It's small comfort, but sometimes that's the best you can hope for. Taking my seat and looking at the happy, half-buzzed faces around the table, I realize the atrocities that occurred here are in the past. They are ghosts in the background, representatives of the moments in time that should occasionally be acknowledged anew but should not be allowed to interfere with hope for a better future. It could be argued the exploitation and repression across Africa is different now, more corporate in its intentions and more subtle in its applications, but this is not the time or the place to contemplate any of that. We're just a bunch of guys who climbed a really big mountain and are now celebrating together.

I think it's probably time for more beers, and it's my round.

11

LIONS AND TIGERS AND BEARS, TANZANIA STYLE

After coming down from Kilimanjaro there is an adjustment to be made. Climbing the mountain wasn't the singular goal for this trip, but it was an important part of it, and now that it's done I've got to figure out exactly how I want to approach the rest of my time here in Africa. In a way, I guess the weight of expectation has been lifted. Even if nothing goes well for the rest of my visit I have at least accomplished one big thing in my travels, which is a relief. Following that line of thinking, I can probably also mail it in from the physical effort standpoint for the rest of 2019. Clearing away all those ridiculous New Year's resolutions about getting more exercise by 6:30 a.m. on January 7 is a refreshing change from how my year usually starts, that's for sure.

After a long leisurely breakfast, I look forward to my walk into town. I'm comfortable with the route now, and at Cemetery Memorial Park a full company of young military cadets are being drilled in small groups across the entire open field, while just across the road an open-air bicycle repair shop has set up for the day. Other than that, it's mostly tuk tuks and motorbikes and cars that provide distraction as they scurry about on their daily commutes. The tuk tuk drivers are keen to slow down and offer a ride, but I'm happy to walk.

At Union Café, where well-off locals, expats and tourists have once again gathered for lattes and Wi-Fi, I settle in at one of the outdoor tables on the charming veranda that wraps around two sides of the building. It's a good spot to people watch, and perhaps to ponder the implications of time, now that I have a little of it to burn. For the adventurous souls out there, a trip to Tanzania revolves around climbing the mountain. Or, if strenuous physical activity is not your thing, then a safari to see the animals out on the Serengeti Plain. Either one would qualify for a place on most people's "Trip of a Lifetime" list. I am fortunate, I have the opportunity to do both. But we are a culture that corrupts time, and I want to make sure I understand its true worth before continuing on. I believe we pervert time with a fundamental misunderstanding of its purpose. We do this by insisting it be endlessly productive, even when we're travelling. I've just done a big thing and want step back from the sucking abyss of non-stop activity long enough to properly appreciate what has just passed.

In a thoughtco.com article published on November 26, 2019, called "What Is Time? A Simple Explanation," Anne Marie Helmenstine explores the concept of time. The strict definition is straightforward: "Physicists define time as the progression of events from the past to the present into the future." Nothing in there about measuring it with deeds, as far as I can tell, but the link is all but inescapable in the modern age. The short article goes on to talk briefly about The Arrow of Time, Time Dilation, Time Travel and The Beginning and End of Time. What I find most interesting in the piece is that "scientists believe memory formation is the basis for human perception of time," and from the Time Perception section comes this little tidbit:

"Psychologists believe the brain forms more memories of new experiences than that of familiar ones."

My question for today is, does rushing through experience alter our ability to consolidate memories, even the new ones? And is that why it can be difficult to live in the moment, as time rushes by?

At its core I have always believed time should be used as an opportunity to explore the unknown in order to learn a thing or two about life, not as part of the measure of how many items can be checked off a To Do List. X number of things in Y amount of time is an accomplishment-based formula. As I have already mentioned, I'm hoping for a memory-based journey. A pilgrimage of discovery if you will, but I do still struggle to balance my social programming. Most westerners, when faced with the possibility of an impactful personal journey, can usually scrimp and save in order to make it happen, but often fail to carve out the necessary time to properly explore their surroundings, or reflect on the greater implications of their trip.

We rush to destinations and then rush home again because that's all the time we think we have to give. Maria Coffee explores a variation of this concept in *Explorers of the Infinite*. "Humans were once surrounded by wild time, until they began to chart time, to clock it," she writes. "As humanity overtook wilderness, so western societies' peculiar time-marking has become the norm and wild time the exception." In the end I simply couldn't see the point of coming all this way for a week or ten days. And so I'm trying to settle into another approach, but I admit, it's not always easy to sit still. I often feel compelled to do for the sake of doing, in part because I think that's what's expected of me.

These are complicated concepts to unravel, that require

another latte's worth of contemplation at least, which my waiter brings with a small cookie to dip into the light foam. Returning to the thoughts swirling around in my head, the influence money has on the equation cannot be ignored. Joshua Becker, in a becomingminimalist.com article, gets right to the point in the title, "We Don't Buy Things with Money, We Buy Them with Hours from Our Life." In other words, we buy them with the time and the effort taken from our lives while we're on the clock. Or, as Becker quotes Henry David Thoreau as saying, "The price of anything is the amount of life you exchange for it."

Interesting take. I have often felt out of sorts when it comes to the modern definition of work. I understand the way the system functions, and have manipulated it to my advantage often enough, but haven't always felt comfortable, much less fulfilled, while participating. "The price of anything is the amount of life you exchange for it." When you look at it that way it's no wonder I have occasionally been hostile to the idea. You want me to exchange my *life* for a few dollars an hour? And you want me to be gushingly grateful and ultimately beholden if a couple of extra dollars are offered on top of that? It is an offensive concept no matter how you look at it. One thing I know for sure is you can't put an hourly dollar value on a life well lived. It just doesn't translate.

But Becker sees this theory as a life-changing principle that I'm willing to explore. "When we begin to see our purchases through the lens of exchanging *life*, rather than *dollar bills*, we can better appreciate the weight of our purchases and understand their full cost." Contemplating the hours spent chasing those dollar bills in order to simply exist in my culture is demoralizing, no question about it, but working in order to go and have an experience out in the world makes it tolerable at least. To buy time is a privilege not available to everyone, and I must remind myself to be grateful for that opportunity at least, and I am. Truly.

So maybe it is accurate to say that in modern society time is money, and while we have been fully trained in the simple act of spending the cash, few of us really understand the value of the investment. I have chosen to extend this experience for as long as possible to try and get the most out of it. I have bought a bit of time, in essence exchanging *life* back home for a few dollars to help underwrite a period of *living* here in East Africa. Fair trade, I'd say, and one I'm willing to make as I try to come to grips with the intricacies of the deal.

Following the thread a little further, it occurs to me that Moshi has been consumed by the modern interpretation of time as money, with experience relegated to an afterthought, just as with every burgeoning tourist destination in the world. Staring out at the busy intersection of Arusha Road and Selous Street, I realize maybe that's what I don't like about this place. Everyone is either in a rush or on the make, creating an environment where money is the focus and time is relegated to a linear measure, while experience is left behind as an afterthought.

I have to admit, it sometimes feels like all I do here in town is organize my finances, and I'll be doing the ATM shuffle once again this afternoon in order to pay for my safari trip. There's no escaping it, I've got to pull those funds together so we can *go*. But what I enjoy most about this place is lingering in it. Here on the patio of Union Café with a latte, or later today on the patio at Secret Garden with a beer. In these moments the warm breeze of time washes comfortably over me and I am content in its passing. I suspect it'll be another 20 to 30 minutes before I succumb to the neurotic impulse to get organized and begin the ATM shuffle. Until then, I going to savour every second as it goes.

After all, if Becker is right, then I've already paid for it with little bits of my life. I intend to get my money's worth.

•••

There's a slight chill in the air, it's still dark out, and all is quiet, but I am excited. The dogs are surprised to see someone up so early and slowly unfurl themselves from under the front of the SUV parked in the gravel driveway and make their way over, only to curl up again immediately, one resting on each of my feet. As I sit on the stoop waiting for my ride to Arusha, the faintest of faint predawn glows begins to appear in the east.

When the car arrives, it's yet another new driver I haven't met, and there is a passenger as well. Ben will be the tent mate I thought I was going to get on the climb, and the 75 kilometres to Arusha will be a good opportunity to get acquainted. Turns out Ben is from France and is on a year-long sabbatical from work that he is using to travel the world. He's already been to Japan, the Middle East and South America, to name just a few of the destinations he's visited. This is good news, he's a fellow wanderer, and it's easy to get along with a fellow wanderer. The fear in this situation is you get an incompatible tent mate and spend five days in uncomfortable conversation. Or worse, uncomfortable silence.

Tarangire National Park is our first stop on a five-day tour of the north-central region of Tanzania. About 80 kilometres beyond Arusha, the small town of Makuyuni sits at the crossroads of our route, and about 25 kilometres beyond that on Highway A104 is the access road to the park. Also on our itinerary is Lake Manyara National Park, about 40 kilometres up Highway B142 from Makuyuni, but what I'm really looking forward to is the Ngorongoro Conservation Area and Serengeti National Park later in the trip. Those two interconnected and protected areas are home to some of the best wildlife viewing on the planet, so I expect the *wow* factor to be high once we reach those destinations. Until then, meh. Whatever. How good could it be?

It is with these low expectations that we roll up to the gate at Tarangire, and entering the park is about what I would imagine for the beginning of our tour. A flat, dry, tree- and shrub-covered landscape greets us as we move quite abruptly from an area of cultivated farmland at the edge of the park and into the bush. A family of vervet monkeys, a group of warthogs, a singular giraffe playing peekaboo from behind some acacia trees, and a small herd of impala all feature in the first 45 minutes of our game drive. These animals, seen in the wild as opposed to in a zoo or on a television screen, are a new experience and so are decidedly cool, but it's hardly an overwhelming display of charismatic megafauna of the sort that inspires strong emotion.

In an age of overused superlatives, it is perhaps wise to temper your enthusiasm for fear of being disappointed by reality. It worked on Kilimanjaro. Except for the 15 minutes spent at the top, the crowds didn't bother me much, and that was because I was mentally prepared for the people. Tarangire is about to become the exception that proves the rule. Reality, in this particular case, could not be more superlative.

It's only after we drop down into a small river valley

that things take a dramatic turn and the true heart of Tarangire is revealed. As the sky opens up, a small herd of eight to ten elephants casually graze as they move slowly through their territory. The rain is brief, but heavy, and it transforms the animal's rough, thick skin from a medium pale grey to a darker shade that almost looks brown. The animals have a habit of tossing dust up onto their backs to protect them from irritating insects and the sun, and now that dust has turned to clumps of caked-on mud. At one point, three mid-sized, immature females come together to bump and nuzzle in a bonding fashion about 30 or 40 metres away. As luck would have it, they are turned in our direction *and* happen to be standing in a gap in the underbrush that separates us. Camera at the ready and long lens trained on the three ladies, I end up with one of what will be many cherished photographs of the wild animals of Africa.

These are African bush elephants – the largest land mammals on earth – and to encounter a group of them is both thrill and privilege. Generally, herds such as this one are made up mothers and their offspring, and the males set off on their own after reaching maturity. Sometimes the males form small bachelor groups for company, and only come into contact with the females during mating season. This herd has little interest in, or concern for, our presence, and it's enthralling to watch them move about as they interact with each other and feed.

I have always found animal behaviour to be endlessly fascinating, and could spend hours watching this group of elephants, but a game drive doesn't work that way. After the initial thrill of coming into contact with this herd subsides – and the requisite photos are taken – the interest shown by my fellow truck-mates wanes, and our guide appears eager to move us along to the next photo op.

In Arusha, Ben and I traded the pickup car for a proper safari vehicle, and Zebron is a competent driver/guide, with an innate understanding of the sightlines provided by our extended cab Toyota Land Cruiser. There is space in the front for the driver and one passenger, and in the back there is seating for six more passengers, with windows all around. The selling feature that makes this particular model so popular for wildlife viewing is that the roof can be popped up so passengers in the back can stand up as we bounce along the rough track in search of game. It offers a 360-degree raised viewing platform while still keeping us protected from the sun and rain.

Turning my attention away from the three mid-sized adult elephants, I notice there is a larger female on her own just off to our right, not ten metres away. She's casually grazing on some long grasses, and she's so close I can clearly see the veins and arteries zigzagging under the skin of her ears. Elephants use their enormous ears to keep cool by fanning them, and the skin there is comparatively thin to help body heat escape. Just as I'm about to begin contemplating the amazing instrument of dexterity that is an elephant's trunk, Zebron starts up the truck and says it's time to go. There's something we've got to see.

Wait. What? We just got here.

It strikes me that Ben is comfortable just going with the flow, and when I glance over he gives a little shrug, but our two other travelling companions are also keen to see what's next. Our truck-mates are Russian, and although Sergey is enthusiastic and friendly, the language barrier does make detailed communication difficult. His wife is easily the least patient of us all, and at every lull in the action over the coming days will say, "We go?" with her heavy accent. Sometimes it's a question. Sometimes it's a statement, of the type that doesn't leave room for discussion.

Just now, another of the bigger elephants has found the perfectly shaped tree and is rubbing her forehead and trunk in a vertically oriented notch, so of course I don't want to go anywhere yet, but Zebron insists there are lions up on the escarpment.

Sure there are.

Bouncing up the dirt track, I can't help but feel an eagerness to stay with the elephants and do look back to get one last glimpse of them as we go, but Zebron is true to his word. There are lions here. Lots of lions, and lots of other Land Cruisers too. Crowded in on the narrow track there are about a dozen other vehicles, and it occurs to me this is not an accident. Lost in the excitement of our elephant encounter was the unmistakable crackle of a CB radio coming to life, turned down so low I could barely hear it. It didn't seem important at the time, but now it all makes sense. These guys talk to each other and relay information on animal movements and locations. How else could Zebron know there were lions up here on the lip of the valley?

Instinct? I don't think so. He's good, but he's not that good.

Pulling up to the back of the queue of vehicles is not as disappointing as you would expect, because the lions are away from the track to our left, so everyone has a decent view. There are at least a dozen lions in this pride, including a remarkable number of cubs who look to be between four and six months old, and interestingly there are no mature males – with their distinctive shaggy manes – anywhere to be seen. While the *wow* factor has jumped up a few notches, the lions themselves are about as indifferent to our presence as the elephants were. They know we're here, but they just don't care, and so we shoot our pictures and stare in stunned silence as they wait out the growing heat of the day in their casual detachment.

I have three cats back home. They are old and lazy and fully domesticated, but if a fly or a bee somehow finds its way into the condo a remarkable transformation occurs. They reach back into their ancestry to find the hunter within. They move in a controlled and deliberate manner, using walls and furniture as cover. Even out in the open of the hardwood of our living room floor they will crouch down in the non-existent long grasses in an attempt to conceal themselves from their prey. It's strangely compelling to watch, and it seems that some instincts are hard to shake even after generations of eating dinner out of a bowl. No question about it, in those moments they are transformed.

The reason I bring it up now is because the demeanour of one of the mature females in this group has changed ever so slightly. It is a subtle shift, that I might not have noticed were it not for the small pride in my living room. She's onto something but doesn't want to raise an alarm. Moving deliberately, she has walked right through the gauntlet of Land Cruisers lining the dirt track. All the lions in the pride have been to the left of us, near to the edge of the ridge overlooking the valley below. My immediate impression when we drove up, after *Holy shit, that's a lot of lions*, was that all the vehicles would surely scare the animals away, but they appear comfortable in their role as photogenic ambassadors to the park.

What I will come to realize over the next few days is that to them we are neither predator nor prey, but simply an innocuous bit of the landscape that happens to move around for most of the morning, and that is generally gone by late afternoon. It helps that these are professional drivers moving on established tracks, so even when a dozen vehicles show up in a particular spot, the animals can move off and we can't go following them unless they walk along the dirt track.

After she passes through the vehicles, the hunting instinct is now obvious in this big female. She is slinking along more than walking. She's crouching close to the trees and moving very slowly with lots of pauses. It is only now that I see what has captured her attention. Three warthogs, 150 metres away and visible through a break in the bush. The warthogs seem oblivious to the lioness, and all of us for that matter, and she's trying to sneak around to the left in order to come on them from the blind side. There is also another mature female flanking off to the right, a tawny patch of muscled fur intermittently visible in the denser bush. There's also a quiet buzz rippling through the vehicles (and lots of pointing) that indicates a third lion that I don't see from my vantage point making a more frontal approach. And still the warthogs casually graze.

This development is amazing on a number of levels. We haven't been in the park for even two hours, for one thing. I had also never even heard of Tarangire National Park until our briefing this morning, and certainly didn't expect a Mutual of Omaha's *Wild Kingdom* episode would be playing out right before my eyes so soon. On top of everything else it's the middle of the day and getting hot again after the brief downpour. Expending needless energy is not in the lion playbook, but clearly the calculus has been made. This meal might be worth the effort.

When you watch a nature program on television the

majority of the raw footage is edited out, for obvious reasons. Even on the hunt, there's not a lot going on, until suddenly there is. After all the patient buildup, the attack happens incredibly fast. A few panicked squeals are followed by a flash of dark brown through a gap in the thick acacia bushes, followed almost instantly by a larger tawny flash in hot pursuit. The energy coming from the group of human spectators is palpable. It's as if we've been collectively holding our breath in anticipation of this moment, and now that it's here, I panic.

What do I do!? What do I do?! Do I watch? Do I try and get a picture? Which direction should I look toward for a decent sightline? After the deliberate buildup, I'm not ready for the intensity of the action and ultimately miss the shot. Not only that, I'm not even sure what has happened in the end because the animals have all scattered off into the deeper bush.

It isn't until one of the female lions wanders back into view that it becomes obvious the attempt has failed. The majority of lion hunts end in failure. The website africa-wildlife-detective.com estimates that a solo lion will be successful in one out of every six attempts, while lions hunting in a group will improve the odds to one in three. After the dust settles here, these lions display behaviour that hints at an understanding of the odds. They instantly revert back to energy conservation mode. One by one they return to the edge of the pride, but don't rejoin immediately. Instead, they come together to reaffirm their bond as the primary hunters of the group by engaging in an endearing cuddle session.

The first of the lionesses I had spotted on the hunt lies down heavily in a comfortable-looking patch of grass and is quickly joined by her companions. The three of them rub cheeks and jowls and proceed to roll around all over each other, paws splayed in the air, looking not unlike a cardboard box full of kittens waiting for mom to come back and feed them. It is an incredibly tender display for such big, powerful animals. Lions are the only species of big cat that lives in groups, and these displays of affection help reaffirm social bonds and individual status among the pride. As they are cuddling, a male impala shows up off to the right and is understandably startled by what he has wandered into, but the lions are still recovering from their exertions and show no interest in the small, skittish intruder who is too far away to bother chasing, and who wisely retreats in the direction from which he came.

The rest of the day is spent rumbling slowly around the park in search of game. Elephants turn out to be the main attraction, but we also come across some lone giraffes, plenty of impalas and some gazelles, and a lazy leopard passed out in a tree, who never moves a muscle in the 15 minutes we spend waiting for him to do something interesting.

As the afternoon slips away, a more complete picture of Tarangire begins to emerge. While the lions and elephants and giraffes are clearly the highlight of day one, it is the birds and trees and overall landscape that leave an indelible impression. The knob-billed duck feeding in a shallow muddy pool looks like an impossible evolutionary oddity, with his white head dotted with dark spots and his pronounced knobby bill looking like it would be a challenge to see past, not to mention a burden to carry around. The southern ground hornbill we encounter could easily have been named carnivorous demonic turkey. The secretary bird? An eagle's body on a stork's legs that can grow to be four feet tall and weigh ten pounds, that likes to stomp its small prey to death. Totally normal.

This species diversity underscores an important detail that makes this region so important to African wildlife conservation – intact landscapes. Tarangire and Lake Manyara National Parks are not connected, but they are in close proximity, and the Ngorongoro Conservation Area is not far away either. Serengeti National Park shares a border with Ngorongoro. At the edges of Serengeti there are a number of game reserves and game-controlled areas. It adds up to a massive footprint where lesser-known species have kept their place on the land, which helps keep the entire ecosystem healthy and balanced.

We've closed the roof to the Land Cruiser now and have moved back onto the smooth pavement for the roughly hour-long journey to the village of Mto Wa Mbu, where we will be spending the night. Reflecting on Tarangire as we return to the world of the humans and the countryside flashes past at high speed, all I can say about the day is, *WOW*.

All caps.

12

THE LOST WORLD

As it happens, these parks in the northwestern part of Tanzania are sufficiently different to be classified as unique from one another, at least at the superficial level. That first day in Tarangire National Park was an eye-opener to the value of an extended swath of land that has not been overly disrupted by the heavy hand of man. Poaching is still a threat to a number of the iconic species in the region, but a surefire way to decimate an animal population is to destroy their habitat. Seventy large mammal species and over 500 bird species speak to how that widespread destruction has been avoided in both the Tarangire-Manyara and the greater Serengeti ecosystems.

Visiting each park individually has subsequently revealed an amazing ability on the part of the animals to adapt to subtle variations in the larger landscape.

Tarangire has a river cutting through its centre, which gives the land an undulating character that sets it apart from the vast plains littered with the rocky outcrops called *kopjes* that helps to define the Serengeti. Lake Manyara National Park is only a few dozen kilometres away from Tarangire as the crow flies, but has denser forest along the steep western boundary that marks the edge of the Gregory arm of the Great Rift Valley, in addition to a swampy marshland near the lakeshore that provides different kinds of habitat compared to Tarangire. The elephants we saw navigating the dense brush there were smaller and tended to be more solitary, but there were a couple of hippos and some Cape buffalo in the swamp, not to mention a whole new collection of waterfowl, including African spoonbills, lesser flamingos and great white pelicans.

Serengeti National Park off to the west lived up to its advanced billing, offering up classic African savannah scenery that included expansive grasslands, isolated woodlands, the occasional small marsh and of course the iconic umbrella thorn, a tree that all but poses for photos at every fiery sunrise, and then again at every fiery sunset. The Serengeti's great migration – where upwards of 1.5 million wildebeest start to congregate as the dry season begins, before heading north to the Maasai Mara National Reserve in Kenya – is almost four months away, but there were still plenty of wildebeest, zebra, gazelles and antelope spread out across the plains. And of course, there were lions. Lots of lions. Currently, Serengeti National Park encompasses an area of 14,750 square kilometres. The park's beginnings date back to the 1920s when the British established the first reserve. It was an effort to reverse a rapid decline in the lion population resulting from over-hunting. Official park designation occurred in 1951, and while I was having a cup of coffee with Ronaldo before setting out on this safari, he credited former president Julius Nyerere with steering the country in the right direction when it comes to conservation. Ronaldo came across as reverent in that moment and went so far as to call Nyerere "a visionary."

That modern Tanzania can boast 38 per cent of its land area as protected in one form or another (Uganda is second in the region at 26 per cent, Kenya third at 12 per cent) speaks to a commitment to the cause that has endured. And it's not as if Nyerere didn't already have enough on his plate. As president of a fledgling republic, he had to guide his country through the transition from colonial rule, navigate a complicated relationship with Zanzibar in order to create a unified state, and champion his particular brand of African socialism, known as *Ujamaa*. It would have been easy to overlook environmental protections and concerns, especially in the late 1950s and early 1960s, when such matters were not so pressing in the public consciousness.

Nevertheless, the Tanzania National Parks website recognizes a speech Nyerere gave at a symposium on the Conservation of Nature and Natural Resources as a key moment in the development of national park policy. In it Nyerere said:

> The survival of our wildlife is a matter of grave concern to all of us in Africa. These wild creatures amid the wild places they inhabit are not only important as a source of wonder and inspiration but are an integral part of our natural resources and our future livelihood and well-being.

Driving around all day through these parks gives you a lot of time to contemplate the implications of such forward thinking, in between the incredible animal encounters of course, when coherent thought is rightly abandoned and the best you can hope to manage is slack-jawed amazement. In the more mellow moments, when you're surrounded by so much natural beauty, it is hard to imagine the world at large is in trouble. It may seem like an odd time to be concerned with such things, but I believe that being somewhere as extraordinary as northern Tanzania is when we need to think about it most, precisely because this place has not been visibly diminished. It is rugged and wild and beautiful, proving there is still much to lose if we're not careful.

On November 16, 2017, *The Tyee* published an article written by William E. Rees titled "What, Me Worry? Humans Are Blind to Imminent Environmental Collapse: Accelerating biodiversity loss may turn out to be the sleeper issue of the century." In addition to having the longest title/subtitle I've ever seen, the article explores the impact of man on the larger ecosystem, noting that "the overall driver is what an ecologist might call the 'competitive displacement' of non-human life by the inexorable growth of the human enterprise."

Rees lays out some compelling arguments on the importance of protecting the entire biomass and offers this big picture view that I hadn't thought of in quite this way before: "There is a deeper reason to fear the depletion and depopulation of nature. Absent life, planet earth is just an inconsequential wet rock with a poisonous atmosphere revolving pointlessly around an ordinary star on the outer fringes of an undistinguished galaxy."

I love it! Life is what makes planet earth special – not human life, but *life* – and we are threatening that distinctive detail on a number of fronts. According to Rees, "Climate change is not the only shadow darkening humanity's doorstep. While you wouldn't know it from the mainstream media, biodiversity loss arguably poses an equivalent existential threat to civilized existence." Are these warnings exaggerated or alarmist? I somehow doubt it, but only time will tell for sure. Even a system as large as a planetary one can eventually be overwhelmed. Looking to a celestial neighbour for clues reveals another rocky world with a thick atmosphere filled with greenhouse gases and a surface temperature hot enough to melt lead. Venus is a blast furnace. Nothing lives there.

But herein lies part of the problem for the average individual in taking these warning signs more seriously: this world *is* still beautiful, and is remarkably resilient in the face of a decades-long onslaught by man. The slow, creeping change that is altering the global landscape can be hard to gauge, even first-hand. Without extensive personal history and familiarity with an area there often seems little cause for worry. Every first-hand experience is a new baseline for each individual. Every generation sees a location in its current state, which is different from what the generation before experienced. Subtle differences and incremental changes can be easily overlooked, quiet warnings easily brushed aside as fanciful.

The science says we are at a dangerous crossroads, and quite possibly an irreversible tipping point, yet there are still trees and plants and animals in abundance if you look in the right places. This delicate deception of our senses helps feed the nagging disbelief in the possibility that we are hurtling toward the abyss, one of our own making no less, but there is a deeper subtext here and a muted warning that should nevertheless be heeded. These pristine natural environments are the canaries in the global coal mine, and we're still not really listening.

The top of Mount Kilimanjaro seems a world away from the dry open plains of the Serengeti, but is only 300 or so kilometres from here, and is also one of those places I'm talking about. The disappointment of not seeing the glaciers up close, even in their steady and noteworthy retreat, was offset somewhat by the unique, in-the-moment experience that is fresh snow and bitter cold so close to the equator. While being a noteworthy exercise in the study of perception, it is one of those confounding situations where immediate sensation conflicts directly with what you know to be true intellectually. Global warming is a thing, despite what all the naysayers might have you believe, and Mount Kilimanjaro on a clear day is part of the body of proof of that theory. Temperature change is a subtle creep, and the vagaries of weather make it more obscure, but the glaciers *are* wasting away. It's a simple fact that's obvious even from down in Moshi. The raw data confirming this observation is incontrovertible; temperature over time is trending upward everywhere and is having an adverse effect on global systems.

Lions are similar beacons to pay attention to, for biodiversity, not necessarily climate. A large predator population can only survive if a habitat is healthy enough to support the grazers upon which they prey. An intact ecosystem allows the natural dynamic to continue to play out here, much as it has for centuries. This is what makes northern Tanzania so amazing and compelling to visit – it lures you in with its beauty, and then it challenges you to look deeper. It demands that you think harder about what we ultimately decide to save, and what we hope to keep.

In *The Language of Landscape,* Anne Whiston Spirn writes, "The language of landscape is our native language. Landscape was our original dwelling; humans evolved among plants and animals, under the sky, upon the earth, near water. Everyone carries that legacy in body and mind."

As if climate change and biodiversity decline weren't enough to contemplate, the evolution Whiston Spirn is talking about also happened right here, on these plains and in the nearby mountains. It could be another reason people are unconsciously drawn to the region. As it happens, this is home no matter where it is you're from.

As we were rattling along the washboard track of a dirt road leading out of the Ngorongoro Conservation Area and into Serengeti National Park, we passed a sign pointing down another bone-jarring dirt road – Olduvai Gorge. The gorge is where Mary and Louis Leakey did their best work tracing back the human family tree, identifying the remains and chronicling the behaviours of *Homo habilis*, Australopithecine and *Homo erectus* species from the fossils and stone tools found in the gorge. I studied the subject as an elective in college, and knew the gorge was in Africa. The National Museum in Dar was a useful refresher on the subject, but it wasn't until we came upon the nondescript road junction in the middle of nowhere that the geographical puzzle pieces came together more clearly in my head, with an almost audible clang.

How did I not realize this place was right here in the middle of everything else I wanted to come and see? And why didn't I schedule an extra day to go exploring in the gorge?

Cramming all this discovery and insight into a short period of time, I am once again awestruck by the wonder that is Tanzania. This place is amazing. I admit to being overwhelmed by these past two weeks, and the revelations that have come thick and fast. It'll take months to unpack it all, to look through the pictures and comb through the notes and come up with an adequate summation of the experience, but one thing is for sure: without protected status and the strong economic incentive that tourism affords, these animals and this landscape would not look the same. This place would not be the same. It would inevitably have been diminished by now.

It turns out Nyerere *was* a visionary after all. He had it right all along. There is no way he could have imagined the extent to which human industry was going to threaten life on this planet, but he knew enough to realize that in his little corner of the world it was important to save a significant chunk of nature's wonders. The phrase *think globally, act locally* can have no better example to follow.

•••

We've been on some rough roads over the last few days, but this, this is ridiculous. Descending down into the Ngorongoro Crater involves a steep grade, loose rocks and a low gear that all conspire to slow the Land Cruiser to walking speed. There are a couple of spots where it almost feels like we could flip over forward onto the roof of the truck if we hit the bounce juussst right, and you know it's steep when the wheels slip with the brakes fully applied and you *slide* down the track. But straight away after getting into the crater upright and unharmed, the welcoming committee is a lone Cape buffalo grazing in an open field near the road.

A familiar pattern has emerged on our series of game drives. We'll be travelling along, getting our daily "African massage" courtesy of the rough dirt tracks, when someone will yell out, loud enough to be heard above the rumbling engine and rattling chassis of the vehicle.

"Lions!"

Invariably, someone else will shout, "Stop. Stop. Stop!" As if that really needs to be added.

You would think that after some long, hot hours in the truck the exhilaration of spotting a new animal would wane, but even after four days of remarkable moments excitement still takes over at the point of first contact. Bouncing along, it can sometimes feel like your internal organs are going to shake loose. But you also don't want to sit down and rest too long for fear of missing the chance to be the first to see something cool. The anticipation is addicting, and we all take turns with the call, depending on who happens to be gazing off in the lucky direction at the time. It's not always lions – the technique works equally well with other species.

"Giraffes!"

"Stop. Stop. Stop!"

Or, "Elephants!"

"Stop. Stop. Stop!"

We've done it with hippopotamus, wildebeest, gazelle, ostrich and zebra, to name just a few. This morning it's Cape buffalo. This particular animal has dried mud caked on its flanks and a pair of red-billed oxpeckers hitching a ride on his back. The birds are adept at picking ticks off the hides of all the bigger animals in the ecosystem, but at the moment appear to just be resting between meals. The buffalo also appears to have just one eye, although it is hard to tell if this is the result of a birth defect or an injury that has long since healed.

Cape buffalo are part of the famed Big Five. Stocky and slobbery with a face only a mother could love, it's hard to imagine them in the same category as lions, leopards, black rhinos and elephants, but the designation appropriated by the travel tourism industry was originally used by big-game hunters and referred not to the set of animals whose sighting was most coveted, but rather which animals were most difficult to hunt on foot. Cape buffalo are notoriously ill-tempered and, unlike their Asian cousins the water buffalo, cannot be domesticated. The fact that this lumbering beast in front of us can survive out here with just one eye certainly speaks to the toughness of individuals of the species.

Dropping a little farther down onto the comparatively

flat crater floor, we come across a few more buffalo, a lone jackal, some wildebeest, a collection of Thomson's gazelles frolicking in a shaft of early-day sun knifing through the cloud cover, and a pair of spotted hyenas curled up in a small divot in the ground ten feet from the side of the road, that we don't even see until we drive right up next to them. At first the animal sightings are sporadic, but as the sun climbs higher over the crater rim to the east the bulk of the morning clouds begin to burn off. Then, somewhat miraculously, the animals come out in larger clusters. They are all over the place, seemingly from out of nowhere. Wildebeest and zebra and buffalo and gazelle, grazing in the dozens over in that direction, and then in the hundreds off in another.

As I mentioned, by this fifth day it's hard to imagine being astonished by wildlife, but there you have it, in the Ngorongoro Crater they live in concentrations that do still manage to amaze. By some estimates that I found online there are as many as 25,000 wild animals that call the crater home, including 7,000 wildebeest, 4,000 zebras, 3,000 gazelles and 600 hyenas. It is also thought there are 200 elephants, 60 lions and 30 endangered black rhinos. This is a world that continues to exist outside our penchant to diminish and our instinct to consume. It is a tiny intact remnant of the previous glory of the natural world.

It is a lost world.

With its remarkable symmetry it would be easy to assume the Ngorongoro Crater is an impact crater – the visible remains of a violent collision between an asteroid and the earth that has not yet been worn away by the forces of erosion. This would be a mistake. The crater is in fact the collapsed caldera of an ancient and extinct volcano. Roughly three million years ago a mountain at least as high as Kilimanjaro stood here, and then erupted with such violence it collapsed in on itself, leaving behind a divot in the earth 600 metres deep and 19 kilometres across. It remains the largest intact collapsed caldera on Earth that is not filled with water or significantly eroded at the margins. The unique combination of factors that make up the crater's physical geography – and the remarkable foresight of Tanzanians to protect the landscape and its natural inhabitants – make this place one of the most unique ecosystems left on the planet. But I admit, first views didn't leave that big an impression as we skirted the crater rim.

You catch your first glimpse of this natural wonder on the drive out to the Serengeti Plains after touring Tarangire and Lake Manyara parks, on day one and day two, respectively. The road climbs up to the crater rim at its southernmost point early on day three, before traversing to the western edge and descending past the Malanja depression and out onto the vast grasslands to the west. The view from the crater rim viewpoint is pretty enough but is hardly what I would call overwhelming in the spectacular. I expected it to be deeper, more dramatic at the edges and, I don't know, full of animals maybe, but 19 kilometres across in all directions translates to roughly 250 square kilometres where the wildlife can hide in plain sight.

From a height of 600 metres and at a distance of two kilometres a 1000-kilogram Cape buffalo isn't much to look at, even with a telephoto lens. Two hundred of them at three kilometres are just a bunch of ant-like specks in the grass. Beyond that, it's just lots of grass with barely a hint of the beasts hiding within. It isn't until you get down into the crater on the return trip from the Serengeti that the true nature of this place begins to reveal itself.

From below, the rim does appear a more formidable barrier, creating the unusual impression of a wide-open yet contained space. It kind of feels like a giant zoo without the fences.

After passing through the Lerai Forest, a comparatively small, densely wooded area in the southwest corner of the crater, we spend most of the rest of the morning zigzagging across the open ground, searching for game, but, in a way, the crater continues to be an enigma. There are so many animals one moment, yet there are surprisingly large areas devoid of wildlife the next, until you drive around a long sweeping bend or come up over a low rise and all of sudden the numbers skyrocket again. In amongst it all are a remarkable number of lions. Forget about Shark Week on PBS, today is Lion Day in the Ngorongoro Crater, and we seem destined to see them all.

Zebron spots the first group of the morning and sounds the alarm as he slams on the brakes.

"Lions!"

Reflexively, Sergey shouts, "Stop. Stop. Stop!" in his heavy Russian accent, even as Zebron skids us to a stop, and Ben, with his signature understatement, adds, "Sure. More lions. Why not?"

The group of three adults – one male and two females – brings our rough count total this trip to about 40 individuals so far, so we're already feeling spoiled, but this trio is hardly an exciting find. One of the females is passed out cold in the short grass and never moves a muscle as we watch. The big male is similarly inert but is asleep on his back with his forepaws in the air, which is nothing if not adorable, and the second female is awake and is casually grooming her front paws. After a minute or two she looks directly at us, yawns, gets up, and wanders over to go to sleep next to the other female. That's it. Thanks for coming out. Show's over.

After Zebron starts up the truck again, we begin to make our way over to the north side of the crater, hoping for more lions. Interestingly, this place hasn't always been off limits to human habitation. According to Wikipedia, Adolph and Friedrich Siedentopf leased a small corner of the crater from the German East Africa administration prior to the First World War that they then turned into a farm, and the Maasai have been herding their animals all over this region since the early 1800s, when they pushed out the Mbulu and the Datooga people.

Implementation of the National Park Ordinance in 1951 created Serengeti National Park, effectively displacing the Maasai from a large portion the plains, and in 1959 the Ngorongoro Conservation Area Ordinance was enacted in an attempt to separate the conservation area – which the Ngorongoro Crater is a part of – from the new national park to the west. The Maasai can occupy the land and graze their cattle in the conservation area, but cannot live in or graze livestock in Serengeti National Park. But the Wildlife Conservation Act of 2009 further restricted land use in the crater, effectively displacing the Maasai again, this time from this small part of the conservation area. Tensions persist between the conservation authorities and the local Maasai communities, but the crater is now for wild animals only.

Over on the northeastern side – near where the Siedentopf brothers had their farm a century ago – the Munge River flows into the crater from the only comparatively low point in the rim. The land is rolling and the grass is longer than in the area around Lake Magadi and the edges of the Lerai Forest, and splayed out in the grass by the side of the road is, surprise, surprise, a pride of lions. Why not, right? There are approximately 15 individuals in the group, and the herd of Cape buffalo nearby don't seem to be of much interest to the pride. The lions are either laid out in the grass asleep or are lounging contentedly, staring out into space and waiting for something to happen that would be worthy of concentrated attention.

Panthera leo is the only big cat that is social by nature, and prides are generally extended family groups. Females do the majority of the hunting, while males are tasked with protecting the group from intruders. The thing is, those jobs don't take up a lot of time, so lions spend most of the day resting. Lions spend upwards of 20 hours a day sleeping or lounging around, looking positively indifferent to the world around them, but I have to admit, even in repose they are about as charismatic as they come. I could watch them all day and never get bored. As the lazy dynamic of this extended family group slowly plays out in front of us, a lone jackal appears suddenly in the tall grass after trotting up the hill. He has come up short 30 metres from the lions, his ears piqued in a gesture of surprise more than alarm. A jackal would be no match for even a single yearling lion, but he's quick, and could bound away down the slope before any of the lions even got to their feet. Making the situation even more interesting is a group of six zebras that are also finding their way slowly up the same slope, and they don't yet see the lions.

As it happens, zebras are my second favourite of the animals that we've come across, which is a bit of a surprise. I thought for sure it would be giraffes or elephants or leopards, but zebras are great subjects for black and white photos, and with their spiky manes they project a frisky, slightly badass attitude that is nothing if not endearing.

Boisterous and playful, they strike me as the adolescent punk rock horses of the equine world, but I fear their youthful, devil-may-care outlook on life might not serve them well just now. A few of the lions have caught wind of them, and have crouched down flat in the thick grass, hoping not to be seen.

Amazingly, the lead zebra in the mini-herd has also smelled lions on the breeze, but continues to come upslope, as if hoping for a better view of the developing situation. He stops eventually, about 20 metres beyond where the jackal is standing and watching, as he continues to wait and see how this all plays out. The five other zebras quickly tuck into tight formation around the lead, and then, counterintuitively, nothing happens. The zebras keep a watchful eye, but don't back away down the slope as I would expect, and only about a third of the lions even pay them any attention. The rest of the pride continue to sleep in the grass or gaze out across the crater in completely different directions.

The inherent tension of inevitable conflict slowly bleeds away as the minutes pass without incident, and after half an hour and all the photos we can possibly take, the inevitable question is put forward, "We go?" Sure. I guess. There really isn't much reason to linger, but as we drive away I realize we've learned a very important lesson about wild animals in wide open spaces without much cover: everybody knows *exactly* how fast everybody else is, and conducts themselves according to that simple calculus. There is no panic, and nobody wastes energy unnecessarily. One of the zebras even turns its back and begins to graze while waiting for the next move. A gesture that borders on defiant, but what are the lions going to do?

As we slip away back down the slope to the floor of

the crater it occurs to me that Zebron has been an exceptional guide. He has led us to all the best spots for viewing wildlife, and has been noticeably respectful of the animals themselves. In fact, over the course of this safari one of the things that has impressed me most is the professionalism of all the drivers. In an effort to reduce damage to the landscape caused by vehicular traffic, drivers must stay on established tracks. This, in turn, reduces stress for the animals. The rough gravel roads and off-road dirt tracks are murder on the trucks, but the ruts and potholes and divots help reduce speed and limit accessibility to certain areas. This gives the animals reprieve from what could easily become incessant harassment from well-meaning but not always enlightened-to-the-nuances-of-animal-behaviour visitors.

If an animal is visible in the distance on the savannah or is within camera range through a break in the forest cover then by all means, stop and enjoy the spectacle. But if the leopard escaping the heat of the day up in that acacia tree is obscured by the branches, well then, tough luck. You *cannot* drive in closer or circle around the back in hopes of a better sightline. Some animals, like zebras and lions, are remarkably indifferent to the attention and will continue to display natural behaviours within a few feet of the vehicles. Others, like ostriches and warthogs, are more wary by nature, and keep a greater distance no matter the circumstance.

An excellent example of this ease of manner is a second big pride of about 15 lions – not two kilometres from the group having the Mexican standoff with the zebras – who walked right through the collection of Land Cruisers stopped on the road as if the trucks were simply a grouping of rocks impeding a straight-line traverse from Point

A to Point B. The lions never even gave any of us a second look, even as we leaned out the top of the trucks to point our cameras and camera-phones straight down on them from above. That was half an hour ago, and as an added bonus, we've just seen our first black rhinos off in the distance.

The rhinos couldn't care less about us either.

To be fair, we're a long way off, and by all accounts rhinos don't see particularly well. There's two of them on the visible horizon, five or six hundred metres away on top of a minor bump on the crater floor. At that distance it would be difficult to identify them as anything other than more Cape buffalo moving across the landscape, except that they're dark grey, not black. I'm happy to point this out to the group once I figure it out.

"Hey, gang, are those rhinos off in the distance?"

Zebron is all over it. But responds in the manner of a professional who has already spotted the animals and knows we'll never be able to get anywhere near them in the time we've got left. No sense getting us all excited about it.

"No, no. Buffalo," Zebron says.

"No, I see the buffalo," I reply, I little irritated my spotting ability hasn't been more warmly received. "Out beyond the buffalo, there are two grey lumps."

Zebron pretends to be unconvinced, but humours me by stopping the truck and reaching for the binoculars.

"I don't see them," he says.

I understand his reticence. Coming across the full width of the crater from the northeastern side to the accent road on the southwest side has been a meandering journey filled with animal sightings, and we're already well past our pre-agreed exit time. The problem is we've stumbled into yet another example of the remarkable biodiversity that makes the crater so compelling. We've been hanging around instead of getting out of here because a female lion and her three yearling cubs are loping slowly toward the Lerai Forest in order to find some shade as the heat of the day approaches. The scrubby grassland they're moving through makes them easy to spot, and it just so happens that a ridiculous number of other animals happen to be grazing in this corner of the crater at the moment. Thomson's gazelles dot the landscape, and dozens of zebras and wildebeests congregate in small groups all around us. Out beyond all of that a big herd of Cape buffalo is on a path that bisects the lion's route, maybe 100 metres behind where they passed five minutes ago. Another handful of buffalo are walking much closer to us, on an intercept course with the bigger herd.

Not a single animal seems overly concerned by the lions in their midst. Aware? For sure, but not concerned. They simply move off to a respectable distance from the line of travel and watch as the apex predators lope past slowly. The lack of alarm displayed by the prey species is counterintuitive to my preconceived notion of predator and prey and how they would react to each other. I would expect them to be more distressed by the appearance of lions, but the zebras in particular seem downright antagonistic as they stand right at the edge of sprinting range and stare. Punk rock horses indeed.

At the far edge of this life-or-death action that refuses to play out yet again there are rhinos, I'm sure of it, and I voice my opinion a little more forcefully this time.

"There's a group of zebras watching the lions. Then a few buffalo. Then a couple of wildebeests. After that, rhinos."

There is murmured discussion about the voracity of

this sighting as everybody reaches for cameras and binoculars in order to better scan the horizon. The problem is, the four lions have walked right into the middle of all the zebras and wildebeests and antelope and are passing within 20 metres of our truck. The scene is more than a little distracting and it's hard to concentrate on the possibility of distant rhinos we'll never get close to. In the end, the rhino debate becomes moot as we follow along with the lions and make our way to the exit road up and out of the crater. Truth be told, we should have been on the road back to Arusha and Moshi an hour ago.

All day I have struggled to make sense of this place, and this latest display of predator-and-prey chess encompasses that struggle. The topography makes Ngorongoro Crater a uniquely intact and compelling habitat, even when held up to the spectacle that is Tarangire or the Serengeti. My early impression was a bit off, though; this is no zoo, it is far too dynamic for that comparison. An oversized game park with no fences is kind of close, but still misses the mark somehow. The only thing I'm sure of is that it's unlike anything I've ever seen before.

I guess what is so perplexing to a westerner is that at its core the crater is inconsistent with how the modern world works. That's part of what makes it so alluring, I guess. It is a huge counterpoint to our unbalanced and consumptive habits. There is clearly abundance here, but that abundance is not exploited or used up. It is simply lived with by the natural residents. There is enough good grazing to support thousands of herbivores. Lake Magadi and a handful of natural springs provide water, and the jackals and hyenas and lions chip in with population control. Everyone knows their place, and everyone plays their part. It's remarkable to imagine the wild as so perfectly in sync with itself because modern society can't seem to manage the same simple grace. This ecosystem operates just fine without the clumsy participation of man and is a microcosm of what the natural world once was. We used to fit into that dynamic, but now we've been relegated to the role of confused and destructive voyeurs.

Earlier this morning, at one of the watering holes, a family of geese, including eight small goslings, made their way across the road and into a group of zebras who were taking a drink. One of the zebras took offence at the intrusion and snorted and swung his head toward the miniature interlopers. The adult geese would not be intimidated. They squawked and flapped their wings and held their ground against the much bigger animal. Clearly, you have to be both tough and fearless to survive in the crater.

Later in the day, off in the distance away from the track, a new Cape buffalo calf had been born within the last few hours, not all that far from a pair of lions we had recently passed. The group of adult buffalo had made a circle around the mother and new calf, horns pointed outward, protecting them from potential predators just long enough for the baby to learn to walk. Just prior to that we came upon a pregnant hyena who had found an old bone and was crushing it to bits with her powerful jaws in order to get to the marrow inside. Her loud and oddly contented growling let it be known she was quite pleased with what she had found.

Any one of these moments alone would be instructive as to how life in the crater works, and it all happened over the course of a few hours. Baby geese and baby buffalo shouldn't stand a chance with 600 hyenas and 60 lions roaming around, and yet they're all here. When things do go wrong for animals lower on the food chain nothing is left to waste, not even the bones. Taken as a whole, it's an amazingly humbling and remarkably grounding experience. This is the world as nature intended.

Turning up the ascent road, Zebron punches the accelerator in order to overcome the steep grade, but the rolling is smooth because instead of the bumpy, rocky dirt of the descent road, the ascent road has been paved in cobblestones. It's basically an ornate driveway set at a ridiculous angle that's two or three kilometres long. I can't even imagine how much time it took to lay it down. Watching wistfully as the crater retreats to that somewhat underwhelming vision I remember from a couple of days ago, I worry the sense of naked awe will fade too soon. Already the crater is transforming into a pretty landscape that barely hints at the wonders and mysteries it contains. Except now I know what's down there.

After cresting the rim and beginning the long drive back to Arusha, there's a part of me that's happy we didn't get to see the rhinos up close today. The Ngorongoro Crater is their world. It is a place where the romance and intrigue of nature endures. A place where humans can visit, but that can never be fully understood by a species so distracted by hubris and self-importance. We are not allowed to live there. Not allowed to farm or hunt anymore. Our connection to place has been rightfully reduced to eager spectator confined to the edges, because to allow more would inevitably lead to the destruction of yet another of the natural world's great wonders. It is what we do, but from here on I will always imagine the Ngorongoro Crater as a world apart. A lost world.

Having seen it first-hand, I can only hope it stays that way.

PART THREE

RWANDA

13

100 DAYS

As I wake up from a short power nap, it takes a second to remember exactly where I am, but the rwandair.com lettering emblazoned on the cowling of the landing gear just outside my small window is a ready reminder. Rubbing the sleep from my eyes, I can't help but notice the Bombardier Q400 NextGen Turboprop from Dar es Salaam to Kigali has begun its slow descent to our destination, and there it is, right down below. Rwanda, Land of a Thousand Hills. My evening flight was cancelled yesterday and I haven't slept much in the last 24 hours as a result of the altered schedule, so all I can think is, *Hey, cool, Rwanda.*

There is still 20 minutes of flying time left to go, but no matter how many times I get on an airplane I'm always amazed by the final approach to a destination city. The raw energy and excitement associated with travelling is still there after all these years, and it's during the long, slow glide before landing when the feeling really starts to take hold. It says, "I'm going somewhere." The feeling is even more acute when I'm going somewhere new. Somewhere I've thought a lot about, but haven't yet been to. Rwanda checks that travel box nicely.

As we drift effortlessly through space, the sun is beginning to come up behind us and is casting a soft glow on the landscape below. From a height, the rolling hills seem to stretch out forever, cut consistently by any number of small streams and occasionally by a more substantial river. As we near Kigali, wispy fingers of mist drag over what are, from this vantage point, low ridges. Rwanda has suffered a tumultuous recent history, but this morning she appears peaceful, and beautiful. By the time we land near the eastern edge of the city a light fog envelops us, but the sun is a soft orb hanging just above the horizon, determined to burn off the mist.

Kigali International Airport is small but modern, and vaguely reminiscent of Victoria International Airport on British Columbia's Vancouver Island in the areas that have been recently renovated. Once again clearing customs is an easy go; a cash-on-the-spot visa with no photo requirement, and no check of the vaccination records I endured so many needles to obtain. In all, it takes less than three minutes. You almost expect some minor hassles at border crossings and points of entry in foreign lands. I look forward to it even as part of the exotic nature of distant travel, so I'm a bit disappointed. Sure, a security guard has taken interest in the large black soft-shell bag containing my bicycle and wants to look inside, but the interest appears to be entirely personal, and I am quickly waved through.

After I've exchanged some money, my taxi ride into the city is along excessively clean streets with exquisitely manicured verges, fully operating traffic lights, and a minimal amount of traffic. In my sleep-deprived state, it's all kind of surreal after the rough and tumble feel of Dar es Salaam. Reaching the city centre, we turn down a cobbled side street, make another quick turn, and come quickly to the Hotel Okapi. I know this is the place because there's a giant okapi painted on the side wall. Endemic to neighbouring DRC, the animal is closely related to the giraffe, and looks not unlike a mashup of a zebra's body and a baby giraffe's head. The body is brown, with white zebra-like stripes along the legs. This artist's rendering is four storeys high and is beautifully executed.

As I approach the front desk I realize I'm about 12 hours late checking in, but the lovely young woman at reception doesn't miss a beat. She adjusts my reservation so I don't pay for the unused night, but then makes the room available immediately so I don't have to wait all morning to get settled. She even insists I partake in the complimentary breakfast set out in the dining room. After a 1:45 a.m. wakeup call for a three a.m. check-in to a five a.m. flight, the kindness is appreciated more than I could ever express.

I chose the Hotel Okapi at random from the options available on Trivago but know immediately that I've found another one of my favourite temporary homes-away-from-home. The dining room is at the back of the hotel, with an open-air view overlooking the northern reaches of the city and some of the hazy hills beyond, and breakfast is what I've come to expect. Multiple cups of coffee or milk tea (coffee this morning – definitely coffee), insanely fresh fruit, and fried potatoes and peppers. As a bonus I can get a small omelet *and* hard-boiled eggs. It has been a long travel day already, but the temperature here after sunrise is cooler than it was in the middle of the night in Dar. After getting settled in and fed, I'm feeling comfortable and relaxed.

To be completely honest, I fully expected to be ready for a nap after breakfast, but the prospect of a new city is irresistible, and I am drawn to explore. The undulating topography that Kigali is built on leads me to believe one of the sights I want to visit might be within walking distance. Easy walking distance even. I don't yet have a proper map of Kigali, or Rwanda for that matter, but an examination of the downtown core from the map in the Lonely Planet guidebook reveals a small arrow pointing north off the edge of the page – Kigali Memorial Centre (1.5 km). By my reckoning, my hotel is on the last road skirting the top edge of the map.

Not wanting to wander off blindly into a strange city, I pick up my phone and consult one of the map apps available on it. Sure enough, the digital version confirms where this hotel is in relation to the city centre, and that the memorial is just across the valley, albeit via a circuitous route. I check the route multiple times and commit it to memory – once I lose the Wi-Fi I'll lose my digital map – and compare it with what I can see out there in the real world. It looks like a doable half-day trip. It looks close even, at least as the crow flies, and I try and imagine which building or complex might actually be the memorial over on the opposite hillside in the distance.

Boulevard de Nyabugogo is just down the street from the hotel and is the main artery into the downtown core for the northern part of the city. The boulevard is two lanes in each direction separated by a wide verge, and the sidewalks are also wide and well maintained. Tidy shops line one side of the road and a high retaining wall lines long stretches of the other. The retaining wall holds back the steep hill that the rest of the downtown core is built on, and as Boulevard de Nyabugogo sweeps down along to the left it doesn't take long to pass *way* below where my hotel overlooks this valley.

At the junction with Route nationale 3, I take a hard right and continue down into the valley bottom. The going continues to be steep, and along the way a small side street intersects the larger thoroughfare. Sixty metres down the side street a decent-sized flat area has been carved out of the slope and is being used as a driving school. A handful of compact cars and an equal number of motorcycles are either practising manoeuvres through a maze of orange traffic cones, or are waiting for their turn to do so. As a small car makes its way up to the intersection, the driver struggles to engage first gear and enter the steady flow of traffic on RN3. My overall impression is that this would be the worst city in the world to try and learn to drive a manual transmission in, San Francisco notwithstanding.

Down in the valley bottom the route gets a little more complicated, and after crossing the bridge that spans a small creek and Avenue des Poids-Lourds, I find myself in a rougher part of town. There are a number of what look to be betting parlours sprinkled in with a couple of seedy bars and takeaway restaurants. I get a few hard looks from some tough characters hanging around as I walk along the busy sidewalk, but the uniformed police and military presence is what is notable. There were a lot of security guards and police in the bigger cities and towns in Tanzania, so it's not as if seeing guys walking around with rifles is a new thing, but a few of these soldiers are next level. Very obviously highly trained, and unusually focused as they scan the neighbourhood for any potential trouble.

All that being said, most of my fellow pedestrians don't even acknowledge the mzungu in their midst, or they give a subtle nod *hello* if we happen to make eye contact. As for trouble in the neighbourhood, the vibe in the air does not comport with the hyper-serious demeanour of some of the security personnel. When I stop and ask one of them for directions it is confirmed. Yup, this is the right way to the memorial.

Veering off at 14th Avenue is the beginning of the

walk up the opposite side of the valley. I have to regain some of the altitude lost in order to reach my destination, which thankfully is only halfway up the opposite slope, as it turns out. After entering the grounds to the memorial there's an overflow parking area that offers a wide-open view of the city centre. Much like Tanzania, Rwanda gained its independence in the early 1960s, and the modern downtown district features fewer (and shorter) high-rise buildings than Dar es Salaam, but their placement on top of a prominent hill makes for a dramatic cityscape, especially at night.

Turning my attention away from my walk and over to the reason I've come here today, I find I'm suddenly out of sorts. I did have every intention of calling in on this important site but hadn't planned on it being my very first visitor experience in Rwanda. It's pure coincidence that the hotel and the memorial are in the same neighbourhood, and maybe I should have put some thought into how best to ease into the heavy subject matter before setting out this morning. Exploring a small corner of the city is part of getting acclimated to my new surroundings, but noting the minor differences between Kigali and Dar is a decidedly superficial exercise compared to gaining insight into one of the largest massacres humanity has ever seen.

I wonder, am I ready for the strong emotions this visit will surely stir up? I have my doubts.

The Kigali Genocide Memorial opened in April 2004 to commemorate the ten-year anniversary of the Rwandan genocide, and the grounds are tidy and well laid out, in the manner of a Zen garden, so I spend a bit of time wandering around without purpose or direction as I try to get my head in the right place. The memorial should be approached with an appropriate amount of reverence and respect, and as I pass through the rose garden I remain hesitant to take the tour of the museum. Perhaps in a vain attempt to avoid the heavy slap of history that's surely coming.

On April 6, 1994, a plane carrying Rwandan President Juvénal Habyarimana was shot down on approach to Kigali airport by a surface-to-air missile. Everyone on board was killed, and the power vacuum that resulted opened the door for one of mankind's more horrifying chapters. This memorial was built to honour the victims of the atrocities that followed Habyarimana's death, to educate visitors as to the causes and consequences of genocidal acts, and to offer support to survivors. The memorial is free to visit, but there are options of hiring a guide, or alternatively, renting a small audio unit complete with earbuds. The individual recordings it contains correspond to specific sections within the museum and are designed to augment the visual displays.

Completely out of sorts now, I decide to skip these options and enter the first of the three major exhibitions – The 1994 Genocide Against the Tutsi – hoping to read about the important details directly off the well-presented displays. It doesn't take long to realize this is a mistake. After two or three displays it becomes apparent that audio is essential to a full experience, so I backtrack out the entrance and cross the courtyard to the building housing the front desk. The helpful woman manning reception sets me up with the appropriate equipment and gives a brief explanation of how all it works, before mentioning that an introductory film is about to start in the next room.

Taking a seat in the front row before the movie begins gives me an opportunity to take a breath and gather my thoughts. The sombreness of the experience is setting in, and I don't quite know it yet, but one of the most profound and moving three hours of my life has already been put in motion. My conscious mind just hasn't caught up to that sobering fact. Once the short movie starts, there is no going back, and the film is so captivating I stay and watch it a second time. The raw emotion openly displayed by survivors up on the screen, as they talk about loved ones lost, is beyond heartbreaking and I can't help but cry both times.

It was after Habyarimana's death that the Hutu majority began a campaign of systematic violence against the Tutsi minority as part of their version of a "final solution" to the ongoing tensions between the two groups, 50 years after the horrors of Nazi Germany. Over the course of the next 100 days between 800,000 and one million Tutsi, moderate Hutu, and marginalized Twa villagers were murdered by the Hutu-controlled army and genocidaires, whose goal was to advance Hutu power by any means necessary. One million is a difficult number to make sense of in the context of lives lost, especially in a time period of just over three months. Being made aware of the general details of events and putting the numbers in perspective compared to other mass atrocities in history is nothing when held up to listening to someone up on the screen talk about what happened to them, to their friends and to their families. It's next to impossible to imagine what that experience would have been like.

Returning to the museum proper, I find there are a dozen or so other visitors at the moment, evenly split between western tourists and local Africans. Everybody maintains a quiet and respectful social distance, in order to give everyone else space to process what they're experiencing. It feels like a weird thing to say given the subject matter, but the museum is excellent. The displays and the audio descriptions are informative, and it's clear a lot of time and effort was put into them. Even the soft lighting helps create the appropriate aura for the overall presentation. The early displays focus on life in Rwanda before colonization, a time when Hutu, Tutsi and Twa became the established groups in the region. In the 15th and 16th centuries a clan system slowly gave way to small kingdoms, and the minority Tutsi often held high positions in the power structure, but by all accounts, serious conflict was rare.

In the late 19th century the area became part of German East Africa, and after the First World War Belgium extended its influence from neighbouring Zaire (now the DRC), and began taking a more active role in regional affairs, with a focus on instilling western values on African culture. They favoured the ruling-class Tutsi, and a key moment in the developing narrative came in 1935 when an identity card system was put into place, creating hard lines between different members of the population. By the time of independence in 1962, those divisions were firmly entrenched. When the Belgians left, the Hutu took control of the country and scrapped the monarchy in favour of a republic. A large number of Tutsi fled over the border into Uganda.

As the story progresses up on the walls of the museum, the planned nature of the mass killing is made apparent and no detail is spared in describing the horrors of those 100 days. Large-format photos and video segments hold little back. Tutsi and sympathetic Hutu could not escape persecution, and sexual violence was rampant. Even those who sought refuge in the many churches throughout the country were not safe. The army and local militias fired guns and rifles indiscriminately when ammunition was available, and they tossed grenades through windows. Or, they simply locked the doors from the outside and burned the churches down with everyone inside.

Holy fuck. What a nightmare.

As I continue on slowly through the museum my emotions ebb and flow as I try to make sense of it all, and one of the more personally moving displays in Exhibition 1 ends up being "Amaphoto y'umuryango," or "Family photographs" in Kinyarwanda, the native language. Up on a slightly raised platform around a dimly lit, medium-sized circular room, six triangular-shaped cubbyholes are brightly lit for effect. Clipped in neat rows on thin wires along the two walls of each cubby are dozens and dozens of 4x6 inch snapshots of people lost to the genocide.

From the centre of the room, each wall resembles an old video store display, with VHS tapes set up in neat rows. But up close the photos prove to be a collection of head shots and candid pics in a mix of both black and white and colour. On the open side of each cubby, a small leather ottoman sits in wait for those survivors who want to spend a bit of time with friends and loved ones lost. There are approximately 2,000 photos in all, and "Amaphoto y'umuryango" is essentially a large group family photo album of the dead.

•••

Sitting in the café after exiting the museum, I have to rest for a while before making my way back to the hotel. There's no way I could eat anything, but lingering over a bottle of water is welcome as some of the details begin to sink in. I have to admit, I've been rattled.

The second of the permanent exhibitions, Wasted

Lives, documents the other prominent massacres of the 20th century, including a few that international law has failed to recognize as genocide. Along with the Holocaust, mass murder in Namibia, Cambodia, Armenia and the Balkans is examined. Exhibition 3 – Children's Room, focuses on the young lives lost, and the biographies and stories of the fates of a handful of preteens and toddlers are especially gut-wrenching. How do you justify the killing of children under any circumstance?

It's all a lot to take in, and you can never properly prepare yourself emotionally for something like this, so maybe it was better to just show up instead of agonizing about the details too much beforehand. I suppose there's also a part of me that did not want to face the hard realities of what happened here in Rwanda, at least not head on. Quite frankly, it's upsetting to contemplate death on such a massive scale, and the fact that this all happened in my lifetime adds to the sense of unreality that surrounds the devastating series of events. Sifting through the details is not a wholly historical exercise in this case. Examining the actions and critiquing the behaviour of generations past is an easy thing to do from a distance of both time and space. It's much harder to admit that we, as a species, are still capable of something like this in modern times.

In 1994, I had recently entered the workforce after finishing university, and was preoccupied with trying to figure out what I was going to do with my life. I knew about what was happening in Rwanda in a vague, disconnected kind of way. Africa was a long, long way away at the time, both in terms of physical distance and as a priority for my attention. Twenty-five years later I think maybe I had wanted to experience the recovery of the country (which is truly remarkable) while not getting too bogged down in the horrors of its past. There was never a thought to skip the memorial or downplay the serious nature of events, but maybe I could see it without feeling it too much. This is impossible, of course, and is an affront to the past, not to mention disrespectful to the estimated one million dead. To say nothing of the countless survivors who lost family and friends.

And I think that is precisely why the Kigali Genocide Memorial is so good – it doesn't pull any punches. You have no choice but to have your reality shaken to the core. You have no choice but to feel the gut-wrenching truth about what happened here deep down in your soul.

Before I leave the grounds, I take a second tour of the gardens. There are a number of distinct areas where one can engage in quiet reflection, including the Rose Gardens and the Gardens of Division and of Reconciliation. And then there are the mass graves. An estimated 250,000 of the victims of the genocide are buried here on site. Set up in three main rows, remains continue to be transferred from unmarked graves all over the country for a proper, dignified burial. The tombs themselves are subtle in design, rising maybe ten inches above the surrounding walkways, but the footprint of each concrete slab is chilling. A huge number of the corpses they contain will never be properly identified. Near the "Amaphoto y'umuryango" exhibit from earlier, there were four large glass cases filled with human skulls, some of them with round holes or long gashes cut right through the bone. When proper weapons were not available, farm implements and household tools were used. These were clearly fatal injuries made by hammers, hoes and machetes. In the adjacent small room, there were two large cases filled with femurs and other long bones. The collection of that many unidentified remains gathered together in one place was sobering enough; a quarter of a million more skeletons buried out here in the grounds is both heavy and heartbreaking.

As I begin walking back to the hotel after nearly four hours at the memorial, the weight of history is lifted just a little bit, and I find everyday Rwanda has moved on from those dark days in 1994. No one will ever forget, but the city continues to go about its business in the here and now in 2019. There are still people waiting for the bus or hanging out in front of the betting parlors and restaurants, or simply walking from one place to another. Many are out on errands perhaps, or heading to or from work, and as I make my way slowly up the hill past the driving school, there are still young people swerving around, trying to develop the skills necessary in obtaining a licence. In the background the security personnel are still on patrol, keeping a watchful eye on things.

At the junction with Boulevard de Nyabugogo, the afternoon traffic has intensified, and there are more pedestrians walking the sidewalks than there were this morning. Interestingly, I've been in the country for about eight hours now and can't say that I could pick out any single Tutsi or any single Hutu. President Paul Kagame was the commander of the Rwandan Patriotic Front prior to and during the genocide, and when the RPF overthrew the genocidaires he became vice-president and minister of defence. A shrewd politician with a military background, he assumed the presidency in 2000. A key plank in his efforts to unify the country has always been that there are no Hutu and there are no Tutsi, only Rwandans. At least superficially, that goal seems to have been accomplished.

Overall, there is an underlying vibe here, to be sure, but it does not come across as a simmering tension. Paul

Clarke, a reporter at the local newspaper in Canmore, the *Rocky Mountain Outlook,* spent three months working in Rwanda in 2012 and described the feeling to me as collective PTSD. This is an accurate assessment, and in my admittedly limited exposure, that feels like a simple and deep underlying sadness that 25 years has not been able to shake.

Back at the hotel I take a quick shower, and then head down to the restaurant. Securing the same table as this morning at breakfast, I'm hoping to take some notes while the experience is still fresh in my mind, but end up gazing out at the northern hills more than anything else, because emotion remains more dominant than any kind of conscious thought. As time passes, night falls and the lights of the northern neighbourhoods begin to flicker on. Wispy clouds have drifted in, obscuring the stars to create an inverse nightscape, with all the points of light on the lower third of the horizon. It has been a big day, filled with a mixture of sadness and outrage, and yet beyond the horrors and beyond the atrocities I think one of the important things I will take away from the experience is the capacity for forgiveness, even as I doubt in my ability to embrace it. Amazingly, in amongst all the horrible details that came to light today there was also hope. Hope for reconciliation. Hope for a collective healing. Hope for the future.

I was simply not prepared to see movies featuring the survivors of the genocide, and their vulnerability and candor caught me completely off guard. I can't remember the last time I cried so much in a single day. The feelings they inspired with their words would well up and then spill out over my ability to contain them, so I would sit and quietly sob, and then struggle to regain my composure. A shocking feature of those 100 days was, in rural areas especially, Hutu and Tutsi were often neighbours and friends despite the greater political and cultural unrest. Almost overnight they became mortal enemies. When survivors would look directly into the camera and speak of the need to forgive the betrayal of people from their own neighbourhoods in order to move on, it would overwhelm me. It also impressed me to no end.

The question is, could I forgive in similar circumstances? Would I forgive?

Sitting here, safe in my status as western visitor a quarter of a century removed from what happened, I can't help but think of my friends and family back in Canada. I imagine a group of people from the next town over coming and raping and killing those people who are dear to my heart. Just the thought of it brings my blood to a boil. Guns from a distance and grenades tossed through windows is bad enough, but using hammers and machetes is next level terror. It is execution at close quarters. It is inescapably personal. You have to look your victims in the eye and finish the job as they try in vain to protect themselves. Emotionally, the thought of it rips right through me, and even now, in this moment where history meets hypothetical, my hands instinctively close into fists because anger is the only thing that keeps me from tearing up for the umpteenth time today. Retribution seems the only solution, and yet the survivors here insist otherwise.

Intellectually, I can't make it make sense either. How in that moment of ultimate cruelty could a person wielding a machete not pause and say, *Wait. I can't do this. It's wrong.*

So I wonder once again as I gaze out at the reversed night sky, could I forgive, knowing the grisly details of how my friends and family died? And could I manage the survivor guilt? Could I carry on after being spared even as so many were lost, without succumbing to the overwhelming urge to seek revenge? And what if I was on the other side of the equation, caught up in the hysteria of runaway populism and a racist ideology? Could I live with myself after committing the atrocities that inevitably come with adhering to that kind of world view?

Staring out at the lights of the city, I honestly don't know if I could do either of those things.

14

THREE WEEKS

After the emotional – and at times overwhelming – experience at the genocide memorial a couple of days ago yet another new question has to be asked now that I've managed to collect myself. What do I do from here? I've got roughly three weeks to go before returning to Canada, but fear everything I might experience going forward will surely pale in terms of resonance and impact. I have been challenged in ways I could never have prepared for and have been wandering around in a daze ever since, unsure of what to make of these things I've seen. There is a deep sorrow lingering in my heart for all the victims and the survivors of the genocide, and I can't say I'm especially proud of being part of the human race, knowing what we're so easily capable of.

Visiting Hiroshima had a similar effect on my psyche, as I imagine Auschwitz would in the event I ever travel to Poland. I spent an afternoon in Hiroshima back in 1995, and haven't thought about the visit in years, but this recent experience has triggered some of those memories. As I wandered around the Peace Memorial Park and explored the main museum, a desire to learn more about what happened at that spot gradually formed. An innate curiosity grew sombre as the gravity of the consequences of the first targeted atomic bomb ever to be dropped, on civilians no less, began to weigh on me.

In that split second on the morning of August 6, 1945, 80,000 people died instantly, and tens of thousands more succumbed to radiation sickness in the months that followed. The bombing was a wartime act, and arguably saved hundreds of thousands of lives by helping to shorten the Second World War, but the point to be made here is a lot of people died who had very little to do with the larger conflict that swirled around their daily lives. The Hiroshima Peace Memorial Park and the Kigali Genocide Memorial are examples of the darker side of humanity, laid bare for all to see. A reminder that for all we are that is good and decent and just, we are also, at times, heartless monsters.

As I sit and gaze out over the northern reaches of the city this morning I'm clearly feeling reflective, and not particularly motivated. The coffee is good, and it takes close to 90 minutes of lingering over breakfast to put down the notebook and finally get moving with my day. Going for a bike ride to shake off the melancholy before it gets too hot, I see the city is also just beginning to shift into gear. It's cooler here than in Dar by four or five degrees Celsius on average, but with any physical effort at all, like, say, powering up and down the hills the capital is spread out over on foot or by bicycle, that difference is negligible. I believe I can also say this with some confidence, were someone who walked the streets of Kigali every day so inclined, they would be prepared for an attempt on Mount Kilimanjaro with no further training whatsoever.

As for the city itself, it has been transformed in recent years. The horror that was 1994 destroyed lives and families, alienated communities and sent the whole country into a state of shock. It also decimated the economy. The country ground to a halt. The website nationsencyclopia.

com reports that within a year of the genocide the economy contracted by 50 per cent and per capita income bottomed out at US$80 a year.

With no historical point of reference, you would never suspect this was so recently the case. Modern Kigali is modern in every sense of the word. The cars driving past are almost without exception either brand new or well maintained and buffed to a high-gloss shine, and the pedestrians walking around downtown are all sharply dressed and moving with a sense of purpose that is instantly recognizable in any major metropolis. International investment also appears to be improving, and new construction projects are springing up all over the place.

As a fan of the English Premier League, I note that an obvious indicator of this international interest is the partnership between Arsenal Football Club and the Rwanda Development Board. Visit Rwanda is the current tourism campaign, and the logo appears on the sleeve of the north London club's jersey. It is their first official sleeve sponsor. Meanwhile, the Arsenal badge is everywhere here. In my travels in Africa and Asia there has been one English club that has dominated the replica jersey market, and that's Manchester United. Chelsea comes in a distant second, and Arsenal an even more distant third. In Rwanda, however, Arsenal is king. Whenever I spot an EPL jersey or a hat, it inevitably has the Gunners logo on it. Even the local sporting apparel shops, of which there are a surprising number, have jumped on board and painted the Arsenal logo right up there next to the shop name.

At the moment Kigali is a-movin' and a-shakin', no question about it. This gleaming city on the hill has rough neighbourhoods at the edges like every modern metropolis, but overall the downtown core borders on picture perfect with its litter-free streets, well-maintained roadways and manicured verges.

Heading out onto those streets, my fortuitous choice in hotel location has come in handy once again. The points of interest I want to visit today are relatively close by, and this time I don't have to go all the way down into a valley bottom, only to climb another steep hill on the other side to get to my destination. A short, steep climb to Place de l'Unité National – the major roundabout here in the city centre – leads to a mostly flat ride following the contour of the hill on Avenue de la Justice to Kandt House Museum, which also doubles as the Museum of Natural History.

According to the official visitrwanda.com website, Richard Kandt, a German, was the first colonial governor of Rwanda, and what makes this site important is that it was the first European-style brick and mortar building to go up in Kigali. The year was 1907, according to the Institute of National Museums of Rwanda sign erected outside in the yard, and at the time Kigali had a population of 2,000 people, including 420 foreigners. Most of them were Indian or Arab, and there were only nine Germans. Apparently, "Kandt choose the site because of the good climate and its central location in the country."

This intrigues me in a number of ways. First of all, I find it amazing that only 112 years ago there were no buildings at all in this now bustling city. Second, I'm trying to imagine Kandt wandering around the hillside and deciding, "Right, let's do this thing right here." And third, how do you properly administer a largely unexplored territory that's 9000 kilometres from your home country with only nine of you? I can't help but think history is a peculiar thing sometimes, but overall the museum does a good job documenting the pre-colonial, colonial and post-independence history of what is now the capital of the country. I especially enjoy the black and white photographs and the maps that help walk me through the past. Behind the main building a cramped live reptile display that pretty much makes up the entirety of the Natural History Museum is probably an unnecessary add-on, but you can be sure I won't be rustling around in the forest once I leave town. It has come to my attention that there are some *big* snakes out there.

After Kandt House, Avenue de la Justice begins to climb the contour of the hill, and veering left on L'Hôpital Road carries me up to the Belgian Peacekeepers Memorial. The compound is small and does not have the same overwhelming weight as the genocide memorial, but the violence is immediately obvious. The whitewashed front wall of the one-storey building is pockmarked with dozens and dozens of bullet holes, and over half of the bullets fired also tore right through the first layer of cinder block beneath the whitewashed facing. President Habyarimana's plane going down on April 6 opened the door for what followed, but what happened here is cited by many as another key event in the descent into madness. I cannot describe the details any better than what is stated on one of the plaques erected at the site, which I will quote here:

> On April 7, 1994, while assuring the security of the Rwandan Prime Minister, 10 Belgian commandos were surrounded by members of FAR (Forces armées rwandaises) who ordered the commandos to disarm in exchange for safe passage to a UN base. Instead of being taken to the UN base the 10 commandos were brought to a military camp here, at this site. On arrival the commandos were attacked

> by a hundred soldiers from the camp. Against this overwhelming force the commandos took refuge in this building and, with two side-arms they managed to conceal, resisted for several hours. They fought till their death while hoping for help that never came.

This camp is also known as Camp Kigali, and the genocidaires rightly calculated that a brutal attack on the Belgians, who were the largest and among the best trained of the forces that were part of the United Nations peacekeeping mission, would wreak havoc on the peacekeeping force as a whole. A number of prominent Rwandan government officials not sympathetic to the violent cause were also executed, further clearing the way for the army and co-operating militias to do anything they wanted. The Belgians did indeed withdraw the remainder of their troops, and the mission was further hampered by Chapter 6 of the UN Charter. It was a Canadian who was in charge of the UN force, and to commemorate the 25th anniversary of the genocide cbc.ca posted a partial transcript of the Sunday Edition radio broadcast with retired Lt.-Gen. Romeo Dallaire and host Michael Enright, with the title *'My soul is still in Rwanda': 25 years after the genocide, Roméo Dallaire still grapples with guilt.*

Dallaire was deployed to Rwanda in 1993 and quickly realized the stated mission of overseeing a truce between the Hutu and the Tutsi in the simmering civil war that erupted in 1990 was not likely. He repeatedly warned the UN Security Council that trouble of much higher magnitude was brewing. The reply to the warnings was clear and unequivocal, as stated in one fax from UN headquarters in New York: "You will not intervene. You will not put troops at risk."

His hands were tied by those higher up the chain of command.

"You were supposed to be a facilitator, not a soldier, and the use of force was purely for self-protection," Dallaire said in the CBC piece.

It should be noted that international politics also played a part in the decision-making process at the UN. According to the CBC article, the Security Council and then American President Bill Clinton were reluctant to get too involved because of the events that had transpired in Somalia the previous fall. An American-led raid in Mogadishu resulted in the deaths of 18 Americans, two UN peacekeepers and hundreds of Somalis. The story was dramatized in the film *Black Hawk Down*, which was released in 2001.

Dallaire has subsequently endured a lot of criticism for his actions – or more precisely perceived inaction – in 1994, and as if to accentuate the point there is a blackboard on the wall of one of the rooms the Belgian commandos sought refuge in. The blackboard is riddled with bullet holes and is covered with notes left in chalk. Prominently displayed is a drawing of a large skull-and-crossbones. In capital letters next to it is the name, DALLAIRE. Beneath that the name, MARCHAL (the senior officer in the Belgian force) also appears in all caps. Scribbled in French beneath their names is a set of rhetorical questions, "Avez vous des oreilles? Yeux? COEUR?"

"Do you have ears? Eyes? A HEART?"

Three weeks into the slaughter over 2,000 peacekeeping troops were *withdrawn* from the country, reducing the contingent to under 300, thus making anything more than observing, reporting and sheltering terrified citizens who did manage to find their way to UN camps next to impossible. In mid-July the RPF, led by future president Paul Kagame, took control of the capital and the genocide was over.

Dallaire took the failure of his command to do more for the victims – despite limited resources and a crippling mandate – personally, and has suffered from depression and other PTSD symptoms in the years since. The CBC piece mentions four suicide attempts. It's a lot for one person to bear, but I think the subtitle from his book about the genocide is instructive in the wisdom of trying to assign individual blame. Dark forces throughout the country did unspeakable things and the warning signs of impending catastrophe were years, if not decades, in the making. The international community then mismanaged its responsibility to protect the most vulnerable in their most desperate time of need.

Most telling of all perhaps, is that Rwanda is not a one-off. Throughout history, nation building and civil war have been used to justify outrageous acts of cruelty, and what happened here is but another occurrence in that pattern. Dallaire's book is called *Shake Hands with the Devil: The Failure of Humanity in Rwanda.*

In the end, I believe this belongs to us all. Once again.

• • •

The Tanzanian bike experiment did not go as well as hoped, obviously. I only managed about 225 kilometres, in and around Dar es Salaam, and then up to Bagamoyo and back. With a one-way excursion to the black cotton soil near Saadani that ultimately scuttled the Kilimanjaro sea-to-summit plan thrown in for good measure. I do, however, love having the bike in places like Dar and Bagamoyo and Kigali for exploring. Unfamiliar neighbourhoods and outlying points of interest are more easily accessed and explored by bicycle. You can get out of an uncomfortable situation quickly if one does arise, and you don't have to deal with touts and street hustlers trying to take you for a buck. Wave, smile, ride away. Problem solved. I'm just not sure about the longer-distance touring anymore.

It's a much bigger commitment, for one thing, of both time and energy. To say nothing of the dubious joy that comes from muscling all your stuff around with you instead of simply chucking a backpack into the hold of a bus. Clearly, I'm still trying to figure out the pros and cons, but I do feel strangely obligated to have a second go of it now. After lugging the bike all this way, I should try and get some miles in to justify the effort and expense of bringing it with me.

It does help that Rwanda is not a big country – it ranks 46th in area out of 54 countries in Africa – so exploring the northwestern quadrant (between 400 and 500 kilometres of biking, I figure) should be sufficiently ambitious without deteriorating into a mindless grind against a never-ending landscape. That's the hope anyway, and a two-day ride to the northern city of Musanze seems a fair introduction to the idea.

There's no elevator at this hotel, so step one of today's adventure is holding back gravity as my loaded-down bike wants nothing more than to bounce wildly to the bottom of the stairs. Once in the lobby, however, I find I'm feeling remarkably eager to take this on. After climbing Kilimanjaro I find my fitness levels are as good as they've been in years, and the initial apprehensions that were swirling around while I was packing my bags have subsided somewhat. All of a sudden, I'm kind of excited to get out on the road. The road will be a chance to clear my head of all the death and despair that comes with examining the genocide up close, and it will provide the opportunity to see how a transition to "rapidly modernizing country" is going in rural areas.

In order to check out I have to pay American dollars for the room, which I put on my credit card, and Rwandan francs for the laundry service, which I have in cash. Once again, I'm dealing with my ever-present front desk clerk, who, to my great shame, I have not properly introduced myself to, and so don't even know her name. But she's been great these last few days. Always cheerful and always helpful and possessed of a personality and sense of humour that I'm sure would make us great friends. As I'm flittering around with nervous energy and double-checking every zipper and every strap on my bike before departure, I catch a bit of a vibe from the clerk as she watches me prep the final details. She seems a mixture of amused and concerned.

"Do you have enough water?" She finally asks, and I instinctively interpret this as a warning that supplies might be hard to come by.

"Why, are there no shops along the way to Musanze?"

"There are," she replies hesitantly, which is somewhat confusing, so I go with the only other thing I can think of.

"Is today a public holiday?"

"Sort of," she says. "It's the morning set aside for community work. It's called Umuganda. You're probably not going to find anything open until after noon."

I've heard about this collective work project commitment but didn't know any of the details, including the name. Umuganda is a word in Kinyarwanda that means a coming together for a common purpose. On the fourth

Saturday of every month the morning is set aside for community projects both big and small. If a school needs to be built in a rural area then everybody pitches in, but the initiative is also used to clean city streets and rural roadsides, helping to explain why Rwanda always looks so tidy. If there isn't a drainage ditch to dig or a fence to build, then people collect litter. The problem is that most businesses are closed as a result, and I had no idea it was Saturday.

This puts a sudden damper on my enthusiasm. There was a billing snafu in connection to my safari trip, which delayed my return from Moshi by a day, and then the bus ride to Bagamoyo was longer than I was anticipating. I got in late, so the next day was wasted collecting my bike and getting my gear together at Funky Squids before setting off for Dar. Flight to Rwanda cancelled. Another day disrupted. I suddenly feel like I'm running out of time, and I don't want to waste another day. The thing is, tomorrow is Sunday, and who knows what that will mean in rural areas. Small businesses might be closed then too. I might as well just go now. Besides, I have ZERO interest in lugging all this junk back up the stairs.

Once again, I take Boulevard de Nyabugogo to start, and the traffic is indeed incredibly light because of the Umuganda. After the long, speedy descent to the valley bottom the boulevard turns into Route nationale 1, and for about a kilometre travels along flat ground to the junction for Route nationale 4. It's a nice little warm-up.

Almost immediately after making the turn, however, I begin the climb into the surrounding hills. I'm still not used to being on the right side of the road – as opposed to being on the left side while in Tanzania – but out on the highway there is almost no traffic at all, so it won't be an issue even if I stray. The road itself is more than I could have hoped for. A single lane in each direction, and the black-top is well maintained and is lacking even a single pothole. The smooth surface is wide, with six to eight inches beyond the white line indicating the outside edge of the lanes. Most important to the touring cyclist is the generous three feet of shoulder beyond that.

The shoulder is not as smooth as the main surface, mind you. It's a coarse black asphalt aggregate of visible pebbles, but it's firm and also free of any potholes. It appears that the aggregate layer was laid down as a base, and then the smoother layer was laid over top, but was not extended all the way to the edge. The inch-high lip between the two surfaces is startling if you manage to hit it while pedalling along and daydreaming, but overall the road is exceptional. Come to think of it, if the main transport route between Msata and Korogwe in Tanzania – the one that I wisely decided to avoid – were this good, riding it would simply have been a long, hot and sweaty effort, not a suicide mission.

Pedalling slowly along, the only discernible problem with this road is the grade, which over time becomes increasingly more difficult to manage. For the first six or seven kilometres it's hard work, but doable, but then as the clock moves into the second hour things get more challenging. As I get a little bit tired the hill gets a little bit steeper and turning the pedals gets harder to manage. As tired and harder increase over time, I have to calculate the wisdom of burning off too much energy just to keep rolling. Interestingly, I have also noticed I have a bad habit of unconsciously pushing hard into the pedals until my heartbeat spikes and my breathing becomes laboured and I'm forced to ease off. A more comfortable pace lasts for only as long as I'm paying attention, then I catch myself pushing too hard all over again. Wherever the eight- or nine-degree grade tips up to ten or 11 degrees (or more) I can't keep pedalling and have to get off and walk.

Not good. Not good at all.

Normally, I'd start to freak out right about now. It's a long, long, long way to Musanze on foot from here, but instead of thinking about it too much I simply put my head down and get on with the task at hand. Having biked around Kigali for a few days I figured this might happen. Even without any extemporaneous travel items to lug around I struggled on a few of the inclines. These are all hills with no towering craggy peaks at the top, but they're still really, really, *big* hills.

After about a kilometre of slow, determined effort on foot, I'm pleased to find there is a part of me that doesn't mind this walking and pushing business. Sure, it exposes my shortcomings. I'm fit enough for the steep bits, but not as strong as I was in my youth, so I can't just power up the *really* steep bits without dumping a painful amount of lactic acid into my thighs. I also don't have the energy to hold on to my ego's wistful musings about efforts past for long. The goal of this trip is to travel across the landscape in order to see what's there. Doing it quickly was never part of the equation – that's just a weird parameter stuck in my head that is better off ignored. There is a simple joy in this effort, when I can manage to check my ego long enough to settle into it, that is.

And it should probably also be noted that this whole ridiculous development is not without precedent. While I was in Nepal a few years ago I pushed my bike up some hills too. In fact, there's a remarkable similarity between what I'm up against today and the journey from Kathmandu to the trailhead for the Mount Everest Basecamp trek at

Jiri. The same effort and ego struggles apply, but much more interesting from an avid traveller's point of view is the mirrored landscape. The steep aspect of the road is a near match, as are the terraced hills supporting small farm plots. The growing heat as the morning progresses and the ever-present haze lingering in the mid-distance are also hauntingly familiar. On the second day of that particular adventure a number of mechanical troubles set in to make things even more difficult. The rack that I had was insufficient to the task at hand and had to be readjusted every five kilometres or so, and the gear ratio on the bike was probably more suited to a 25-year-old me.

I was determined not to suffer the same fate again this time around, so I brought the bike into the Bicycle Cafe in Canmore a week before leaving for Africa, and the manager Jay had a few suggestions to help make this tour as trouble free as possible. A new heavy-duty rack was an obvious upgrade, as was a swap-out of the entire crankset in order to accommodate better climbing gears. Spinning at higher revolutions wouldn't be fast, but at least I wouldn't have to walk uphill. He also recommended fat touring tires that would be more resistant to puncture and more stable on dirt roads that lean toward the sandy side of the scale. The best part? They could get the upgrades done in a couple of days.

Perfect.

The next afternoon my phone rang.

"Hello."

"Jamey?"

"Yes."

"Jay here."

"What's up?"

"We've got a problem. We found a crack in your frame."

Stunned silence on my end.

"Specialized will replace it, but it'll take two weeks."

After a long pause, all I could manage was, "But I leave in six days."

"I know. What do you want to do?"

"Well, shit. I don't know."

I'm sure there was more stunned silence at this point, but I can't say for sure. What I do know is my mind was racing through a number of options all at once, not the least of which was I didn't have two grand to spend on a replacement ride. Then it occurred to me, I had an old touring bike that I never used anymore. Maybe I could dig it out of storage and we could tune that up.

"I've got an idea. I'll be down to the shop in half an hour."

In the end Bicycle Cafe went above and beyond. In a couple of hours, they replaced all the ratty old brake and gear cables on the 12-year-old bike, lubed up everything that needed lubing, and adjusted everything that needed adjusting. They put the new rack and touring tires on there as well. What we didn't get to in time for the flight was organizing a new gear ratio on such an old bike, and that's why I'm walking now. But this hill can't go on forever, and the handful of locals with bikes I do come in contact with are also walking and pushing the loads they're carrying, so I don't feel completely out of place.

Labouring on through the rest of the morning is both simple and humbling. Sometimes I can get on and ride, and sometimes I have to walk, but it's all part of the same job. To make it to the next corner, and then decide whether to take a break in the shade or push on to the next corner after that as the road relentlessly ascends the hillside. In the effort the world gets pleasingly small: the road at my feet, the view down into the valley as it gets progressively farther away, and the occasional local villager walking by with bundles of firewood or huge yellow jugs filled with water are all that exist. Everything else is tomorrow's problem. When I finally accept that it's going to take a while to make it to the final crest of this massive hill, the slogging effort transforms into an acceptable challenge, to be approached with dogged determination. The next-level motivation that was lacking near Saadani has revealed itself.

Bring it on. I'm ready this time.

•••

For all the advancements in the last two decades, Rwanda still relies heavily on subsistence agriculture, and a huge percentage of the workforce farms. Coffee and tea are the two main cash crops for export, but most of the small plots and terraced fields I've seen today are dedicated to growing things like potatoes, cassava root, wheat, corn and bananas for local sale. The country is fertile – the volcanic soil is fecund, and when it rains, it rains *a lot* – but that fertility also extends beyond the natural ecosystem to include the human population, which makes feeding the people an ongoing challenge.

It is estimated that at the time of independence in the early 1960s the population was roughly three million. In the years leading up to the genocide it was slightly higher than seven million, and for obvious reasons that number didn't increase significantly until after the millennium. In 2010, the population hit ten million, and now it stands at roughly 12.5 million, give or take. In a country roughly the size of Massachusetts, that makes Rwanda the most densely populated nation on the African continent.

The thing is, it doesn't feel crowded. Kigali has only

about a million people, not a big city compared to most, and the slope so far today has been too steep for villages or towns to set up by the roadside. Maybe once I get up over the crest of this hill things will get busier. And since we're back on the subject of this hill...

For a good long while it was beginning to look like this acceptable challenge was going to continue in perpetuity, which would have been unacceptable. But, as I'm beginning to get properly tired – and fear I'm going to run out of water – an oasis appears on the horizon in the form of the Sheraton Pub Resto-Bar Lodge. After two and a half hours of climbing, the anticipation of finally reaching the top of this hill is palpable. One of the key parameters of the *I wonder what's up around the next corner* game is that eventually the top is there, not just a rise that leads inevitably to another rise, and then another after that. As I trudge slowly up the sweeping right-hand bend, this looks like it could finally be the one.

Could it be? Is it? Come on, please, please, please. Every step makes it seem more likely, and after gaining the sightline near the top of the curve there's no discernible incline in the near distance. The road flattens out and actually begins a small descent around the next bend. Fuck ya! It's the one. What a relief, and on the opposite side of the road the Sheraton awaits. Obviously, it isn't part of the international hotel chain, but it will surely do.

Rwandans love to paint their buildings given half a chance, and this traveller's oasis is a bright red beacon of marketing. I'm not sure how the deal works exactly, but it looks like in exchange for prominent branding companies provide exterior paint for a business's storefront, or in this case a small building complex. Individual cell phone companies have specific colours, as do beer companies. Mutzig beer is under the same company umbrella as Primus and Heineken, and from the looks of things the brand is keen on expanding its visibility in rural areas, because every conceivable surface of the Sheraton is painted red and the Mutzig logo is everywhere.

Sadly, it's too early for a beer, but a seat on the patio and a bottle of Coca-Cola, paired with a 1.5-litre bottle of water, does sound divine. I demolish the Coke in no time flat, and eventually pour the last half of the water into one of my travel bottles and continue on.

For the next few kilometres the road follows the top of a ridge and is beautiful riding. There are no cars and it's fun to be going fast again. As I'm soaking it all in I come up on a solo rider struggling along as best he can on a flat rear tire. He's got a large hard plastic crate – not unlike a milk crate back in Canada, only bigger – strapped to the rear rack of his bike. Clearly, he uses the bike for work, and it must be unpleasant doing that work on a perpetual flat. Pulling up alongside, he seems very happy to see me and puts extra effort into each pedal stroke in order to keep up, while managing a huge smile the whole time. He doesn't speak English very well, but when I point to the wheel and mime a pumping motion he seems to understand the question and shakes his head *no, I don't have a pump*. I wave him over to the side of the road, and we try to fill his tire with my pump, but it won't hold air no matter how hard we try. I think he knew it wouldn't and was humouring me in my effort to help.

Not long after, the road begins another grinding ascent, which I was not expecting, but it's followed by a tremendously steep and speedy downhill section, which in turn is followed by a picturesque and easygoing stretch along a valley bottom. The tightly terraced hills and slightly more open valley floor follow a river that looks like pale chocolate milk that needs just a little more syrup added.

Cruising the valley bottom is exceedingly pleasant riding. There are few cars or buses and no big trucks, but lots of pedestrians and bicycles moving between villages. Many of the bikes here are used as bicycle-taxis and are creatively tricked out. Funky paint jobs are common, as are reflectors and stickers. Some have fancy fenders and mud flaps, and there's even the occasional set of streamers of the type the kids in my neighbourhood had fluttering from their handle bars when we were 10. Anything to get noticed and maybe pick up a fare. All of them have heavily padded, super-duty racks for their clientele to sit on.

In around the villages the bike-taxi riders and their passengers get a real kick out of pedalling along with me on the flat stretches, but a couple of gear changes on any gentle incline allow me to drop all but the strongest riders, since they're all on one-speeds. It truly is fantastic riding after the long grind of the morning and I find myself infused with new energy and enthusiasm with every passing kilometre. There's even a thought of pushing all the way to Musanze in a single day. At the far end of an anonymous little village, I'm making good time with a bike-taxi rider determined to keep up no matter what. He's chatting amicably in Kinyarwanda with the woman sitting side saddle on the reinforced rear rack, but neither of them makes any attempt to communicate with me, even though we've been keeping pace for almost a kilometre. I glance over from time to time, but they just smile and continue on with their conversation and then, abruptly, they're gone.

In my distraction I've not been paying attention to the road ahead, and coming into a sudden steep downhill section I let momentum get away from me. The road hugs the uphill slope to the left as I begin to turn into the hard right-hander. On the valley side a stand of tall pines obscures the road ahead, but doesn't make the corner completely blind, and coming up the hill in the opposite direction there's a dump truck being overtaken by a local bus. This is notable because they're taking up both lanes.

All I can think is, *What are the chances? There's been hardly any traffic all morning and these idiots are passing each other uphill through a section of tight turns. Seriously? Are you kidding me?* To add to my troubles, I'm going very fast now.

It's amazing how brain function accelerates when disaster is imminent, and the calculations in my head are suddenly working triple time. The obvious solution is to pull off to the right onto the shoulder and let them go by, but the corner is exceedingly tight and I'm going way too fast, AND there's a section of two-inch-high rumble strips hugging the full length of the corner. Each of them is set two feet apart on the rough shoulder. I'm not sure I can cut the corner any closer and survive the exit off the smooth pavement and across the rumble strips.

Forty metres to impact.

For a split second the idea of swerving across the road to the shoulder on the opposite side seems like a good idea, but there's rumble strips over there too, and a tough angle to manage at speed before hitting the guardrail.

Thirty metres and coming up fast.

Maybe this dummy will realize he's on the wrong side of the road and will hit the brakes and tuck back into his lane.

Twenty-five metres.

Nope.

Well, shit. Twenty metres and time to make a decision. Fortunately, I'm through the worst of the bend and feel more confident in giving option number one a try. Cutting right, it's a rattle-crash-bang exit onto the shoulder, but I'm able to keep the bike upright and under control, and most importantly have made it with seven or eight metres to spare. After clearing the rumble strips I'm also able to suck in a deep breath and properly express my feelings about the whole incident, while raising and pumping a clenched fist for emphasis.

"You stupid... MOTHERFUCKERS!!!!!!!!"

As the steep slope levels out, my speed bleeds away and crisis mode quickly fades, allowing the world to slow back down to normal. Needless to say, it takes a while to regain my composure and stop my hands from shaking, but there's no sense in stopping and dwelling on the incident, so I ride on in an attempt to drain the adrenaline from my system completely. By the time I make it to the next village calm is restored. Every once in a while bad things happen, and you just have to be grateful that it wasn't a worse thing that happened. That probably applies to life in general, not just travel, but when you're all alone in the middle of nowhere in a strange country it's wise to talk yourself down from the "what if" ledge as quickly as possible, or else you'll just go home.

In the village there's a fantastic deli-style takeaway shop, and realigning my blood sugar levels helps put the recent traffic incident further into the past. There's another monster climb out there before my ultimate destination, but it's still too early to stop for the day, so I stock up on supplies and water just in case and get back on the road. Forty minutes later I pass the 55-kilometre roadside marker (the markers have been a regular feature indicating the distance from Kigali), and just beyond there's another bright red Mutzig-branded Bar-Resto Lodge.

Perfect.

As I pull in the driveway, a couple of instructive thoughts on the day come to mind. One, don't speed recklessly downhill no matter how tempting it is to let gravity take over; you never know what's coming around the next corner. And two, when you commit to just going somewhere, and don't focus too much on getting somewhere, this amazing thing called living in the moment happens. Yesterday morning I wasn't sure about having three weeks left to go on my trip. I was feeling raw and unsettled and wasn't sure what continuing on would be like. Thirty-six hours later I'm in the middle of another unique adventure within the larger adventure that has been East Africa so far, and apart from the brief brush with death on the roadway, I'm loving it.

15

VALENCE AND JAMES

Climbing again to start off this morning was inevitable. While the map I bought on a street corner in Kigali is woefully inadequate in giving any significant details of the route, the bikemap.net website does have a helpful elevation chart that expresses the verticality of this road in a way contour lines on paper never could. Studying the web page thoroughly before setting out yesterday, I learned that in the roughly 90 kilometres between the Hotel Okapi and the town of Musanze there is an elevation gain of almost 2400 metres (nearly 8,000 feet), split mostly between two significant climbs, which I have decided to take on in two separate days. By my best guesstimate, 16 of the first 20 kilometres yesterday were nothing but up, up and up. Today's effort will be shorter in both vertical and horizontal distance, but ten-plus kilometres straight uphill is still nothing to sneeze at, and I expect it will surprise no one to learn I'll spend about half of that distance walking. But it's another beautiful day, and it's not as if I've got anything else to do.

At the top of the hill there is a small village, but I've got plenty of water, so instead of stopping at one of the shops lining the road, I pull over next to a small football (soccer) pitch that is trying to take advantage of some comparatively level ground near the hilltop. Comparatively being the operative word, of course. There's a drainage ditch right behind one goal, and one-third of the field is wildly uneven. The grass is patchy, and the goals themselves are two stout saplings, with a longer, thinner sapling nailed on top as a crossbar.

As I soak up the sunshine and have a well-earned drink of water, some of the local kids are drawn to the unusual visitor in their midst. Even though this is the most direct route from the capital to Musanze – a popular tourist destination and the takeoff point for gorilla tracking in Rwanda – a white guy on a bicycle is decidedly out of the ordinary in this neighbourhood. Since I've been in the country I've seen a grand total of zero other westerners on bikes, and so far, my unannounced appearance has brought mixed reactions from children 12 and under. Some kids are positively dumbstruck and stare at me with little to no expression, as if they're thinking hard on the question, *What, exactly, is going on here?* Others appear frightened and hide behind their mother's or father's legs as I pass. And then there are always a few brave little souls with ready smiles and shouts of "mzungu, mzungu, mzungu!" or, alternatively, "good morning," no matter what time of day it is. This group of kids by the football pitch are shy at first and ball up like a school of herring, cautious of the shark, before venturing too close. Eventually, the brave ones do come to the front as I stand and sip my water.

"I play football," one of them says, rather matter-of-factly.

"I play football too. Is this your field?" I reply, pointing to the small and uneven patch of grass before us.

"Yes. I play football here."

"I play football!" another one shouts, as we stand and admire what is the local equivalent of Emirates Stadium, Arsenal's home ground. And then another young boy shouts, and then another. The floodgates opened, I'm happy to report about half the 20 or so kids who have gathered play the beautiful game, including some of the girls. The shyer kids just stand and stare, wondering, *What, exactly, is going on here?*

I didn't have talking points prepared for this eventuality and we quickly run out of ways to express our appreciation for the sport and their humble little field, but this is why I love football so much. I can go anywhere in the world and there will be people there who either play the game or watch the game. More often than not, it's both, and it's always an opportunity to have an exchange with locals about a subject that is universal like few others. Young or old, male or female, there will always be football fans in any group you meet. It doesn't matter if Judaism, Christianity, Islam, Buddhism or Hinduism is the dominant religion in the country you're visiting, there will be football fans there.

At home, I have made friends with people from all over the world and learned about their lives and their culture and their language (mostly the swear words, to be fair) because we played football together. I've spent some of my best – and worst – sporting moments with Dutchmen and Germans and Czechs and Japanese and Turks and Chileans and Brits of all stripes – along with too many others to name – because we were teammates. I count many of them as friends still. I never would have had those experiences or built those relationships without football.

As I'm trying to think of something more to say, while simultaneously reminiscing about the joy the game has brought to my life, things take an unfortunate turn.

"Give me money."

One of the brave boys has blurted it out without

preamble or expectation or even emotion. It's just a dead statement, dropped randomly into what was a cross-cultural interaction that had potential as a teaching moment for all involved, myself included. It's the harshness of the delivery that destroys the rapport that was developing and brings a sour taste to my mouth.

This will be my singular disappointment about Rwanda – it's children under the age of 12 who are most likely to emotionlessly view westerners as walking ATMs. Street vendors working the hard sell is an expected part of the travel experience, but there is almost always an effort to engage. Hustlers and legitimate independent small businessmen alike, they all have strategies to enter into "negotiations" with visitors. Simple begging happens in every big city in the world, regardless of cultural, social or economic factors. A desperate request for alms is hard to misinterpret no matter where you find yourself and is easy to accommodate.

This is different. It's so blunt and off putting. So direct and harsh. "Spare some change?" and "Give me money" are disparate approaches. One is a request, the other a demand.

"Give me money," the brave boy says once again, without actually looking at me. He was originally the most engaged and outgoing member of the young group, but now he's staring off blankly into the mid-distance. His eyes suddenly a void where animation and excitement were only a moment ago. I don't know how to deal with it. With adults there are so many options, including a simple wave-off, an uncomfortable "please don't bother me," a lighthearted and grinning "nice try," or a flat-out irritated "piss off," depending on the situation. But these are kids. There's no playbook I'm aware of. I'm sure they don't know exactly what they're saying. If I learned a single phrase in Kinyarwanda it's unlikely I would get the nuance right. Without an appropriate way to react I quickly stow my water bottle in the cage fastened to the frame of my bike, tuck my camera-phone into the handlebar bag with my proper camera, and wheel out to the road. All the while stewing in a mixture of disappointment and confusion.

Out on the road the asphalt drops away immediately. Before I can even tuck my feet into the toe clips I'm on an awesome runaway downslope once again, and the disappointment is quickly whisked away. Despite the nearly overwhelming urge to let it rip, I'm much more careful this time. A reckless downhill is just reward for the hot, sweaty work of the morning, but I've got to keep the speed in check and have an eye out for the potential of another motherfucker passing on a blind turn. Regardless, it's still great fun cruising along without having to pedal, even with the systematic application of brakes factored into the equation.

As the long, sweeping right-hander develops, the bulk of the hill is to my right, obscuring a long view in the direction I'm headed. As the road hugs the contour of the slope, the valley to the left begins to open up as I make my way into the next drainage. The view is intermittent through the trees roadside, but then at the completion of a harder right-hand bend the view opens up even more, and *boom*, just like that, there are suddenly volcanoes on the horizon in the hazy distance. It takes a minute to realize exactly what I'm seeing – because I'm concentrating on the road ahead and all – but once I figure it out I swerve across both lanes and skid to a halt in the gravel next to the road.

Until this moment all the views from up high have

been of robust hills rolling off into the distance, one leading into another and then another so that the horizon appears as a collection of rounded humps with no dominant features commanding attention. These volcanoes are more substantial and distinct, and quite abrupt on the skyline due to the distance and the haze, which is enhancing a two-dimensional quality to the view. The entire footing to the collection of peaks is elevated, the result of centuries of volcanic deposits, and the roughly conical mountains sit perched above. There are eight mountains in the range, with elevations of between 3000 and 4500 metres, and all but two of the Virunga volcanoes are dormant. The range itself is well known beyond the confines of this part of Africa, largely because of the work of Dian Fossey.

Fossey was an American primatologist who came to the Virungas in 1966 to study the mountain gorillas who live in the forests below the peaks. The work she did from a remote camp set up in the col between Mount Karisimbi and Mount Bisoke almost singlehandedly changed the way the world viewed the great apes. The terrifying beasts of King Kong–style lore proved to be highly intelligent, surprisingly social and remarkably gentle animals. Fossey was murdered at the camp at Karisoke in 1985 in suspicious circumstances, but her work helped save a species that was on the road to extinction, through misunderstanding as much as from poaching and habitat loss. The camp is gone now with the exception of a few ruins, but Fossey is buried in a small graveyard there, along with some of her favourite gorillas. In time, I hope to hike up and visit the site.

After I put my camera away, the cruising continues to be hard and fast into the valley, where I find another unexpected climb awaits (naturally), but then a final speedy descent leads to some easy and fast miles along the Mukungwa river valley. The beautiful pastoral scenes and the sun beating down are both energizing, and my legs pump the pedals with a smooth ease. There's a big local weekend market in the largest village I pass, and as a result a steady stream of people are using the shoulder of the road as a footpath. There are the expected bike taxis, but there are also a lot more bikes carrying goods to market, and still hardly any cars at all. Some enthusiastic hellos and the occasional thumbs-up are augmented on this stretch of highway with high-fives and fist bumps delivered at speed as I pass. I feel like a celebrity, and this section of the Mukungwa river valley is easily one of the favourite ten or 15 kilometres of bike riding I've ever done in my life.

There's one last hot, grinding accent into Musanze, which I end up taking partially on foot, and after I've cleared the last of the grade and come onto the level ground the town is built on, an interesting street layout is revealed. The main drag is noticeably wider than the main highway, and for a couple of blocks in the central district is split up by a grassy verge carefully landscaped with shrubs and ferns. It feels kind of grandiose for a town of this size, especially since most of the actual town is laid out to the north and the west of this "central" hub.

Cruising back along the main street after a quick reconnaissance as far as Kigombe Stream, I need to get my bearings if I want to find the hotel. Secret Garden in Moshi was such a winner that I've decided to follow the recommendations of previous travellers once again but am not sure where the Sainte Anne Hotel is. The Musanze Modern Market is a big shopping mall on the main street, and pulling up and leaning my bike in the shadow of a statue of a full-sized silverback gorilla leaves little doubt as to what the tourist attraction is around here.

Once I've fished out my Lonely Planet for direction, it doesn't take long for a group of kids in that troublesome 10-to-12-year-old age group to spot me, but unlike with the rural children there's no hesitation, they simply crowd in and start asking questions. What's your name? Where are you from? Why are you here? Where is your wife? Never mind that I'm clearly engaged in a task and not inclined to chat. But I also notice that these kids are already wise to the subtleties of this kind of interaction. They don't immediately ask for money and are working hard to begin a dialogue first. Emanuel, the oldest of the group, leans in as I'm looking at the simple town map laid out on one of the pages and asks, "What are you doing?"

"Trying to figure out where my hotel is," I reply, while turning the page level with the ground and twisting it this way and that, trying to match the street layout I can see in front of me with the map layout I can't make any sense of.

"What's it called?"

"The Sainte Anne Hotel."

Emanuel points up the block without hesitation.

"It's up that road. At the first corner turn right."

I pivot the page, and it suddenly makes perfect sense. I had the orientation wrong. Realizing that none of these boys asked me directly for money, but did provide a service, I figure that's worth a couple of hundred francs for sure. So I express my gratitude and hand over some coins before they scamper off to spend them somewhere. The beauty of it is they have no idea how reaffirming the simple interaction is to my faith in people's motivations.

Thanks, guys.

•••

For the first time on this trip – and maybe ever in the

entire history of my hiking and bicycling adventures – the distance I needed to travel today was actually shorter than anticipated. After showering and changing clothes, I grab my notebook and head out to explore Musanze. As I walk back down to the area around Kigombe Stream I take a few notes along the way, but am ultimately lured by the prospect of some shade and a chance to rest my legs at Migano Café. A western-style coffee shop and restaurant.

After the latte break I'm standing at the corner, unsure of what to do next, when Valance and James make their introductions. They are 17 and 18 years old respectively, and disarmingly charming. Normally, I'm wary of people approaching me on the street, but they penetrate my defences with ease, and in no time at all we're taking selfies together and discussing the merits of supporting Chelsea versus supporting Arsenal (Valence is for Chelsea, James is an Arsenal man through and through). As I turn back toward the hotel, they decide to follow along and we walk awkwardly for a while, having already burned through the first round of small-talk options. I admit, idle chit-chat is not my strength, but I do have one undeniable skill in my bag of travel tricks. The ability to sniff out a good dive bar. In this case that bar is yet another Mutzig-branded place on the way back to the hotel.

The bar is on the upper floors of a multi-storey building, and the entrance is not immediately obvious, but I'm hoping for a view of the volcanoes, so I make my way to the rear of the building and find a stairway there. Valence and James are not inclined to join me, and wave from the street as I turn at the end of the alley and head up the stairs, still unsure if it is the way. Fortunately, it is. The bar has multiple rooms and is spartan in its appointments, and there are a bunch of guys at a pool table with the felt almost completely worn through, waiting for the next game. More importantly there's an open seat at the wood, which is where I prefer to sit when I'm on my own. Unfortunately, the outdoor patio seats set on a small balcony overlooking the street below are taken, but the sightlines don't clear the surrounding buildings and trees anyway, so I grab the open spot at the bar. A 33cl bottle (the rough equivalent of our standard 341ml bottles in Canada) of Skol Malt is less than a dollar Canadian and could prove to be trouble at that price if I'm not careful.

As I get halfway through my second, I can't help but notice a waiter going up and down another set of stairs a few metres from the entrance.

Leaning in, I ask the bartender, "Is there a rooftop patio?"

"Yes, up those stairs," he says, pointing vaguely in that direction.

Fantastic.

"I'll take one more beer, please."

The patio is also spartan in its appointments – the number of red Mutzig-branded plastic patio chairs and tables is not nearly proportional to the available space on the roof – but the skyline is more than I could ever ask for. The view skims the tops of the other buildings in the neighbourhood, and most of the trees as well. The Virunga volcanoes sweep majestically across the horizon, and are much closer now than the first sighting earlier today. Muhabura and Gahinga are dead ahead, with Sabyinyo positioned a little to the left. Farther left, some shifting cloud and an unfamiliarity with the mountains makes it harder to pin down Bisoke, Karisimbi and maybe even Mikeno in behind, but they're out there playing peekaboo.

What is immediately apparent, after getting over the

initial awe inspired by the landscape, is how far up the slopes the patchwork of cultivated fields go. Even from here – a distance of about 13 kilometres – Volcanoes National Park looks very small, and it's difficult to imagine a significant population of gorillas would have enough space to roam. But the latest census indicates there are currently 1,004 mountain gorillas in the interconnected territory that makes up the national parks in Rwanda, Uganda and the DRC. Thanks to the pioneering work of Dian Fossey that started in the late 1960s, and the tireless contributions of countless individuals and conservation organizations that have joined the fight since, gorillas are now the only species of great ape with a population that is increasing in the wild. It is a hopeful story.

As another beer arrives I realize I'm tired, and maybe a little heat-stroked as well, but the broken cloud continues to be entrancing as it brushes over the collection of peaks that extend 120 degrees across the horizon. The beer is beginning to work its magic, and after the big effort of the last couple of days I'm happy to catch the buzz and wait for the coming sunset. As I'm contemplating how great life is in this exact moment, my mind can't help but drift to Barry Lopez's new book, *Horizon*. There is an opening quote by French writer, poet and aviator Antoine de Saint-Exupéry in it that is nothing if not beguiling: "To travel, above all, is to change one's skin."

I have to wonder, as the end of this journey begins to draw near, have I changed my skin? I admit, I absolutely do feel different, but I don't know if I'm changed. I'm still essentially the same person I was two months ago when I came to Africa, but maybe what I've done is return to a skin that's more comfortable. One that's more natural. It's not a full transformation, I'm still too often anxious, and fall too easily into the "western shoulds" as my default position when I'm not sure what to do next, instead of being patient and allowing the right option the chance to present itself. I long to get truly comfortable with the idea of letting the day guide me. If it doesn't amount to much, so be it. We're not there yet.

But overall, I am better here, out on the road looking to satisfy a hunger to experience and to explore in order to learn and to know things first-hand. There are powerful glimpses of peace and purpose in that process, and that is why I'm drawn helplessly forward by the idea. It's not about escapism, or the avoidance of everyday life in western society; I'm simply trying to find my best life. Perhaps travel is an acknowledgement of my true self. This is the curious me, the adventurous me, the thoughtful me, the hopeful me. I like this me. If Ngoda were here I'd be sure to let him know that everything is poa.

After getting up and moving to the edge of the roof to take pictures of the volcanoes in the distance as the light slowly changes, I am drawn to chat with the six local businessmen sitting at the next table. The beers are coursing full speed through my system now, and I'm feeling gregarious and outgoing. These guys were here when I sat down, so I'm sure they're feeling no pain either. After the obligatory hellos and where-you-froms, the obvious question arises.

"What do you think of Rwanda?" One of them asks.

As it turns out, there is no easy answer.

I like *me* here, but I also like *it* here, and am not sure how to properly articulate why. Giving a reasoned, fact-based answer that captures the extent of my feelings proves surprisingly difficult. I'm trying to make it make sense intellectually, when the real reasons are much more complicated in that they carry a heavy element of emotion. Sure, Rwanda is clean, the people are friendly, and the hills and mountains are beautiful, but those are all stock answers. I've encountered variations of these themes all over the world.

At a more personal level, I like the bikes all over the place. Bicycle taxis and bicycles used to move freight from village to village and the Rwandan national cycling team ripping across the landscape (the Africa Rising Cycling Center, the team's home base, is here in Musanze and I've seen groups of guys out on high-energy training rides on both days up from Kigali). These are all things that make me smile when I think about them. A bicycle-based culture is more intuitive to me than a society dependent on motor vehicles. I deeply appreciate this country halfway around the world that makes more sense to my core being than my home province, with its jacked-up pickup trucks and a rabid commitment to a shitty type of dirty oil that has no future in a global economy that is destined to wean its way off fossil fuels one way or another.

DodgeRamistan (a.k.a. Alberta) is brash and blustery and loud, and not always terribly enlightened. But I digress.

Another thing I like about Rwanda is the countrywide commitment to addressing a difficult past. To acknowledge the failures in leadership and the atrocities committed, in order to at least attempt an effort at reconciliation after the genocide, is admirable. Nothing is being swept under the rug. I remain beyond impressed with the survivors who have stated a desire to forgive in order to move on. This is not my home, I do not belong here, but I have mad respect for this place and the efforts being made to reunite a country. There is a common purpose here that I don't always experience in my own community, let alone in my province or in my country as a whole.

That's all a lot to dump on a bunch of guys having after-work beers, so I end up giving the stock answer. For no better reason than if I try to say more, I'll end up blathering on nonsensically. I have had a few.

"I like Rwanda. It's clean, the people are friendly," and as I wave vaguely out at the volcanoes, "and the mountains are beautiful."

So ... freaking ... lame.

Oh well, the businessmen seem appeased if not necessarily impressed, and after taking a few more pictures and returning to my plastic patio chair, I am reminded of Tim Cahill and his extensive library of stories that have influenced me over the years.

In "The Platypus Hunter," a story that appeared in his book *Hold the Enlightenment*, Cahill laments on the prospect of getting older. Writing in the third person, he contemplates the point of it all: "He feels the seasons of his life slowly flapping in front of his face like the beating of some great dark wing. You're born, he thinks; you live, you die, and to what end?"

To what end? In an evening of Skol Malts and questions, that's another good one.

Cahill admits to being clueless about the greater purpose of an individual's existence, but muses that a series of "small, highly defined quests – seeing a platypus in the wild for instance – will one day accumulate into a critical mass and there will be a blinding light like the collision of suns." For dramatic purposes, he imagines in that radiant moment he will be able to see into the Very Core of the Universe.

I first read "The Platypus Hunter" in my 20s and reread

it about once a year, whenever I'm feeling unsure about the path I've taken. Or when I need to be inspired to go out and have another look at the world first-hand. I, too, have no fucking clue about the purpose of existence, but the older I get the more convinced I become that a series of "small, highly defined quests" is a good idea. Each journey is part of changing one's skin. Or returning to a better-fitting skin at the very least. In spite of a few missteps along the way, I've somehow managed to pile of few of these "quests" into a single trip to East Africa, which is no small accomplishment, I guess.

The revelation deserves a final beer, and as I drink it the rest of the evening fails to impress in the way I had hoped. The clouds settling in as nightfall approaches wash out the scene. There's no fiery sunset blazing across the volcanoes, and so no great photo op to round out what has been a pretty perfect day so far, unfortunately. Walking back to the hotel for dinner, I don't have huge expectations for what tomorrow might bring either, and that's okay, it'll probably be a rest day anyway. But going to see the gorillas in Volcanoes National Park later this week will be another new, and unique, "quest."

Maybe I'll get a glimpse into the Very Core of the Universe then.

•••

As I'm sipping a latte at Migano Café with a thumping headache, the Universe is dull and uninspired and is unlikely to reveal its Core, but the café really is a lovely spot for an early lunch. The tunes coming from the speakers are hip and modern, and the décor is similarly appealing and stylish. As I was sitting here yesterday it occurred to me I could be anywhere in the world while inside. Montreal,

Paris, Sydney, Hong Kong, Buenos Aires, who would know, but the universality of café culture is comforting when you spent the previous evening drinking too many beers while contemplating the meaning of life.

So, for today, I'm going to try and sit with a mellow appreciation of the journey so far, and take some time to reflect on it without the distraction of schedule or the self-imposed need to accomplish. There's nothing to do today, and no rush to go and do it. I'll tackle what comes to my mind, and then try and let it go just as easily. It's what Cahill would do. After a couple of lattes and a really good pesto chicken sandwich, the plan is no more complicated than walking back to the room for a nap.

As I'm shielding my eyes from the sudden brightness of the sun, Valance and James spot me from the opposite corner and come across the street with big grins on their faces. A quick chat is welcome, since they're the only two people I know in town. They seem like nice enough kids, but I can't help but wonder how they've managed to penetrate my defences so easily. We've already done selfies together and exchanged email addresses. Now they want to accompany me on my walk. I was about to find an excuse to brush them off, but sure, why not.

Instead of heading straight back to the hotel, we head farther up the main road. It's a bit awkward walking at times, because even though their English is pretty good, there's an accent that doesn't sit well in my ear to factor into every exchange. I was hoping things would be easier here in Rwanda. I had it in my mind Swahili and French would dominate where English wasn't spoken, but of course Kinyarwanda is the native language, and French has fallen out of favour because English is the language of tourism, and increasingly business, in the rest of East

Africa. Rwanda has made the transition in order to keep pace.

As we make our way slowly uphill past the main hospital and the Karisoke Research Center – home to the Dian Fossey Gorilla Fund International – we chat as best we can, before turning around at the Musanze District Office. Taking another route through town back to the hotel, we also pass the local stadium and the farmers market. The boys dutifully point out the landmarks along the way and I share a little bit of my experience as a foreign visitor, with the hope that they can use the information to secure future guiding gigs. Tourism is big business in this part of the country, and there are good jobs to be had. Then they rattle off a few questions that I don't actually know the answers to, or at least the specific answers to.

"How big is Canada?" James asks.

"Big. Especially compared to Rwanda."

I know Canada is the second biggest country in the world by land area, but can only venture a ballpark guess as to the number of kilometres that translates into. Nine million square kilometres comes to mind, but I'm not sure.

"What are your exports and imports?"

Hmmm. Wow. Not a clue. I'm used to questions like *What is your job?* And *Do you have kids?* I end up winging it with my answers. I would expect Canada to export lots of timber and grain. As for imports, geez, electronics and oil maybe.

(I am embarrassed to report that I did not represent my country well in the pop quiz. Canada's top two exports in 2019 were mineral fuels, including oil, and vehicles, according to worldstopexports.com. Wood was seventh on the list, and agricultural products didn't even make the top ten. On imports I did slightly better – vehicles was number one [don't even get me started on how it makes any sense to export US$61.4 billion worth of a product, and then turn around and import US74.4 billion of the same basic product, but what do I know] and machinery, including computers, was number two. Mineral fuels, including oil, was fourth. And not for nothing. Canada covers an area of 9.98 million square kilometres. Rwanda is only 26,338 square kilometres in size. *Big compared to* is something of an understatement.)

The more we walk the more I can't help but warm up to these kids. Maybe I've been out on the road alone too long, or maybe I see something of myself in them when I was their age. I'm hungover and it's hot and I really need to lie down for a while, but maybe I can hire them for a few hours sometime. Embrace the opportunity that has presented itself. Instead of constantly fighting off the advances of older and more experienced men looking to land a freelance guiding job, I can turn into it and see what the experience brings. Once we reach the hotel, I make them a deal: be back here at ten a.m. tomorrow and we'll do this again. They accept the job offer, but I am insistent on this next point: "but we've got to see something I wouldn't see otherwise." They agree, and I get the feeling they might already have something planned.

The next morning, as I'm having breakfast, I do wonder if Valence and James are actually going to show, and what we're going to talk about if they do, because they caught me off guard with their questions yesterday. But, as I'm leaving the hotel, I don't get three steps outside the gate before I see Valence and James down at the corner, smiling as always. The hellos and handshakes are warm – bordering on affectionate – and they have brought a friend with them. Edison is also 17, and before we can even begin the walking tour we get into a street corner interview about their families, their schooling and future job prospects. I'm not a very good interviewer – I prefer to sit back and observe and then report – but this is an opportunity to practise my skills while learning a thing or two about their lives. As we chat, a couple of older guys try to draw my attention away, but I brush them off with a wave and an annoyed look. It's only after a particularly aggressive tout requires the *hey, fuck off, I'm not talking to you* treatment that we begin to walk.

As we head off, the idea of visiting their home comes up once again and I resist. James brought it up yesterday, but it seems intrusive to me. I explain as best I can that it would be too personal, and I would be uncomfortable, but they are insistent. I guess it is an experience I wouldn't find on a normal tour operator's agenda, so after some further discussion I relent. The problem is their home is a two-hour walk away, and a four-hour round trip was not what I had in mind for today. Not to be deterred, the boys suggest a motorcycle taxi, but after the experience near Saadani National Park another wild piki piki ride is out of the question, and the boys look genuinely disappointed when they find out how much a proper taxi ride is. They want to treat me, but it's more than they can afford. In the end I agree to include the fare in the three-hour tour package, and we negotiate a good deal for an out and back in the taxi, with the driver to wait for us while we visit their family.

I have no idea what to expect from the outing, but it turns out the boys live near Kinigi village and the road up is in tremendous shape. The national park headquarters are in Kinigi, and some of the money collected from entrance fees goes to the building and maintenance of public works in the area. The pavement is smooth and pothole free and trees line the route for long stretches. There are also a lot of people out walking the wide sidewalk. On the far side of the village the driver turns off onto a dirt track at James's direction, and before long it gets too rough, so we get out and walk. We pass the primary school they all went to, and then cross a small stream on a log bridging the gap. Along the narrow dirt path there are a number of compact farm plots and modest clapboard or mud and stick homes, and in one of the yards a small outdoor church service is in progress.

It's obvious that the wealth filtering down from the tourism industry is not necessarily making its way to the subsistence farmers living here, just below the park, to the same degree as the community infrastructure is being funded, and as we leave the dirt path I am immediately invited into James and Valence's home. The boys are half-brothers, and their father passed away a couple of years ago, so I am introduced to their mother and a couple of aunts. The living room is basic, a hard-packed dirt floor, dried mud walls with the bamboo supports showing through in places, and a few simple wood chairs and benches, but everyone is gracious and welcoming. We talk for a while about the boys' schooling and the crops in the field, but English isn't the first language spoken in the household, so James fields most of my questions about life here in the shadow of the famous volcanoes. I'm trying hard to be casual about it all, like this kind of interaction happens to me all the time. The older ladies are a little more reserved, but the kindness and openness of these people is endearing.

Valence and James and Edison all have smiles that are infectious, and at the end of the conversation, when they produce a brown paper bag and pull out a wood carving of a silverback gorilla as a thank-you gift for spending the morning with them, I have to drag the three of them in for a group hug to keep from bursting into happy tears in front of everyone. After two months of having my traveller's guard up, these young men have stripped it down in the matter of hours. Meaningful travel should always be a search for the memorable and the uplifting. Mission accomplished, and then some.

The Very Core of the Universe has not been revealed, but an important element of its basic structure has been exposed – and just like that.

16

AGASHYA, ISANO AND DUSANGIRE

There are no surprises on the 13-kilometre bike ride up to Kinigi. Having just driven it with Valence and James and Edison, I find everything exactly as it was yesterday. The grade is much easier than on any of the big hills on the road from Kigali, but it's still 13 kilometres uphill, so I shift into a low gear and simply settle into the slow, steady effort of it. This gentle pace gives me some time to think about that first visit, and I find that the disparity in income opportunity, based almost exclusively on birthright, is what made me so uncomfortable while visiting the boys' modest home. My privilege in this world is guided to an overwhelming extent by the country I was born in and the parents I was born to. When we were that age, my friends and I were just like Valence and James and Edison. We laughed a lot, we liked sports, and we enjoyed the simplicity of just hanging out together when there was nothing else to do. As I recall, we also imagined ways to make some money, so we could do things and buy stuff.

As high school was coming to an end most of us got our act together and started to figure out tolerable ways in which to make a living as adults. Almost all of us went to university, and many of us managed to scrape together some extra cash in order to travel, with the hopes of expanding our experience and our general frame of reference (when we weren't getting drunk or stoned, as is the tradition of youthful exuberance that's found itself far from home). A few of my friends were rich, but most of us were regular old middle class, yet that still afforded us great privilege in this world, which I'm sure nobody fully appreciated at the time.

I suspect the path through life will be much different for these guys, and opportunity may not be so forthcoming. I feel bad about that. Not responsible, but certainly concerned for their future. Everyone should get the chance to see it all. To do it all. Are we all not worthy? Are we all not deserving? So maybe there's a challenge to be met here when it comes to making any further comparisons between the country I call home and the countries I enjoy travelling to. As I gain an even deeper understanding of how lucky I am in this life for the opportunities it affords, that would seem to me to be my responsibility.

As I enter my 50s, I can confirm the modern western world can sometimes feel like a series of exhausting tasks, to be juggled and managed and adapted to. Job, mortgage, kids, this is the standard routine. I don't have kids but do have the other two, and that's more than enough for me to handle most days. These responsibilities slip easily into a routine where everything is imposed from outside the self, based on a need to live up to financial commitments. At times I have done well playing the money game, but when the shine of minor affluence wears off a harsh reality sets in. The pursuit of it didn't actually satisfy. Many people get caught up in the mindless hunt for more affluence in the mistaken assumption that it will justify the means, if they can hang on just a little bit longer. They hope it will bring value to the effort, and maybe make them happy one day, somewhere in the future. This is the myth of unrestrained capitalism, that more is better. This is my point of reference because it is what has surrounded me my entire life.

But these kids I've gotten to know a little bit are operating from a different background and a different set of circumstance. Just like everyone's, their world view is informed by the set of conditions that they experience daily. Basic education, adequate health care, ready access to food and clean water, shelter from the elements. Things I have sometimes taken for granted as a Canadian have a different calculus here. My expected normal is not necessarily as straightforward for everyone. These are universal human needs. In point of fact they are human rights, but we are not evolved enough as a species to guarantee that for the entire populace of most countries, let alone the world at large. Let's face it, there are many in the so-called First World who cannot live up to the lifestyle to which I have become accustomed. There are moments when I can barely manage it. Work, work, work, and then more work. To what end I don't know, but we continue to collectively aspire to the malfunctioning western dream that only more will ever be enough. And the rest of the world is hell bent on catching up.

Once I reach Kinigi a quick stop for a drink of water is in order, and then at the town's only significant intersection I make a right for the final kilometre or so to Kinigi Guest House. The road is steep at first, and a couple of the local fellas take the opportunity to join me, as I can only manage a walking pace as I pedal. They work the now familiar routine of wanting to practise their English language skills as introduction, and what am I going to do? They have a captive audience. We banter back and forth for a few dozen pedal strokes, and as the grade relents they have to break into a jog to keep up. By the time they get around to suggesting an email address exchange in order to stay in touch they are at a dead run. Then the road levels out even more.

Sorry, guys, gotta go.

A little farther along I pass a huge open field to my left and Mount Sabyinyo comes into view. The mountain is no longer obscured by the roadside trees and is close now, and the jagged multi-peak top is a departure from the classic conical shape of Bisoke. I'm tempted to linger on the view, but there's also a heavy storm cloud coming in fast and I don't want to get caught out. At the end of the field the road takes a hard left and turns back uphill. I can see the Kinigi Guest House grounds, tucked in the upper right corner of the huge fallow field, but don't know if I'm going to make it in time. Picking up the pace, I find the last 200 metres is a painful sprint that sears my lungs and fills my thighs with lactic acid, and when the first ponderous raindrops smash the pavement with 100 metres left to go I know I've lost the race. I'm soaked in seconds when the sky opens up, but at least it isn't much farther, and thankfully it isn't until I reach shelter that the hail starts.

After waiting out the rain over a leisurely lunch on the covered patio, I'm able to check into my room in one of the outbuildings on the property, and after freshening up, I decide to walk over to the park headquarters to inquire about a gorilla tracking permit and find out when I might be able to go see the animals. I went to the main tourist information centre in downtown Kigali and was told there were permits available for later in the week, and that I could get them in Musanze, no problem. At the satellite office there, I was told there were still permits available, and that I could get them at the park headquarters, no problem.

Now that I'm here there's not a soul to be found. The parking lot – a truly unique black flagstone style expanse made up of porous volcanic stones – is empty, and the immaculately manicured grounds are devoid of any activity at all. There are two large gazebos for visitor orientation, and a few small one-storey buildings for administration offices and toilets and guide locker rooms. My guidebook indicated the offices would be open until four p.m., but at three p.m. it's deadsville. The place is shut up tight. I even go so far as to rattle a few doors and peer through a few windows, but banker's hours are obviously in play today.

In the outdoor foyer of the main building, however, there is an amazing mural along two of the walls. The sprawling painting runs across the top of the doors and windows of some of the offices. The background is bright yellow, and in varying shades of green and blue the volcanoes of the park appear in rough scale, with peaks identified, including height in metres. Along the base of the mountains the approximate territory of each of the habituated gorilla groups is marked, with a small silverback painted above each group name, in case there was any doubt who the boss is. Apparently, the Kwitonda group likes to hang around near the base of Mount Gahinga, the Agashya group is fond of the western slope of Mount Sabyinyo, and the Titus group prefers the area between Mount Bisoke and Mount Karisimbi. As a whole, the display is incredibly helpful in getting oriented to the surrounding landscape, and I can't help but wonder which of the 12 groups I'm going to get to visit. For some reason, one of my favourite parts of it all is the anchor point, written in bold capital letters: PARK OFFICE – YOU ARE HERE!

Yes. Yes, I am. And I am suddenly very, very excited about it.

Stepping back out onto the road, I see the world around me is green and damp in every direction and there's a slight chill in the overcast air. About 40 metres beyond the park headquarters the well-maintained asphalt gives way to a dirt track, and if I've got my bearings right (that's a big if) Valence and James's home will be somewhere down that track, now that I find myself at the opposite end of it compared to yesterday. As I turn toward the guest house, the anti-poaching patrol staging area is in the yard next door, and there are a handful of rangers next to the small building gearing up to head out into the park. I'm tempted to wander over and talk to them about what the plan is, but there is a military level seriousness to their preparations, so I decide it's best to leave them be.

A little farther along (and right across the street from the guest house) the gorilla-naming ceremony site sits in another large field. Once a year, the Kwita Izina is performed, and baby gorillas born in the previous year are named. The ceremony is a national celebration, but today the field is empty except for the gigantic bamboo statue of a mother gorilla with a baby riding on her back. There are a few smaller (comparatively) animal friends also made of bamboo scattered about that are not all endemic to this part of Africa, including an elephant, a giraffe and a rhino, but other than that, all is quiet.

The armed park rangers aside, what strikes me about this part of Kinigi, away from the village centre, is how peaceful it is. There's nobody on the road, and I've only seen the occasional local walking through the surrounding fields. There's little, if any, mechanical noise intruding from anywhere in the neighbourhood, and at the guest house, there's only the manager, a server, a cook (that I've yet to actually see) and one other couple who are planning to go gorilla tracking tomorrow.

It's an astonishing counter-narrative to a busy country ramping up efforts to pull itself fully into the modernized world.

• • •

This morning I hope to have better luck securing a permit. It's only a few hundred yards from the guest house to the headquarters, so first thing I begin to make my way over to see if anything is open, making sure to detour down through the huge field first. It's still peaceful and quiet up here. There's a sharply dressed young man who comes over to chat briefly while I take photographs, and an old man with a walking stick making his way through the field, but other than that I have the whole thing to myself as I enjoy the dawning of a new day over the rolling hills to the south.

At 6:45 a.m. a handful of Land Cruisers come tearing up the road to abruptly disrupt the morning calm. From the direction of Kinigi village, across to the turn leading up to Kinigi Guest House, and over to park headquarters, the road is three sides to a square with the field in the middle, and I've got a pretty clear view the entire way. The vehicles are in tight formation and are speeding along at a pace that feels excessive under the circumstances. Check-in time for park activities is seven a.m., and the information sessions do take a bit of time to complete, so it's not like anyone is going to miss the last train to Clarksville or anything. Yet it's still a NASCAR style race to the finish line.

It's all a bit strange, but suddenly I feel like I should hurry up too, and park headquarters is decidedly busier than yesterday when I arrive. There are tourists having coffee and watching a video about gorillas that is set up in one of the gazebos, and there are plenty of guides in freshly pressed uniforms scurrying about as they prep for their pre-trip briefings and figure out which tourists are going to be paired with which gorilla group. Checking in at the main office, I'm relieved to find I can get a permit for tomorrow, but as I go to pay Visa decides once again that they're not sure I am who I say I am. A quick international phone call clears up the matter, but it's going to take a few minutes for my payment to be processed.

While I'm waiting for my paperwork, Anaclet Budahera agrees to an interview out in the grounds. I want to talk to someone in the know about how gorilla tourism works, and Anaclet is the man. He's the Tourism Warden for Volcanoes National Park, and as such is in charge of the day-to-day operations here. There are roughly 200 people working in this park, including rangers, trackers, guides and administration and sales staff. Anaclet is hesitant to be recorded, but is happy to chat about the program, and doesn't mind if I take notes. Straight off it's clear he has a passion for his work, and I envy him that. My day job is okay, I guess. It pays the bills and has some great perks (not the least of which is disappearing for months at a time when I want to go do research for a new book), but this is next level. Working to help save an endangered species, while simultaneously helping to improve the lives of the people who live in the immediate vicinity of the park.

Now that's cool.

I suppose this is what is referred to as a career, not a job, but to hear Anaclet tell it the journey was not entirely straightforward. As a young man he became aware of the foreigners passing through his village and wondered, *Who are these people? What are they doing here?* That early interest developed over time into a desire to work in a tourism industry reborn after the genocide ended. It was everyday curiosity that led in this direction. Hard work got him here.

According to Anaclet there are 12 habituated gorilla groups in Rwanda's Volcanoes National Park, as well as two groups of habituated golden monkeys. Gorilla tracking excursions have a maximum of eight people per group, and contact with the animals is restricted to one hour. An important detail in limiting the impact felt by the animals is that each group of gorillas only sees one group of visitors per day. For the other 23 hours they are left alone to go about their business undisturbed. In Rwanda there are currently 300 animals that are monitored almost constantly, and in Rwanda, Uganda and the DRC someone is keeping a close eye on approximately 600 mountain gorillas total. As I have mentioned, the latest census indicates there are currently 1,004 gorillas in the three countries, and this number has been steadily increasing in recent years. Every time I think about it, I get goosebumps. In a world where most things natural are diminishing in one way or another, this is an encouraging counterpoint to that narrative.

The recovery is not without its challenges, however. Rwanda's population and the gorilla population face a common obstacle – lack of habitat. For the gorillas that means undisturbed tracts of forest filled with suitable foraging, and in an agrarian society dependent on productive land to feed a rapidly growing populace, that means farms. Lots of farms. That field I enjoy so much for my morning and evening walks, the one right below the park with the long views – that used to be gorilla habitat. Now the trees are gone. Part of the ongoing gorilla recovery effort does include expanding the park, which contracted significantly after the genocide, when tens of thousands Tutsi refugees were repatriated. That means buying back the farmland that abuts the park boundary and letting it go wild. Twenty-seven hectares have been added to date, and a buffer zone offers some flexibility for both animal and human. Anaclet reports firewood and honey collection is permitted in the buffer zone, and there is a compensation program for crop loss due to animal activity. In addition to gorillas, Cape buffalo and other ungulates do wander down into the fields for a snack from time to time.

To support such an expansive program, the Rwanda Development Board decided to increase the fee for gorilla tracking from US$750 to US$1500 in May 2017 (which is why Visa is so interested in what I'm up to today), and the argument Anaclet offers up is that the lower impact that comes from fewer people can still have the same financial benefit. My counter-argument on this point is that we are pricing these wonders out of the reach of regular people, something I also discussed at length with Ronaldo back in Moshi. But there's no doubt that a key aspect to the success of the program is addressing local needs in order to create a partnership, and that takes money. If electricity is installed more extensively, then the use of firewood is reduced, and the forest is spared. Improved health services means a decrease in the harvesting of traditional medicinal plants from the park. The thinking goes that if every citizen is benefiting from gorilla protection then the job becomes much easier. The big picture plan is to develop a model program that can be effectively implemented wherever fragile ecosystems are under threat. Anaclet is understandably proud of that prospect.

It's a ton of information, and I can't take my notes fast enough. As we've been talking Anaclet has become more passionate and animated. The professionalism required of an employee in an important government job is eroded ever so slightly, and clearly, he is inspired by his work. I am happy to sit and listen for as long as he is inclined to explain the current state of affairs in the park.

Eventually, Anaclet has to get back to the office but gives me a quick rundown of gorilla development before he goes. Newborns are considered babies until the age of 3. From ages 3 to 6, the animals go through their "troublemaking" phase as juveniles, and are considered subadults until they are 8 years old. At this point females can conceive, and males are considered black-backs until around the age of 12, when they reach full maturity and develop the silver-white fur that is so distinctive to the species. The average lifespan for a gorilla is 35 to 40 years. And finally, poaching is currently under control, but vigilance is key. The goal is to have zero losses, and to that end protection activities are exceedingly well organized. Those guys I saw yesterday, the ones getting prepared to go out on patrol, are part of a larger group of protectors that uses the tactic of heading out on a random and rotating schedule, so that poachers can't predict the whereabouts of any of the patrols at any given time.

As our conversation draws to a close I find I'm stoked, and almost forget about the exorbitant price tag associated with the coming adventure. Almost. After my paperwork is approved and delivered, Anaclet and I wrap things up, and I head back to the guest house with a mind that's reeling in a swirl of excitement and anticipation. Needless to say, all I can think about for the rest of the day is gorillas, gorillas and gorillas.

• • •

A great many people have written about the magnificent creatures of this contemporary Garden of Eden. George Schaller did groundbreaking work in the area of field biology with numerous species around the world, including mountain gorillas. In 1963, *The Mountain Gorilla: Ecology and Behavior* helped begin to shift the public's understanding of the animals who lived high in the jungles of equatorial Africa. Dian Fossey's book about her time in Rwanda, *Gorillas in the Mist,* was also made into a feature film, and fellow Canadian Will Ferguson writes about visiting them as part of his thoroughly enjoyable book *Road Trip Rwanda.*

And then there's my man Tim Cahill. No one has had a bigger influence on me standing here at the edge of Volcanoes National Park than Cahill. In point of fact, there has been no one who has managed to inspire my wandering spirit in general quite as much as he has. Cahill is an adventure travel writer based in Livingston, Montana, and is a founding editor of *Outside* magazine. I've never even met the man, but such is the power of story that it has the ability to motivate you remotely, across both time *and* space. A good story can also get you moving physically if you are so inspired. Thanks for the push, Tim.

In the 1980s Cahill wrote two articles about this place that were especially impactful, "Love and Death in Gorilla Country" and "Life and Love in Gorilla Country." I found them in his books *A Wolverine Is Eating My Leg* and *Jaguars Ripped My Flesh.* Much of what I know about gorilla behaviour and Volcanoes National Park – known back then as Parc National des Volcans – comes from Cahill. I have read other stories and books about the subject, but it was Cahill who planted the seed. I thought,

There's an experience in life I have got to have one day. In his words I found profound experience, felt viscerally. Thirty years after first reading his work, here I am at the edge of the park, ready to experience this place for myself.

Although I don't quite catch his name, my driver for today is very friendly, and right on cue at 6:45 a.m. all the other tour vehicles come charging up the road toward park headquarters. This morning I'm part of that charge, for all of the 45 seconds between the guest house and the lava stone parking lot. When we arrive, I find roughly 40 other tourists already waiting, all freshly scrubbed and eager for what may come. There's an air of anticipation within the group, as nervous energy prevails over all attempts to appear calm and collected. It's a good thing there's coffee and tea and a video to distract as the gorilla groups are allocated and guide assignments are handed out. Almost all my fellow visitors are middle-aged and older for obvious reasons (the price tag), and by my reckoning only a small handful of people are under 30. There are zero hippy-traveller-types mixed in.

I am designated to the Agashya group, with seven other westerners: four Belgians travelling together, two American women and a New Zealander named Dave. At first, I am hesitant to engage beyond the expected pleasantries. I'm here to take in the experience of gorilla tracking, not make new friends. But everyone is pleasant enough, and after the pre-trip briefing we all amble out to the parking lot before rocketing away down the sleepy road en route to our designated trailhead. After getting back to the road junction in Kinigi, we turn right and head farther up toward the ridge that marks the border with the DRC, where we finally encounter the first potholes I've seen since getting to Rwanda. Gradually, as the route crests the hill and then runs roughly parallel to the park boundary, the road deteriorates further, until we make another right turn for our final approach to the trailhead, where it pretty much disappears completely. We're now on a pathway, or a rough track, or an off-road access. One thing it is not is a proper road.

"Are you ready for your African massage?" my driver says with a big grin as we make the turn.

I had forgotten about the African massage. Volcanic soils are rich in nutrients, which is why this area is coveted as farmland, but the underlying volcanic rock is rough and wildly uneven where it pokes through. That makes for an extremely bumpy ride for the last kilometre or two. A working field is real estate far too valuable for a road along this stretch, especially because pyrethrum – a natural insecticide and important export – grows well here, so the track runs over the exposed rock wherever possible. At the trailhead we leave the vehicles behind and begin to walk, first through the farmers' fields that border the park, and then up into the jungle where the gorillas live. What is immediately notable is how much land up here is field and how little actual jungle is left. It was obvious from the bar rooftop in Musanze, and is even more so now. Once again it is very difficult to imagine a significant population of animals thriving in such a small space.

Cahill often travelled with photographer Nick Nichols on his adventures, and I am fond of a scene from another one of his travel yarns where Cahill describes Nichols' attempt to capture this striking juxtaposition, while Cahill himself embarks on one of his more ridiculous misadventures in discovery (find the story if you can – in "Gorillas in Our Schools," from the book *Hold the Enlightenment* – it's so funny). I have not seen the Nichols photo in question, but the idea of it has stuck with me after all these years, and my version stops our group midstride, because I *have* to pull out my camera and capture the image. Sorry, gang. Mount Muhabura sits as a low silhouette in the distance, and the pyrethrum field at our feet leads to a ridge in the mid-distance with terraced plots cut into it. Abruptly to the left of the farm plots a wall of green marks the edge of the park. The transition is jarring up close, and David, the New Zealander, says something to the effect of, "That's the shot, you figure?"

Oh, yes. The one that affirms Nichols' original instinct, anyway.

As we leave the fields and enter the park proper we stop in a shady bamboo forest, and one of our guides, François, gives us a short briefing on what to expect from here. Our senior guide, Fidel, who delivered the main briefing back at headquarters, is more serious and reserved, but François is a big bear of a man, and is animated and funny in his delivery. I try to listen closely, but my attention keeps drifting into the surrounding jungle, mostly because it is so beguiling.

I love the word *jungle*, it has a mysterious, wild, slightly dangerous connotation that automatically makes me think *adventure*. Growing up exploring landscapes covered in the temperate forests of eastern Canada and the northeastern US, I always imagined jungles were where the real action was. Sure, there were bears and beavers and moose and wolves out there in the forests of home, but I imagined the jungle had all manner unknown creatures lurking in its murky and mysterious depths. Jaguars, giant snakes and improbably coloured birds all come to mind, not to mention poisonous caterpillars and poisonous frogs and, of course, crocodiles in any of the marshy bits. But here's an inconveniently bland reality: a jungle is simply a forest in a place where it rains a lot. Realizing this fact kind of takes the romance out of it. It dulls the exotic edge ever so slightly, but make no mistake, there are still mysterious creatures to be found. Enormous apes that make a grown man seem like a teenage boy by comparison, for example.

After passing through the tall bamboo, we plunge into the deeper underbrush, and then begin to move up along a narrow, steep and occasionally muddy and slick trail. The stinging nettles aside, the walking is pleasant enough in the diffused sunlight, and apart from the small clearings, it's an absolute riot of vegetation. Gorillas are vegetarian with the exception of the occasional feast of ants, and there is an abundance of tender bamboo shoots, thistles and wild celery everywhere. These plants all have high concentrations of water in their cells, which makes up for the fact there are no streams or creeks this high up on the ridge.

A little over an hour after leaving the vehicles, we catch up to the four advance trackers. (Including one with a serious-looking rifle, who *always* stands 30 metres above us on the hill, in the direction of the DRC border. Protection from rogue animals? Or from would-be kidnappers from across the international boundary? I have my suspicions.) The advance trackers are waiting for us at the edge of a clearing, and there is immediate consultation with Fidel and François. Dropping my daypack and pulling out my water bottle for a drink, I can't help but notice there are no gorillas, but catching up to the trackers means they must be close by.

"I hear the sound of gorillas," Fidel says as he turns to address our group, as if to confirm my suspicion.

At first, I think he's joking. Pulling our legs to build the tension – although that's more a François kind of move – but I've been listening for animal noises. What I should be focusing on is the sound of breaking branches and rustling underbrush, which makes sense when you think about it. Big animals moving through thick jungle are going to cause a ruckus. Now that I'm properly focused, it's obvious the Agashya group is moving downhill in our general direction, feeding and bashing as they go. Twigs, sticks and even the occasional branch of considerable heft is but a minor impediment to the next patch of good forage. Nothing but a considerable tree trunk is enough to deflect the advance of an adult gorilla.

After another brief consultation, Fidel and François move our group onto an intercept course, in the direction of a slightly larger clearing above us through the trees. The slope is very steep now, and the footing is treacherous. Often, you're not actually standing on the ground, but on the flattened underbrush that constitutes "the trail." In fact, a good part of the coming hour will be spent in and around this next clearing, that upon further inspection is less mountain meadow and more battered-down bushes. The gorillas are keenly adapted to this terrain. They walk on all fours, which gives them extra stability, and although their hands are very much like ours (only tougher and way stronger), they also have opposable big toes, which offers next-level grip that hiking boots can never hope to match.

Our first contact is with a juvenile, who is not much more than a dark tuft of fur moving through the underbrush, but it doesn't take all that long for things to go from anticipatory to exciting to surreal. Within ten minutes or so we're surrounded as the gorillas continue to move diagonally downslope. It's a slow start, but it seems like every time we make our way to a new spot a new animal appears out of the surrounding jungle.

What is amazing to me at the beginning of the encounter is that the attitude of the gorillas appears to be – much like that of the animals of the Serengeti and Ngorongoro – *Oh, the humans are here again, big whoop.* To us the gorillas are a great many things, including close cousins, beautiful and powerful creatures, a threatened species in an increasingly diminished global landscape, a once-in-a-lifetime opportunity to visit one of the rare creatures who continue to live in the Garden, and symbols of hope for the future. To them we're no big deal. *Saw a parade of odd-looking upright apes yesterday, I'll probably see a similar parade again tomorrow. Somebody pass me some bamboo.*

As if to reinforce the point, we come across a young gorilla that's maybe two to three years old, feeding alone up on the slope a few metres from the trail. My first thought is a nervous, *Where's Mom?* But the little guy or gal seems perfectly comfortable on his or her own, and doesn't appear terribly concerned about us either. François offers up a few grunts to reassure we are no threat (François speaks excellent gorilla – a remarkably nuanced "language" made up of various grunts and coughs), and the miniature ball of fur returns the greeting and then continues on with the task at hand, which is picking out the most succulent leaves from an extensive set of options laid out by nature's hand. The baby gorilla is literally sitting in a bed of food.

As the visit goes on the contacts begin to come thick and fast, and the now familiar gorilla noises erupt from everywhere, up the slope in the trees, off to the left, in the bushes over to the right. It can be hard to keep up with it all, and that's how Isano managed to sneak up on me, the rascal. One minute you're marvelling at a ball of fur not much bigger than a cocker spaniel while he chomps casually on a bed of vegetation, and ten minutes later you're face to face with over 400 pounds of lumbering muscle coming straight at you down a hill.

After Isano completes his exhilarating drive-by and disappears into the undergrowth (and I finally manage to pull myself together), we make our way to the edge of a particularly steep bit of ground that marks the edge of a small gully. The view is partially obstructed, with the jungle stretching off to the right toward Bisoke, and a few of the farms visible below to the left, but in the foreground another one of the silverbacks is casually feeding. With less than an hour of exposure under our belts it's hard to identify individual animals with any accuracy, but he's absolutely enormous and so I think it must be the top dog, Agashya. He's sitting four metres or so up off the ground in a mess of dense vegetation that is overgrowing a grouping of small stout trees and some immature bamboo. Every time he moves in search of the next tasty morsels the entire green platform sags and shakes anew, but his considerable weight is not enough to crash through to the ground below. Grazing on bamboo, in front of such a picturesque background, he appears perfectly at ease with the state of the world, or at least his little part of it. There is food in abundance, the family group is stable and secure, and it'll be a few years yet before he is usurped as the dominant of the three silverbacks. Life is good. Everything is poa here in the Garden.

As my attention turns upslope, without actually having to move an inch, peaceful is now playful as four young gorillas roughhouse amongst themselves. My guess is they range from 2 to 4 years old, and there's lots of rolling around, playful biting and some poorly aimed slapping.

They are not unlike human children in a snowy school yard at recess as they use a pair of hanging vines in a spirited equatorial bout of King of the Mountain. Just like human kids, they are high energy, easily distracted from the game, and, at times, ever so slightly and inappropriately aggressive.

After a time, one of the vines breaks off and two of the gorillas disappear into the jungle. With a shortage of players the game disintegrates, but the hour is almost up anyway. As we start moving back the way we came across the small clearing, the adrenaline drains from my system and I suddenly feel exhausted. In that moment when C$2,062 (the equivalent of US$1,500) clicked into the negative column of my credit card account I feared one solitary hour would not be enough to justify the expenditure, no matter how cool the experience ended up being. But when Fidel finally informs us it's time to go I'm just about ready. The slope is tiring to stand on for any length of time for one thing, because it's so steep and slippery and covered in broken sticks and branches, but more importantly, wandering into a big gorilla group is the very definition of sensory overload. So many novel sights and sounds in quick succession are impossible to immediately process. I have described a few scenes here but could easily burn up 50 pages talking about what we saw in one short hour.

Turning to David, whom I have spent the most time talking to since we left park headquarters, I say, with genuine sincerity, "You know, I never thought I'd admit it, but that was totally worth fifteen hundred bucks."

David and I are at the back of the group, and while we're musing over the dollar value of the experience as we enter a stand of tall bamboo, our conversation is interrupted when Gasozikeza, the oldest male black back (who, according to Fidel, will probably turn full silverback sometime this year) appears from out of the surrounding underbrush. He's coming up the slope toward us and seems agitated. François sounds the pre-arranged alarm, "no photos, no photos," and we all squat down to try and make ourselves appear small and unimposing while clearing the path. But instead of continuing on up the trail past us, Gasozikeza reaches over and grabs a rather substantial stalk of bamboo. With terrifying ease, he shakes what is basically a small tree back and forth a couple of times before breaking it off at the trunk with a thunderous crack. Mature bamboo is as tough as it comes, with a strength-to-weight ratio similar to most hardwoods. Even with a big rock it would take me an hour of bashing to bring this thing down, and David and I have to jump out of the way to keep from getting hit by the upper branches as they fall toward us.

To be fair, we have been lingering, the five-minutes-to-go call from Fidel was ten minutes ago, and all I can think is, *That's it, we've done it now. We've overstayed our welcome and are going to pay the price. And hey, I didn't know gorillas could tell time.* It does seem an overreaction to a minor bending of the rules, but Gasozikeza is pissed off about something. What an inglorious epitaph it would be: Here lies Jamey Glasnovic, part of the first tourist group to ever be mauled by a habituated gorilla. Sadly, he was the only one who didn't make it.

As it happens, Gasozikeza is simply trying to get at the succulent leaves that would have otherwise been out of reach. Reminding us he's as strong as any gorilla out there – and that he'll be the boss of this group one day – was probably just a bonus. After moving a few metres upslope in our direction to get at the shoots, he sits down and begins chomping away with very little regard for the jittery audience still trying to make sense of the display. When they're resting, gorillas often have a far-off look in their eye, and it is amazing to me how quickly Gasozikeza can go from terrifying King Kong caricature to cuddly stuffed animal that would never hurt a fly. He's now sitting comfortably in the underbrush ten or 12 feet away with a mouthful of bamboo leaves hanging from his lips. He's sporting a thoughtful, almost innocent gaze that somehow spreads across his entire face, and he is nothing if not adorable in this moment. I just want to go over and give him a big hug, but think that would probably be pushing my luck.

My friend and co-worker back in Canada, Geoff, has an 8-year-old son named Tatum. Upon seeing some of the photos from today, Tatum will contend that the gorillas look sad. It is certainly one interpretation. The far-off look is not an easy one to pin down. Sad, contemplative, confused, thoughtful, pensive. They all work, but none are exactly right either. It's part of what makes spending time with the animals so thoroughly absorbing. Their vocalizations, their body language and their facial expressions all contribute to an amazing level of inter- and intra-species communication. I'm just not yet fully up to speed on how to translate the messages. There is no doubt we are close cousins on the evolutionary tree.

Earlier on in this visit, we spent some time in the company of one of the three silverbacks. For symmetry's sake, let's just say it was Dusangire, but I don't know for sure. He was lying back comfortably on the steep slope and staring out through the gaps in the jungle at a small part of the growing spread and sprawl of Rwanda – and by extension the rest of the modernized world – below. He looked positively serene, and it was then that I was struck by the notion of the Garden being real, and that I was getting a brief glimpse of it. Then serene suddenly appeared as thoughtful, and I wondered if maybe this was the idea going through his head: *Wow, you guys are really fucking things up down there.*

Maybe that is sad after all.

17

A TWA PERFORMANCE AND FOSSEY'S GRAVE

I'm still vibrating at breakfast. It turns out the four Belgians from yesterday's excursion are also staying here, so we go through the obligatory pleasantries required after sharing a profound life experience – much as we did last night at dinner – but they are the very definition of fast friends. After breakfast, I'll never see them again.

Sitting down to my coffee, I find I've watched the video I took of Isano during his close pass a hundred times already and still can't get over it, so I hit PLAY three more times before my fruit plate arrives. As I watched him while looking over the top of my camera-phone I hoped beyond hope that the video stayed properly in frame. It did, and by some miracle I also managed to keep my hands steady as he made the turn and sauntered off into the bush without a care in the world. I get goosebumps all over again now, and I'm glad I was able to capture the 17 seconds of footage because memory is not the most accurate of recording devices, not compared to digital video anyway.

When my omelet and toast arrive, I finally put down my phone and start to think about what to do next. There are other options in the park that aren't nearly as exorbitant from the price perspective, but the finances are getting seriously strained, so I can't do them all. I'm going to have to choose just one. There are two habituated golden monkey groups in the park, and a visit with them costs

US$100. You can spend the day climbing Mount Bisoke for $75, and there is an extensive underground cave system nearby that can be toured for $50. A two-day trip up Muhabura-Gahinga goes for $200, including camping fees. In the end I decide on visiting the ruins at Karisoke and Dian Fossey's gravesite, and head over to headquarters to book a spot for tomorrow. It's a simple transaction, US$75, and Visa shows no interest in making me call them to talk about it.

Walking back to the guest house, I find three familiar faces waiting at the edge of the driveway. I can't say I'm all that surprised, Valence and James were very good at tracking me down in Musanze whenever I went out for coffee or a meal, and there aren't that many places to stay up here in Kinigi. Edison hasn't been there for all of our walks, but he knows a good thing when he sees it. There are handshakes and hugs all around, and the boys have a new idea they want to share. They want to take me to see some traditional dancing.

I have a number of character traits that peg me as an empath. Four of the top ten in a piece by Steve Mueller for planetofsuccess.com resonate deeply as I read them. I am inquisitive by nature, and am also both intuitive and introverted, but number nine jumps off the page in the current circumstance: empaths have an innate desire to better the world. I may come across as a grumpy old bastard in person – if you happen to catch me during the eat, sleep, go to work daily routine part of my life anyway – but it's true, deep down I do want to help everyone. I want everyone to have equal opportunity at the very least, and today that means giving the boys another job in the field they seem intent on pursuing, as tour guides.

At the same time, I'm also getting tired of the game.

In addition to being empathetic, I am, unfortunately, something of a cynic. I hate the idea of someone getting something over on me, and am too often suspicious of the motivations of others. Working for years in the bar business and witnessing so many of humanity's less charming character traits first-hand has not helped. It's a conflicted way of viewing the world, so this is not easy for me. What are the cracks in my faith in these young men, you ask? Well, as I said, they've been very good at figuring out where I am.

Am I being stalked? Probably a little bit.

Also, while I was taking photos yesterday evening in the fields over in the direction of Mount Muhabura and Mount Gahinga, two younger kids came by for a chat. In passing they mentioned the difficulties they faced in affording their school fees, except they were maybe 10 or 11 years old. While I was over at their house, Valence and James explained that primary school was free, but high school required additional fees. Curiously, the stories were the same, but the details were different enough to suit each narrative. Am I getting played? Maybe a little bit.

In the end these strategies (including the now extremely familiar *Can we walk together for a while, so I can practise my English?)* are harmless, but it can wear on you after a while. A couple of days ago I was coming out of the guest house before dawn to go down to the big field to take some sunrise shots. Kinigi Guest House has been quiet (only a few other guests coming and going in the five days I end up staying) and the surrounding area is exceedingly peaceful at dusk and at dawn. Without a doubt, it is a beautiful part of the world, and as I was making my way up the gravel driveway in a similarly beautiful and peaceful state of mind a young man and a young woman were passing along the road. They were fully engaged in conversation until he glanced over, saw me coming out the driveway, and pulled an abrupt see-you-later U-turn that absolutely reeked of *Ooo, hey, an opportunity!*

It was incredibly off-putting, much like the brave boy next to the soccer field a week ago, and what I fear is that I'm growing short-tempered about these kinds of interactions. Musanze, especially, is a hotbed for the passive-introduction approach, but Valence and James and Edison have struck a chord with me, and we also have history, so I agree to one more outside the box, off-the-books tour.

As we walk the pathways through the surrounding farmer's fields they point a few things out, like what crops have been planted in each individual field and which volcano is which, and at one point we stop so I can draw a map of North America in the dirt with a stick to help them understand a little bit more about where I come from. Along the way James has been chatting intermittently with some of the locals as we go. He explains that he's speaking in the local language, not in Kinyarwanda, but I don't yet get the implication of this. Eventually we descend through a small gully and come to a more substantial-looking stone home tucked in a stand of trees and low bushes. There's lots of people around now, and one of them is taking it upon himself to shout over to all the neighbours. As we enter the dirt yard it dawns on me that this is the venue for an impromptu dance number, and James has been corralling the performers as we walk.

All cultures use song and dance as part of their self-expression, and during scheduled celebrations or festivals it can be pretty easy to find a performance that communicates the regional style and flavour. The professional performances are often slick and well rehearsed. This is different. These are local folks taking a moment out of their day to come together to share a piece of their culture. As we get settled at the edge of the small open area about two dozen people have now gathered, almost half of them children. The kids are not used to westerners, so they just stand in a bunch and stare at me, but the adults set up around the open space as four of them come into the middle. That's when the singing and clapping starts.

There are no instruments, save one of the older women who is keeping the beat with a stick and an old plastic jug, but the clapping is loud, and the voices soar in the semi-enclosed space. The lyrics are like a high-energy chant and there is plenty of whistling as accompaniment. The dance itself is not choreographed but is also high energy. The two men tend to focus more on the ritual stomping and fast footwork aspect of it, while one of the women (who has a baby strapped to her back with a colourful sarong) is more rhythmic with her body movement and uses her arms to great effect in her particular interpretation of the dance.

Grandma with the stick and jug? She is fairly transported by the exuberance of the performance and keeps the whole thing together with a solid tempo, enthusiastic foot stomping and the vocal lead. Near the end of the impromptu number a lady in a green and yellow sarong cannot contain herself and comes leaping in from the sidelines after a brief moment of self-consciousness. Her style is all hands, with a flowing full body sway as accompaniment. I feel like I'm in a middle-of-the-day rave with no DJ, that has been mashed up with an amateur modern dance troupe in their second or third rehearsal together. It's great.

As I sit with my mouth agape as everyone stops to

catch their breath, with beads of sweat dripping from their brows, the clapping peters out and there's some awkwardness as nobody knows what to do next. It was a wonderfully joyous moment graciously shared, and I am again amazed at how open and friendly everyone is, but another song is not expected. I pull out some francs, the communal tip is accepted, and we go through a series of thank-you's and handshakes.

I admit, I have not been very good at recognizing the difference between Hutu and Tutsi since I've been here, which is a testament to the collective vision for the country's future. Not to mention an indictment of the ridiculous nature of trying to aggressively separate the groups in the first place, but I suspect these people are Twa, the marginalized ethnic minority who are not so much persecuted as forgotten in Rwanda's press to move beyond the genocide.

James confirms my suspicions as we head back out to the walking path. "Yes, they are Twa."

After the dance number we walk for a while down a dirt road and continue with our often halting, ongoing conversation, but after a kilometre or two I suspect the plan wasn't much thought out beyond the visit with the Twa. It's beginning to get hot, so I suggest we turn around and start heading back. Stopping at a small bridge over a dried-out stream bed, we sit for a minute on the low cement guardrail, and James pulls out a handwritten note. All three boys get quite serious as he hands it to me.

The note is an obvious tug at the heartstrings. I've grown attached to these boys, so it's touching that they took the time to write a personal letter celebrating our friendship. As I mentioned, James and Valence are half-brothers, and after their father passed away continuing on with their education became financially untenable. Obviously, I want to help them beyond hiring them for a few hours here and there over the space of a couple of days, but taking on a commitment to further their schooling is a big ask. One that extends beyond my current means. I've strained my credit to the edges already and will be hard pressed to catch up on payments over the coming year, or maybe even two.

It's a complicated situation to explain, and my white privilege has never been laid so bare as in this moment. I can go home, go back to work, and eventually begin to make choices about what to do next in my life with few constraints – a situation based in large part by the fact that I was born white in a prosperous G7 country. Part of me is ashamed that I have, on occasion, complained about my financial circumstance. Not getting a grant in order to travel and write is not exactly a hardship, it's an inconvenience, and in retrospect, being miffed about it is nothing if not tone deaf to the struggles many people around the globe face.

Standing up in order to instigate movement toward the guest house and break up the uncomfortable silence, I promise to think about it, but worry there won't really be much that I will be able to do, at least in the short term.

It's in these moments that I really do wish I could save the world.

•••

After another spectacular African massage, my newest driver Fis parks next to half a dozen other Land Cruisers in a dirt and gravel lot at the edge of a small village near the western end of the park. I had expected to be travelling in another small group today, but there are 16 (yes, 16!)

of us scheduled to walk up to Dian Fossey's old research site in the jungle-choked col between Mount Karisimbi and Mount Bisoke. Karisoke (see what she did there?) was the camp where Fossey spent the better part of her professional life studying gorilla behaviour.

She is buried at Karisoke, along with 34 of the gorillas she got to know so well over the years.

In addition to being a significant location in the annals of field biology, Karisoke is also uncomfortably close to the border with the DRC, but nobody will tell me exactly how close. Although the seven heavily armed rangers waiting for us to get our act together in the parking lot is a tip-off that it's probably really freaking close.

The DRC has been a mess for decades – check that, pretty much non-stop since King Leopold II of Belgium took an interest in the place in the mid-1870s – with ongoing government incompetence and corruption leaving the door open for rebel groups and criminal cartels to operate with near impunity. The country is resource rich but lacking in stable authority, and tourist abductions are not unheard of. Currently the gorilla tracking program is on hold there because of the instability in the region.

This one time, in Tibet, I was at a Chinese government checkpoint on the highway between Lhasa and Kathmandu when a compelling photo opportunity overwhelmed my good sense (such as it is). While my wife Jocey, our guide and our friends Neil and Joyce dealt with the paperwork at the checkpoint, I pulled out my camera and ran back outside past a couple of military types standing guard to take a few snaps of an intriguingly shaped mountain in the distance.

When we got back in the Land Cruiser and drove away, Jocey said, "I can't believe you did that."

"Did what?" was my confused reply. Then it dawned on me. Military instillations, guard posts, and soldiers in general, not usually the best places to be waving a camera around.

Not wanting to repeat that faux pas now, I ask one of our guides if it would be okay to take a picture. He translates the request, and the soldiers nod and immediately strike their best *Yeah, we're hard, you mzungus have nothing to worry about* poses. There's a smaller group of tourists making the climb up Bisoke, which leaves from this same trailhead, so not all seven of these guys will be accompanying us for the full hike, but it's clear that security is a very real consideration when entering this part of the park. More so than farther east where I went gorilla tracking, at any rate.

The hike itself is fairly straightforward. The trail leads up through the pyrethrum fields and into the jungle. At the edge of the jungle there's a buffalo wall made of stone to discourage animals from coming down into the fields, and that's where our extra-big group effectively splits into three. The Bisoke hikers veer off on a separate trail, and our 16 separate evenly into faster hikers and a slower group. The trail is steep in places, muddy in others, and the altitude at Karisoke is roughly 3000 metres above sea level, so we do stop a couple of times to catch our breath and rehydrate. Our lead guide, Bernese, is what we would have referred to in high school as a cool chick. She's perfectly comfortable in hiking boots and standard issue parks camo and light green t-shirt. She also knows her stuff as well as anyone.

At the site where Karisoke once stood there's not much left, and the jungle is reclaiming the scraps that remain. Between 1994 and 1998, refugees of the genocide burned much of the wood from the structures for cooking, and locals scavenged other materials to rebuild homes destroyed in the unrest. The framing for one wall of the Worker's House is still standing, but the actual wall is long gone, as vines and ferns and moss smother the rotting 2×4s. Throughout the grounds, green metal signs have been erected to indicate the previous location of key cabins and work areas. The signs are weathered and faded, and the cabin sites are often just cleared spaces with nothing left but concrete foundations. My favourite sign is for the volleyball grounds. It pokes up out of a mass of ferns and shrubs and it's almost impossible to imagine the encroaching jungle ever having allowed a court as large as one used for volleyball.

In my mind's eye I had imagined having this place mostly to myself for this visit. The guest house has been largely deserted over the last few days and I've gotten used to the comparative solitude of "rural Kinigi." I didn't expect that hiking up into the jungle would be where the crowds are at, but there you have it. Bernese gathers us periodically to give informed lectures mixed with anecdotal stories about the details of this place, but the process is somewhat laboured by the fact everything has to be translated into Polish for the one-half of our hiking group that doesn't speak English.

Still, even in a crowd the small cemetery where Fossey and the gorillas are buried projects the appropriately sombre tone, and manages to convey an underlying sense of struggle, sacrifice and triumph against long odds.

The rectangular graveyard is contained by a low stone wall that rises a foot or so off the forest floor and is overgrown with the same grasses and clover that blanket the graves. Fossey's headstone and plaque are at the north end, and the gorillas are remembered with simple wooden crosses that have been exposed to the elements for decades. Some of the nameplates have fallen off and now sit propped up against the narrow posts that once held them. Many are barely legible after all these years, but all have the individual animal's name carved into or painted on them, as well as the year of their births, and of their passing.

Fossey's metal plaque is simple and subtly elegant:

"NYIRAMACHABELLI"
DIAN FOSSEY
1932–1985
NO ONE LOVED GORILLAS MORE
REST IN PEACE, DEAR FRIEND
ETERNALLY PROTECTED
IN THIS SACRED GROUND
FOR YOU ARE HOME
WHERE YOU BELONG

Nyiramachabelli means "the woman who lives alone on the mountain," and you can say what you will about Dian Fossey. That she was headstrong and aloof and hard to work with, which was her reputation, but one thing is certain, she loved these animals and committed her life to protecting them from mankind's destructive tendencies.

Some of the gorillas buried here were surely killed by poachers, and it's quite possible some were killed by locals seeking retribution for damaged crops as well. Illegal snares set out in the forest for bushbuck and other small game animals can inadvertently snag a gorilla's hand or foot, and a fair few probably died from the complications (mainly infection) of extracting themselves. But others buried here succumbed to old age and natural causes, an outcome that would have been far less likely were it not for one woman's tireless efforts to educate the world about the true nature of these gentle giants.

Fossey's work was cut short when she was murdered here at Karisoke, after someone slashed through the wall of her cabin with a machete and bludgeoned her to death with it. But the tragedy was not the end of the story of the gorillas of Rwanda. The Dian Fossey Gorilla Fund International continues to study, monitor and protect gorillas in the wild, while also delivering programs to educate conservationists and help local communities.

The government runs similar programs through the Rwanda Development Board, and the gorilla tracking program for tourists provides the opportunity for first-hand interaction with the animals (an experience I can confidently recommend). The government is also an integral part of what is perhaps the most important aspect of conservation – habitat protection. Without a forest, there would be no gorillas. Whereas once the park extended over 270 square kilometres, it is now only 160 square kilometres. The goal, as Bernese and Anaclet Budahera both mentioned with pointed emphasis, is to reverse that trend.

Another important partner in the effort is Gorilla Doctors, the Mountain Gorilla Veterinary Project that works in association with the UC Davis Wildlife Health Center in California. After coming back down to Musanze I find myself at the local office, and as luck would have it Kirsten V.K. Gilardi, the US Director of Gorilla Doctors, happens to be in Rwanda, and is gracious enough to sit with me to talk about the work they do.

"Dian Fossey was studying the gorillas in the 70s and 80s," Gilardi says, "and she was getting increasingly alarmed by the number of her study animals that were getting caught in snares."

Shortly before her death, Fossey attended a primate conservation conference in San Diego and put out a plea to veterinarians, that a trustee of the Morris Animal Foundation took up with the enthusiasm necessary to launch the Mountain Gorilla Veterinary Project in 1986. Jim Foster, a vet from the US, was the sum total of the medical team in the early days, starting about a year after Fossey's untimely passing.

"If you fast forward to today," Gilardi says, "we're teams of Rwandan, Ugandan and Congolese veterinarians and in all three countries our core mission is veterinary care for ill and injured Mountain, and now also Grauer's, gorillas in eastern DRC. Our vets do all the work in the forest and we follow up on every report of an ill or injured gorilla."

The majority of these jungle house calls are trauma-related. Injuries from snares are the number one reason vets are dispatched to the field. The number two reason is respiratory illness, and there is strong evidence to suggest the animals are susceptible to human pathogens. It is part of the reason for the seven metre proximity rule. It was not put in place to protect humans from gorillas, as one might think, so much as to protect gorillas from what humans might bring with them to the encounter. Before she passed, Fossey did express concern about the effects increased interactions between humans and gorillas would have on the animals' overall health and reproductive habits.

"In her time there really wasn't any tourism," Gilardi says, "but it was being suggested that gorilla tourism would be what was essential for their conservation. And I firmly believe that. I think that if people couldn't come and see these animals, and they didn't have tremendous value for the government. If they didn't generate revenue that helps manage and protect the parks..." Gilardi trails off to gather her thoughts before continuing. There are a lot of factors in this recovery narrative to consider.

"This is the most densely populated part of all of continental Africa," Gilardi says after the pause. "The pressures on the forest are tremendous, so I do firmly believe habituation for tourism and research is what has saved the species."

George Schaller proved that a gorilla would not attack a human who stood their ground. Dian Fossey proved that gorillas could be habituated to human beings so that we could study them at close quarters to better understand their behaviours. The Rwandan government figured out that in order to preserve the habitat and ultimately protect the animals, conservation efforts also had to benefit the local community, not just foreign visitors and the park itself. Gorilla Doctors seeks to minimize the harm that may come from our active presence in their jungle environment.

Gorilla conservation is indeed a complicated dynamic, with no fewer than seven organizations contributing resources and manpower, but from a low of approximately 250 individuals in the interconnected parks of the Virunga massif in the early 1980s to over a thousand in the most recent census in 2015 (which also includes nearby Bwindi Impenetrable National Park), the system appears to be working.

•••

In some ways, the trip is now over. The primary goals imagined before departure have all been achieved, if sometimes awkwardly, and from a certain perspective it could be said I'm just killing time until I go home. It's impossible to do everything when you go visit a new region, or even a single new country for that matter, and there are certainly some things I've missed here in East Africa. Like Kenya, Uganda and Burundi, for example. But from that Lonely Planet Top 16 list I was poring over back at the Chelsea Hotel two months ago I've managed to experience a fair few. My brief encounter with the gorillas of Volcanoes National Park was an uplifting and hopeful way to finish what has been a long and sometimes challenging journey.

The thing is, there are still ten days until my flight back to Dar es Salaam. While I don't have time to take on another big chunk of countryside, I also can't head straight back to Kigali from here either. I'll end up sitting around the hotel waiting for my flight to Dar, before sitting around the hotel there as I wait to fly home. That would be a lame way to finish off a trip, no matter how ready I now am to just go home.

I have to admit, I'm bordering on travel burnout, where managing the everyday details of being out on the road becomes a chore instead of being part of another mini-adventure fitting into the larger whole. I'm growing weary of finding a new place to sleep, or of finding somewhere for lunch or dinner, or of all the time spent looking for Wi-Fi so I can send messages back home. Unless I'm properly stimulated by the possibility of new experience to go with those daily tasks I'll retreat into the comfort and familiarity of a private room with satellite TV and that'll be the end of it. So instead of two days back to the capital by bike, I'm going to take the long way home via Lake Kivu and the Congo Nile Trail. After all, who knows when I might get a chance to come back to this little corner of the world again. Best to see it while I can.

According to Wikipedia, Lake Kivu is the eighth

biggest lake in Africa, and by the measure of maximum depth is the 20th deepest lake in the world (13th deepest by average depth). None of this makes Kivu particularly interesting or unique, but the real possibility of a limnic eruption sure does. Deep below the surface are massive stores of methane and carbon dioxide – likely deposited there by volcanic activity – that are held in place by the pressure of the water above. Every thousand years or so the balance is upset by an earthquake or landslide, and a violent outgassing event occurs. The released gas would be suffocating to any humans or animals unfortunate enough to be in the area, but modern history shows only two such eruptions on record – Cameroon's Lake Monoun in 1984, and Lake Nyos, also in Cameroon, in 1986. Kivu is due, but nobody really knows when it might happen.

Rwanda's unexploded exploding lake is still a few hours away, however, and the effort in getting there is proving to be more challenging than I anticipated. The Virunga volcanoes are the high point in the region (Karisimbi tops out at 4507 metres, or 14,787 feet), and so I expected that a minor climb over the southern shoulder of Karisimbi would be followed in short order by a massive and largely pedal-free descent to the lake. Silly me. This continuation of Route nationale 4 is not as steep as the two biggest hills between Kigali and Musanze, so I can pedal more and walk less, but it is almost 30 kilometres of relentless uphill travel from the starting point in downtown Musanze.

Fortunately, the highway here is busy with traffic to provide distraction from the relentless incline. Once again that traffic is not vehicular – there are surprisingly few cars that pass over the course of the morning – but there are bicycles all over the place. The bikes are the same one-speeds as the bicycle taxis in town, but they have been repurposed to haul freight. Huge sacks of grain or maize or potatoes or charcoal, it's not always easy to tell for sure what's inside, are loaded up at various points along the route, and are then rushed downhill to Musanze for distribution throughout the region. The burlap sacks are stacked two, three and even five high depending on the contents of the bags and the ambition and skill of the rider.

Bikes without burlap are often loaded with long lengths of bamboo, and only occasionally humans are the freight, but at one point three guys on a single bike come bombing downhill around a corner in a way that strikes me as completely insane. Most riders drag a foot to check speeds on the steeper sections, which must be murder on their sneakers, and I get the distinct impression bike maintenance, including on brakes, is not a top priority. One guy with a full-sized kitchen table balanced precariously on the back rack, that's tied down with simple twine, smiles broadly as he flies past, in a manner that says, *No worries man, I got this.* I must be wide-eyed in amazement to elicit such an unrehearsed yet somehow casual reaction.

Higher up the hill there is some beautiful and lush pastoral countryside, with only a singular negative aspect, which is that the road just keeps going up and up and up. But that's okay, I've settled into the realities of riding a bike in the Land of a Thousand Hills, where this sort of development is inevitable. And oh, if only it were *only* a thousand hills.

Resigned to the parameters set forth by the climb, I have time to think of other things. Last night before dinner I finally began combing through the notes and photos from the trip in anticipation of undertaking the next phase of this challenge, which will be pulling the journey together into something that resembles a coherent narrative. Laying out the chapters and deciding on obvious anchor points to the story has been easy. There have been plenty of experiences worth talking about. I've even managed to name most of the chapters, but a title for the book still eludes me.

Strangely, what I haven't been able to do is sit down and *write* for more than 15 or 20 minutes at a stretch these last couple of months. I've had the time, but not the inclination. It's been all notes and fleeting ideas captured in haste before they disappeared into the ether. I like to think I've been too busy to take on the task but am not so sure if that's true. Upon further examination – as I pedal along without anything else to do but enjoy the scenery and ponder the problem – I realize there's a ton of information to sift through and wonder if maybe I'm feeling a bit intimidated by the scope of the process. It wouldn't be the first time I've avoided taking on the realities of a big writing job head on.

One thing I'm certain of is that it will take far longer to organize my thoughts and get them down on paper than it has taken to travel through Tanzania and Rwanda. Thinking about writing a book is easy. There are ideas floating around everywhere and inspiration only asks to be followed. On the other hand, sitting down to do the actual work is an experience riddled with uncertainty and doubt, and I guess I'm just not quite up to it yet. It doesn't help that I'm also going to have to go right back to work upon my return to Canada, which will steal time and energy from the effort, since there's no grant funding forthcoming.

Suddenly it all feels like too much to wrap my head around. Adjusting to the realities of life back home is not going to be an easy transition after the freedom of the roads and trails of East Africa, where I can do whatever I want with no deadlines or responsibilities or aspirations to fog up my conscious mind. As I finally crest the hill and pedal for a while along a comparatively flat stretch of ground near the junction with Route nationale 11, all the writing that needs to get done remains in the future. My day job is also still a couple of weeks away, so I try and push what is inevitable from my thoughts before making a quick stop at a roadside shop for snacks and a fresh bottle of water.

Back out on the road after a pleasant break from the bike, all there is left for today is the joy of a tremendous sweeping downhill into Gisenyi to pay attention to, with more immediate visions of beers on the beach to lead me on. As gravity takes hold and I begin to glide effortlessly downward, I am reminded of the skateboard scene from the movie *The Secret Life of Walter Mitty*. Sure, the Icelandic countryside is considerably more remote than this particular part of Rwanda, but the adrenaline surge and flush of excited emotion that comes with bombing downhill without a care in the world is universal in its allure, and I can almost hear the music from the movie playing on the wind. At times like this I can't help but feel that the world is a perfectly beautiful place, and so I redouble my efforts to revel in the simplicity of that beauty and forget about everything that has begun cluttering up my mind today. This is why I love to travel. There is peace and purpose in the pursuit of it and I feel completely comfortable in the process – when I can manage to get out of my head, anyway.

Meanwhile, during my distracted musings, a huge storm has developed quickly over top of the Virunga volcanoes to the north, but I'm skirting the southern edge of the chain and only get a little bit wet near the very end of the descent. Coming into the more densely populated area around Rugerero and Gisenyi proper, I notice lunchtime has brought all of the local grade school kids out to the playgrounds or onto the roadside for the short walk home. Many of them wave and shout "mzungu, mzungu, mzungu!" as I pass, and their innocent charm is infectious. I can't help but smile broadly and wave back enthusiastically every time. It appears that I've found that sweet spot once again, where happiness is a naturally occurring phenomenon that I simply have to put a little effort into accessing. I realize this is but another singular moment in time that will invariably fade, but I can still hope for the feeling to never end.

Because right now everything is poa, my friends. Everything is poa indeed.

PART FOUR

EPILOGUE

18

A PANDEMIC, A FESTIVAL AND THE CONGO NILE TRAIL

I lost my job a little over a year after getting back from Africa, and the first ten days were especially tough. Not because I got laid off – I'm sure it's clear by now that I've never really cared about the things I endure for money all that much. It was tough because I didn't know what to do in a time of generalized uncertainty. By March 15 of 2020, the first wave of the coronavirus that causes COVID-19 was ramping up around the world, and all the bars and restaurants in my small mountain town made the sensible decision to close as part of the evolving social distancing measures. By the end of the week those closures were mandated by the Alberta government in an attempt slow the spread of the virus.

I'm not going to lie, a part of me was relieved about not having to go to work for a while. Not because I was afraid of contracting the virus in such a social setting, but because I was desperate for a break. At the time I was having trouble managing my duties. The daily challenges that are an inevitable part of the restaurant business were being too easily blown out of proportion in my mind. I was short-tempered and easily exasperated, and it seemed like every decision I made over the course of the day to help things run smoothly failed to have the desired impact. Problems I should have anticipated simply blew up in my face, and the most concerning detail is that I never even saw them coming. I was loath to admit it, but I was struggling mightily, and for the first time in my life doubted my ability to do the job.

As a result, I found myself mired in a textbook case of capitalist-system burnout, that presented as a toxic combination of stress, anxiety and depression. I knew I couldn't just keep on keeping on, but also couldn't afford to throw my hands up in the air and quit either. I hadn't even paid off the last of my trip expenses yet. Africa suddenly seemed like a long way away, and the lessons I learned there were slowly slipping through my grasp. Bludgeoned into irrelevance by a return to the work-a-day routine. There was a small part of me that said (with that inside voice we're not supposed to use out loud), "Thank God for COVID-19."

A few days after being laid off my world caved in completely. I was so lethargic and unmotivated I could barely get out of bed for more than a couple of hours at a time, and my depression sank in deep. I wondered if maybe I had the virus, but I didn't have enough of the major symptoms to meet the criteria for a test in those early days. I had a minor cough, but no fever, no chest pain or trouble breathing, and no contact with anyone who had recently travelled outside the country. The not knowing what was going on filled me with even more doubt and uncertainty.

It was a dark time.

As those first difficult days began to transition into a month, and eventually two, I started to come out of my funk. I slept a lot at first, but also committed to a new exercise regime that helped get the blood flowing and the body moving (a big shout-out to my brother Jesse for being a dedicated workout partner – while observing proper social distancing protocols, of course). With rapt attention,

I followed the evolving narrative of an entire planet attempting to deal with the destruction of normal while riding out the worst of the storm with my wonderful, caring, funny and perfectly matched COVID-19 isolation partner and wife, Jocey.

We laughed a lot at our own ridiculous jokes, screamed at the TV whenever Donald Trump said or did something stupid (which was also a lot), and most importantly we allowed things to not be okay, without judgment or the expectation of a quick fix. But mostly, I wrote my way through the beginning of the pandemic. I'd been back from Africa for 13 months when the virus accelerated its relentless march across the globe, and this manuscript was a mess, so as I started to feel better I focused on that. Writing gave me purpose and direction at a time when nothing else made sense. Sure, I didn't know what my life was going to look like going forward (nobody did), but my relationship was stable and supportive, my job was in suspended animation, and my mortgage was deferred for six months (thank you ATB Financial). CERB, the Canada Emergency Response Benefit, put food on the table and paid the household bills, exactly as it was designed to do.

With panic averted, writing became an even stronger lifeline. There's a big difference between sitting at the page for five or six or even seven hours – over the course of two or three sessions throughout the day – and waving half-heartedly at a project that's important to you for only 20 minutes to an hour whenever you get the chance, because of work responsibilities and other everyday stressors. For a short time, I was able to focus my attention on just one thing, finishing this book. Even though I was putting a ton of effort into it, it wasn't like work at all; it was fulfilling and fun. Listening to music and reading and thinking and writing, all the things I try so hard to engage in when I travel, were suddenly happening every day right here at home. And, AMAZINGLY, my stress and anxiety disappeared. My battle with depression that had been flogging me for months lifted almost overnight. There was a bolt from the blue one day about three weeks into self-isolation, where I stopped in my tracks in the middle of the living room and thought, *I'm not sure what's going on, but I'M HAPPY.* I think I even danced a little jig to celebrate.

As I was pulling these last pages of a proper first draft together I was reminded of my interview with Kelly back on Zanzibar. Before we got into the details of his project in Kenya, we talked more generally about the lure of travel and of making art, and of clearing the decks every once in a while to do nothing, in order to make space for inspiration.

"I've realized that photography isn't necessarily about going out and coming back with a bull's eye good photo, or an amazing piece of art, or whatever," Kelly said, as our coffee arrived at the table.

"Photography for me has been the ability to look at my environment in a different way. I see a set of linear lines that somebody else doesn't even look at and I think, 'holy shit, those lines are amazing, and that wall and the texture of it, or the light, the way that it's coming across...'"

Kelly paused at the idea of it. I could tell there was an image cast in his head that he wanted to spend a couple of seconds with before continuing.

"Photography has forced me to explore my environment and look at it in a totally different way than if I wasn't a photographer."

"And to interact with it," I suggested.

"A hundred per cent."

It usually doesn't take much, but Kelly had gotten me going and I couldn't help but add this idea to the mix.

"You become more engrossed and engaged in the thing that you're doing because you are now focused on a singular moment or a place in time."

"Exactly!" Kelly said. "Getting a photograph out of it, I kind of look at it as the bonus. You're like 'Oh, neat, that's awesome.' It actually all worked together, but I think even the general idea that I'm morphing my brain to look at my environment differently than I think anybody else would do, that's the benefit of being a photographer for me."

It's not the end goal that's important. What a great concept, that so often needs to be relearned in our accomplishment-driven society. Doing simply for doing's sake has been a recurring theme through all of the travel and effort at the page I've engaged in over the years, and I believe it is my lesson to learn, all over again. What's important is being stimulated by the life that surrounds you, and to throw yourself into the mix at every opportunity. Period, end of story.

When I opened my Instagram account a few years ago I put down Writer/Photographer as a way to express who I am. Mostly because I didn't know what else to say. I love to write, but Writer doesn't fit. Writer, capital W, is a profession. I just love to write, lowercase w. I also love to take pictures, but I'm not a Photographer either. I'm just a guy walking around with a camera, trying to find that texture or some interesting light or those linear lines Kelly was talking about. The rest of it is just noise to me. A desperate and ill-fated attempt to add external value to what are essentially intrinsically motivated pursuits. I do these things because I am inspired to do them, and because they make me feel good.

Back in 1994, on a second bicycling trip across the Canadian prairies (I know, right, glutton for punishment), I was camped for the night at the edge of a small town in Saskatchewan. As I sat in the small cantina late one afternoon taking notes on the day, a woman in her 40s at a nearby table caught my attention and asked, "Are you a writer?"

For some reason I was embarrassed by the thought of it, and probably blushed. I didn't think I had the necessary skills to do the job, for one thing, and had never even submitted a story idea, let alone been published anywhere, for another. But I did love stories. Especially stories about travel. I thought that maybe one day, if I worked hard enough and caught a break or two (and let's be honest, learned how to spell, even 28 years later I'm still a brutal speller), *then* I could call myself a Writer. Until that happened, I was just another guy with a pen and a note pad and a whole mess of ideas bashing around in his head that were looking for a way to get out.

"No, no," I said. "I just like to take a lot of notes because it helps me understand what I'm experiencing."

"Oh, you're definitely a writer," she said matter-of-factly.

I smiled and thanked her for what was to me a great compliment, that I did not feel I deserved. She was right, though, of course, and I simply misunderstood the underlying meaning in what she said. I was thinking Writer, capital W. She was pointing out the deeper significance of the word. As the years passed I chased the dream wrong and got caught up in the idea that unless I could get published, unless I could find a way to get paid for my efforts, and until I could make a career out of it, I would never really be this thing that I already was.

To this day I still falter in this cognitive dysfunction. But, slowly, I am beginning to understand my place.

• • •

Five months prior to modern society coming apart at the seams in response to the COVID-19 pandemic, I was set to participate at the Banff Centre Mountain Film and Book Festival, the biggest and perhaps most prestigious celebration of mountain culture in the world. I was honoured to get the chance to talk about the book I wrote on taking the long way to Everest Base Camp by travelling up through Nepal's middle hills all the way from Kathmandu. As I've mentioned, the story revolved around bicycling and hiking and exploring a foreign landscape, not climbing mountains, but the overall theme suited the ideals of the festival nicely. The outdoors, adventure, mountain landscape and mountain culture. It was a perfect fit.

I replied in about ten seconds flat in the affirmative via email at the invitation a few months prior to the start of the festival, *Yes, I would love to attend.*

My presentation was part of Tales and Ales: A Mountain Reading, hosted by Banff Poet Laureate Steven Ross Smith, and it featured Helen Rolfe and Jenna Butler. Ross Smith was an engaging and entertaining MC, and Rolfe and Butler and I each had roughly 15 minutes to share a part of our latest works. It's patently ridiculous to try and talk with any kind of authority about going to wander around Khumbu in order to gaze upon Mount Everest, when Sharon Wood, the first North American woman to reach the summit, and Pat Morrow, the first person to climb the Seven Summits (including Everest, obviously), are both sitting about three rows back in the audience, but what can you do?

I took a deep breath, screwed up my courage, and launched into my Everest story. No pressure, right?

But here's the thing. We all have a story to tell, and we all have our own way of telling it. I am not what you would call fond of public speaking, but I got through it well enough. The best part of the festival, however, was not my minor brush with fame on a small stage at a very big celebration of audacious adventure and creative endeavour. I'm now 53 years old, and it generally takes me about four years to pull a new book project together. If I was going to have a notable *career* in the business of mountain and adventure writing it would have happened already, so I'm not going to hold my breath waiting for that elusive big break. The best part of the festival for me was the festival itself.

At my core I'm a fanboy of the broader concept of mountain culture, and I was in my element. Over the course of a few days I had conversations with writers and photographers and filmmakers that reaffirmed my affinity for mountain people and mountain places. Contributing just a little bit to the bigger outdoor narrative over the course of a decade, in the form of travel books about the Canadian Rockies, Nepal and now East Africa, is a privilege I will forever be grateful for. But I was also constantly waiting for someone to come up to me, look at the credentials hanging from my neck, and say, "I'm sorry, there's been a mistake, you don't belong here."

Thankfully, that never happened, and out on one of the bigger stages Mark Twight delivered a raw and heartfelt presentation about his abrupt retirement from alpinism, and the challenges of finding direction and purpose down in the valley. *Refuge* is the book and photo exhibition that came from that transitional period.

Next up, Jeff Smoot walked the audience through the history of rock climbing and the inevitable evolution of sport climbing and climbing gyms that he chronicled in *Hangdog Days,* and then Kate Rawles, author of *The Carbon Cycle,* a book about riding a bicycle from Texas to Alaska, gave an inspiring presentation on her latest adventure by bike in South America. There's a book coming out of that epic journey as well. When I spoke to her afterward she admitted to the challenges of trying to figure out what parts of the story to focus on, because so much had happened out on the road.

I feel for you there, Kate.

Interestingly, all three presenters referenced the "day job" as being not-quite-the-right-thing during their talks. It is why adventurous outings and creative pursuits featured so prominently in their lives. They were more than inspired, they were also compelled. Perhaps Smoot said it best: "Nothing happens when you sit at your desk. You've got to go out and do stuff."

Preaching to the choir there, Jeff.

Later in the afternoon, on the same stage as Tales and Ales, legendary Bow Valley outdoorsman Chic Scott hosted Old Style Storytelling, and the four local characters describing their various mountain misadventures over the years were so freaking funny that I still laugh now when the event comes to mind. On Thursday evening, the Eric Harvey Theatre was packed to capacity for the Mountain Book Competition Awards, and afterward Sharon Wood gave a talk about her long-awaited memoir, *Rising: Becoming the First Canadian Woman to Summit Everest.* Her story about climbing the mountain in 1986 had the expected suspense and intrigue, but her admission about how difficult it was to pull the book together, and the description of her process and struggle with the writing struck a deeper chord.

On the mountain she used the mantra *Believe, and Begin* to overcome overwhelming fatigue and creeping doubt near the summit. Sage words for any ambitious pursuit.

After the Wood presentation, Reinhold Messner, one of the pioneers of high-altitude mountaineering, hosted the North American premiere of a new film he produced about climbing in his home region of Tyrol, in Italy, called *The Great Peak: 150 Years Climbing History*. His onstage interview with Geoff Powter at the conclusion of the film was revealing of the man himself. Messner is a controversial character in the climbing world. His prickly reputation speaks of a stubborn man prone to self-absorption. In person, he did strike me as focused and driven in the single-minded fashion of many hyper-successful athletes, but also as thoughtful and capable of self-reflection as well. I especially loved one line Messner delivered during the conversation with pointed clarity: "Traditional mountaineering is an adventure, not a sport."

An adventure, not a sport. I like that, with the underlying theme of *Go your own way. Do what motivates you, and don't listen to what anyone thinks about it.* It's probably why Messner is misunderstood to a certain degree. He followed his own unique instinct for experience, without apology.

On Saturday at happy hour, Rocky Mountain Books (full disclosure, the publisher of my books) held a 40th anniversary party on the second-floor outdoor patio of the Kinnear Centre. It was November in the Canadian Rockies, so there were puffy coats and toques all over the place, but there was also a band and free beer tickets and a mingling of creative minds. Festival attendees rubbed shoulders with writers and photographers, and for a couple of hours stories well told were the only thing in the world that mattered. For a time, I stood against the wall and simply marvelled at the beauty of it. At various points Paul Zizka, Frank Wolf and Lynn Martel, to name but a few of my esteemed RMB colleagues, stopped on their way past to chat and share ideas about their next projects.

I had always thought that a true ambassador of mountain culture required next-level adventure and mountain skills – not to mention off-the-charts strength and endurance – and I have always been intimidated by the collective accomplishments of my colleagues and those who have gone before me. Their abilities, their drive, their vision and their focus have always represented something I thought I could never match. That is undoubtedly true, but what I experienced on that late fall weekend in Banff was their humanity, their vulnerability and their true strength, the ability to do the best they can do to bring a story to life with pictures and in print.

As Sharon Wood said so simply in her presentation, "believe, and begin." The mantra got her to the top of the mountain, but the way I interpret it, it wasn't just about the climbing. It was also about living your best life. That was a revelation.

Hanging out after the party at the Rocky Mountain Books booth at the Mountain Marketplace, I was spent after three days of non-stop stimulation. I felt exhilarated, exhausted and inspired, all at once. Don Gorman, publisher at RMB, was having an intense conversation with another author, when they both sort of glanced over mid-sentence and paused. At that moment I was having a beer while leaning back in a camp chair that a neighbouring vendor had left out after closing up for the evening. Once again, I was deep into the effort of soaking up the energy not only of the room, but of the festival itself.

I guess you could say I was pretty much spaced out.

"Sorry. What was that?" I blurted almost absently.

"I was telling Margo that you also write against the despair," Gorman said.

"Sure," I said, as I tried to focus on a specific subject instead of daydreaming about the universe at large. "And I try to harness it in a way that creates a bit of hope, and a sense of purpose."

I'm not always eloquent in person. That's why I write – it gives me time to figure out what it is I mean to say – but I was pretty pleased with this effort. Then it occurred to me, with a flash of clarity not unlike an epiphany: These are my people. All of them. They think like me. They suffer like me. They hope like me. They are driven to create, just like me. And when I wander off to some far-flung destination in search of my truth – when I wander off on another Cahill-style quest – my people will likely be here upon my return, because they have probably been off somewhere doing the same thing themselves. Until it's time for us to all come together again and talk about what we think any of it means. As time passes the names may change and the stories will be different, but the passion and commitment will remain. The outdoor obsessions that help define mountain culture do not die, they simply find new voices. When I am gone, someone else will take my place.

I find comfort in that, and hope.

• • •

As this story nears a close, I can't help but look back on the last few days in Africa with a special fondness. It was a fitting bookend to a larger journey across time and space that began in the Canadian Rockies before hopscotching across Asia, only to veer south of the equator for the final act. At the time, however, Lake Kivu and the Congo Nile Trail was not *the last adventure I'll take for the foreseeable future,* it was simply an add on. A way to kill time before coming home. It was incredibly hard work, because every riding day had at least one huge climb to contend with, but the shores of western Rwanda also proved a pleasing surprise. Ripping down the hill to Gisenyi was just reward for a tough uphill effort out of Musanze, and Gisenyi itself is not so much a tourist town geared to foreigners as a weekend getaway catering to the Kigali crowd (the capital is a couple of hours away by car). The vibe was distinctly different from Musanze. It was more laid back, in the manner that Bagamoyo and Lushoto were. After a couple of days of wandering around town, I headed south on the Congo Nile Trail. The plan was to ride the northern part of the rough trail, then return to Kigali on blacktop via Route nationale 15.

I met Innocent near the end of day one on the CNT. My map was inadequate (imagine that), the afternoon was a scorcher, and there was a notable lack of guest houses to be had. I was somewhere between the one I should have stopped at and the one I had no choice but to make it to when he caught me up on a steep stretch of dirt and gravel. I was pushing my bike on foot while breathing hard and cursing my life choices in that moment when he introduced himself in the most pleasant of manners, as if we were on a casual stroll in the park.

"Hello, I am Innocent."

There was a joke in there somewhere, but I couldn't find the energy to make it, and so I introduced myself and accepted his help in finding a place to stay for the night. We trudged on up to a village at the top of the ridge, and then left the main trail to descend a steep and often rocky path that immediately gave back all the hard-won altitude of the previous hour and a half. It wasn't the first big hill of the day, and I could barely keep control of my bike on the sections of rough exposed stone on the descent. I literally fell off in a heap of exhaustion when we reached Kinunu Guest House, and then lay in the grass at the edge of the trail until the feeling came back in my arms and shoulders after all the aggressive braking.

Innocent insisted on accompanying me for another day, and while making our way back up to the main trail sucked right off the bat, the rest of the second morning on the trail was an amazing collection of grinding ascents and bone-rattling descents that were punctuated by amazing views out over the lake. I never expected fresh water fiords, but the Kivu shoreline is littered with deep bays and countless inlets that can't help but bring to mind a small-scale version of the traditional oceanic landscape formation. At one point later in the morning there was also some sublime single track along the lakeshore, and it all added up to yet another incarnation of the best couple of hours of riding I've ever experienced in my life. We were exploring a remote corner of one of the most densely populated countries in Africa, but instead of fist-bumping, high-fiving Sunday market goers for company there was scarcely a soul around. I was a million miles from home, metaphorically speaking, and yet felt perfectly at home in the effort. It doesn't get much cooler than that.

Just before lunchtime, the weather closed in and we endured three distinct downpours, holing up in the dining room of a guest house for one, and then in a stranger's home at the side of the trail for another. The heaviest cloudburst caught us out, so we spent 20 minutes sheltered in the forest and used giant banana leaves as makeshift umbrellas. As the rain let up, we continued on and marvelled at the sheer volume of water coursing through a small river floodplain. We were thankful the main channel hadn't yet managed to wash away the small bridge we had to cross, and we laughed like fools as we pedalled through giant puddles and small creek crossings that came up to our cranksets.

The final challenge of the day was a climb up from the river to the village of Bumba, an effort that took well over an hour to complete. Innocent caught a bus from Bumba back to Gisenyi via the main inland road the next morning, and after the return to pavement I veered toward the capital at Rubengera. In the end it took two days to make the 130-kilometre, hill-laden journey from Bumba to Kigali. Like I said, hard work, but by the time I rolled up to the Hotel Okapi there was no mistaking I had been on a proper bike tour. I was hot and sweaty and tired and heavily bronzed from long days spent out in the sun.

It felt great.

• • •

Despite a cautious personal approach to the original wave of the pandemic, I still contracted COVID-19. It was six weeks after my original symptoms had passed, which was weird because I felt fine. I only got tested as a precaution because Jocey was under the weather. Ironically, she tested negative. Go figure. My doctor thinks the test simply picked up some dead virus that hadn't yet cleared my system. That original ten days in March 2020 was by far the worst I felt during my time in self-imposed isolation and the subsequent full quarantine a month and a half later. I don't know what's going to happen from here, but as I work on the final corrections to this manuscript COVID has slipped from the front pages. Out of sight, out of mind, I guess. The genie is out of the bottle and won't be going back in, but a weekly death toll of around 50 across Canada in the middle of 2023 fails to rise to a newsworthy standard anymore. I wonder if we've learned anything from the experience.

Personally, I think we missed the point of these last few years, as we grappled over the finer details of our privilege. It is my opinion that COVID-19 provided the perfect opportunity for humanity as a whole to re-examine, remake and reinvent, well, just about everything. The virus exposed how overextended, vulnerable and inadequate many of our local, regional and global systems are in true crisis. *Normal* is clearly broken, and the pandemic has been a mirror held right up to our face, urging us to take a deeper look at how we do things. The collective compulsion to continually rush back to the defective state of normal as if nothing happened feels like a fool's errand, and I want to stand on every soapbox, rooftop, mountaintop and social media platform and shout, "Jesus Christ everybody, why don't we stop and take a breath! There's more to this disruption of the everyday than just a virus."

But who would listen? Three years after China reported the first cases to the World Health Organization, seven million people have lost their lives around the globe, officially, but that number is almost surely underreported in rural areas and in developing countries where health services are more difficult to access. An exhaustive study conducted by *The Economist* suggests a number two to four times the official tally based on an examination of excess mortality rates that have spiked way above what could have been expected over the time period in question. Their machine-learning model calculates a central excess death estimate of just under 24 million. To put it in historical context, the Spanish Flu pandemic of 1918 lasted a little over two years and somewhere between 20 and 50 million people died.

Amazingly, people's beliefs on how to address this latest pandemic were divided every step of the way. In an opinion piece for CBC News on April 10, 2021 – back when we still had a chance to get a proper hold of this thing – Lisa Young referenced polling data from Angus Reid, which indicated 45 per cent of Albertans thought that provincial restrictions went *too* far!? Only 28 per cent felt the same nationally, but even that minority percentage of the population not taking proper care was enough to keep the virus circulating, and mutating. On the bright side, 42 per cent of Albertans said at the time that the restrictions didn't go far enough, a number only slightly lower than the national average.

It appears that in my neck of the woods at least, lurching back and forth with half-hearted measures that ultimately prolonged the misery was the preferred approach to actually having a serious set of protocols in place that would cripple the virus's ability to spread whenever a certain case threshold was reached. New Zealand did pretty well using that method, and our population numbers are close enough to make the comparison viable. By April 2021 their *total* number of cases mirrored our reported deaths. Going head to head in total cases over time we beat them 80 to 1, and the great irony is that the "draconian measures" conservatives around here were constantly braying about are what allowed that country to get back to a more familiar lifestyle while we floundered. Fast forward to late January 2022 and total cases were more like 30 to 1, but it is worth noting that New Zealand's 52 deaths compared to Alberta's 3,531 is nothing short of a scathing indictment of the attitude we have toward the elderly and more vulnerable members of society. We are a society of me, me, me, and I am appalled by the casual disregard for human life that was exposed here in Wild Rose Country. Not everybody is, it seems.

In the end, the difference between the two jurisdictions didn't have anything to do with the actual virus, but hinged on political will and a commitment from the general public to health and safety. Alberta can boast of neither of those things, preferring instead to minimize the severity of the threat and to grandstand in the name of "personal freedoms." We're not the only ones. The United States of America was an unmitigated disaster with regard to this subject and is barely worth mentioning were it not for one startling statistic: they lost over a million citizens to the pandemic. One million! That's a big number, but not big enough to take things more seriously and put collective health and well-being ahead of selfish interests and economic considerations that are fundamentally flawed and patently unjust. Few seem willing to acknowledge that "the economy" is an artificial construct; it doesn't occur in nature. We could change how it works if we really wanted to. Maybe it will take 30 million, or maybe 50 million deaths before we stop focusing so much on our individual whims and wants, and spend more time strengthening our community connections. Maybe we'll demand more action, accountability and transparency from our elected officials. Maybe we'll pay a little more attention to Mother Earth, and the repeated warnings she keeps sending. If you think COVID-19 was a handful, wait until you see the turmoil full-scale climate disruption is going to bring.

Alas, as it turns out, it could be my empath's instinct to want to save the world that's the real fool's errand here, because a big part of said world doesn't want anything to do with being saved. But I can try and save myself. After an oftentimes contentious relationship that lasted for nearly 30 years, I finally eased my way out of food and beverage in the wake of the second emergency lockdown in Alberta in December 2020. I made the decision, in part, because of the way the collective line of business dealt with the COVID-19 pandemic. An entire industry desperate to rush back to work after every haphazard shutdown regardless of risk in an environment perfectly suited to spreading a virus. Stupid is as stupid does, and in the end I couldn't stomach the counterproductive nature of the job as each new wave washed over town and people continued to aggressively debate the need for mitigation efforts like masks, social distancing and vaccines.

My new gig as a book wholesaler will be a strain on finances until I learn how to live within a budget (you know, like a proper adult), but job satisfaction and overall quality of life has vastly improved in the year since I made the transition. Riding my bike to and from the warehouse adds up to between 25 and 35 kilometres a week depending on the route taken on any given day, and that contributes to a sounder mind and healthier body. Once there, we don't obsessively track hours and breaks and holiday time. We simply get the work that needs to be done, done. When we're having a slow day or a bad day we pack it in early and go do something else to clear our heads. Of course, it would be great to not work at all anymore and just wander the earth in search of memories to be made and interesting stories to tell, but I'm not in a position to make that happen quite yet. At least now my beliefs and my values are more tightly aligned with my everyday reality, and that's something.

This personal change for the better aside, I am forced to concede that we are, as a group, apparently still trapped in an antiquated vision of what society could and maybe should be, despite the ongoing and not-so-subtle COVID wakeup call. I can't alter this disappointing reality no matter how much I rant and rave but will continue to do my best and will say my piece at every opportunity. One thing is certain: I am forever grateful to have been able to escape *normal* every once in a while, in this lifetime at least.

For that I can safely say, it's official: I'm the luckiest man on earth.

AFTERWORD AND ACKNOWLEDGEMENTS

This is my third crack at an acknowledgements page. I can only hope to do it justice but will undoubtedly fall short. I apologize for that in advance. Writing a travel book is a long and laborious process, with lots of people involved through all phases of project development, who are invariably spread out over time and space. As many of my friends are wont to say as we get older, "My memory is good, but short." Amen to that. Any and all omissions or inaccuracies, both here and in the main text, are mine and mine alone.

One of the things I love about travel is that it suits my personality. Long stretches of idle time spent contemplating the universe at large, or Mother Nature's delicate yet resilient contribution to this bigger picture, is never time wasted. I'm also fond of observing human behaviour in unfamiliar circumstances while trying to piece together the effects modern society has on us all, as individuals. What can I say – I find new faces and unexplored landscapes endlessly fascinating as well as intellectually stimulating. Along the way I have come to realize that while I'm a social being in many respects, I'm also something of a loner. It's a complicated internal dynamic to balance. Short, occasionally intense interactions often work best. I really like the idea of "fast friends," met out on the road.

That said, I would like to acknowledge the depth of impact these interactions have on my being. What they may lack in duration is more than made up for with impressions made. In Tanzania and Rwanda, and in Nepal before that, there have been cab drivers and tuk tuk drivers and waiters and lodge owners and guides and street vendors and strangers out on the trail who have all contributed a little bit to my understanding of the world. I have written about these interactions often because the subtle accumulation of wisdom gleaned has had a profound influence on me over the years. I am grateful for that.

From this latest adventure, special mention must go out to Cornel Mushi and Constantino Job. While it is possible I could have made the top of Mount Kilimanjaro without them herding me along on summit morning, it remains unlikely. What is without question is I would still be wandering around the Usambara Mountains in search of Mtae were it not for the route-finding of one Rass Ngoda. Zebron was an excellent safari driver and guide, who balanced proper respect for the animals we had come to see with an innate ability to find optimal sightlines in any situation. It is in the nature of these kinds of friendships, however, that sometimes it's just first names and you get on with it.

In Rwanda, Anaclet Budahera and his team in Volcanoes National Park facilitated a life experience I won't soon forget. I have done my best to convey how powerful and moving it is to spend time with the mountain gorillas of equatorial Africa, but realize words alone cannot paint a complete picture. It really is something that needs to be felt, in person. Thanks to the Dian Fossey Gorilla Fund International, Gorilla Doctors, and a number of other partners in conservation, the opportunity will continue to be available for the foreseeable future. New gorilla numbers have come out since my visit, and 1,063 individuals is yet another gain from what I reported in the main text.

This to me is an astonishing accomplishment, in addition to being an important beacon of hope as we plunge headlong into the Anthropocene, where system disruption will be a persistent reality. Having functioning programs in place that conserve, protect and even expand habitat and regional ecosystems might be our salvation in the end. If we can manage to patch these fractured landscapes back together into a recognizable whole, that is. The decision to act has not yet been enthusiastically embraced on a global scale, as our addiction to carbon-based fuels continues, but the tools are there if we finally decide to use them. Nature has a remarkable capacity to heal, we just have to give her a chance.

As I mentioned in the Author's Note, there was a temptation to tinker endlessly with this manuscript after finally uncovering the story that was knocking around at the back of my mind. English playwright and novelist Michael Frayn once said, "The form chooses you, not the other way around. An idea comes and it is already embodied in a form." That's why I write travel memoirs, because that's how the ideas come to me. When they do, I pack a bag and head out with the intention of bringing them forward. I also believe story knows both what it is, and what it is not. An author needs to respect those boundaries. And so I typed "The End" once I got a handle on things and moved on with my life away from the page.

As COVID-19 lingered and production delays threatened to mothball the entire project, my wife Jocey and I came to some difficult realizations. The first was that local development ambitions were destined to overwhelm sane municipal policy objectives in our beloved small town in the Canadian Rockies. The second was provincial politics had already gone off the deep end. In light of this changing dynamic and an unacceptable trajectory going forward, we up and moved from Canmore, Alberta, to Mount Buchanan, Prince Edward Island. It was the right decision, and we are happy here, but thanks must be extended to those who have been supportive through all three of my big writing projects over the years. I like fast friends, but deep friendships are good too.

One thing I do miss is a kick around with the guys. Long after we got too old for competitive matches, Canmore United stalwarts Frank Vermeulen, Fraser Bowman, Neil Orchard, Libor Kreml and Lawrence White would still get together for some exercise and beers on the bleachers afterward. Sometimes we talked about travel and books, but mostly we talked about life. When Martin van den Akker moved on to Vancouver Island, Jiri Paulik subbed in effortlessly.

My time in Canmore will also forever be linked to the restaurant industry. I spent a lot of time at the Rose & Crown and Tavern 1883 as an employee, and at the Drake and Hy Five as a patron. There are far too many people who made the time spent memorable to name here, but Robert W. Sandford gets special mention. Our "thunderous conversations" at table 62 at the Rose inspired and encouraged many of the thoughts and ideas that ended up in my books. Thanks, Bob. A special thanks must also go out to Heather Lohnes and Tobias Toleman at Alpine Book Peddlers, who gave me a job when I absolutely, positively had to get out of food and beverage, and who are now among the friends I dearly miss after leaving the mountain west. I love you all. You must come and visit if you get the chance.

The team at Rocky Mountain Books must also be mentioned in this little stroll down memory lane. Without them, there are no books. I would like to thank Don Gorman for continuing to provide an avenue for Canadian voices as they endeavour to make their way to the page, and Chyla Cardinal for effective layout and design that makes it look like I actually know what I'm doing. For this effort Peter Enman was tasked with cleaning up the mountain of errors in spelling, grammar and punctuation that are a fixture of my writing. In addition to steering me back on track when I strayed. Peter Norman worked on the first two books. You get to see the polished versions. They were not so lucky. I think it was Stephen King who said, "To write is human. To edit is divine." It's true, and since my skills are lacking in this department, I appreciate the help.

And finally, where would any of us be without family? I'm lucky, I've been lumped in with a group who accept my writing obsession without question, or too many questions for that matter. I dedicated my first book to my mother Dena, and the second to Jocey. This time around Brian, Jesse, Audra, Scott, Haley, Anna, Bob, Chris and Sue get the nod. Life is a weird and wonderful road to travel. It's also exhausting and confusing. It's easier when you take the journey with the people you love.

RECOMMENDED READING

Cahill, Tim. *A Wolverine Is Eating My Leg.* Vintage Departures, 1989.

Cahill, Tim. *Hold the Enlightenment.* Vintage Departures, 2003.

Cahill, Tim. *Jaguars Ripped My Flesh.* Bantam Books, 1987.

Dallaire, Romeo. *Shake Hands with the Devil.* Random House Canada, 2003.

Darwin, Charles. *The Descent of Man.* Penguin Classics, 2004.

Ferguson, Will. *Road Trip Rwanda.* Penguin Canada Books, 2015.

Fossey, Dian. *Gorillas in the Mist.* Houghton Mifflin, 1983.

Ham, Anthony, and Stuart Butler. *Lonely Planet East Africa, 10th ed.* Lonely Planet, 2015.

Krakauer, Jon. *Into Thin Air.* Villard, 1997.

Leakey, Louis. *Adam's Ancestors.* Harper Torchbooks, 1960.

Lopez, Barry. *Horizon.* Random House Canada, 2019.

Marshall, Tim. *Prisoners of Geography.* Scribner, 2015.

Whiston Spirn, Anne. *The Language of Landscape.* Yale University Press, 1998.

We would like to take this opportunity to acknowledge the Traditional Territories upon which we live and work. In Calgary, Alberta, we acknowledge the Niitsítapi (Blackfoot) and the people of the Treaty 7 region in Southern Alberta, which includes the Siksika, the Piikuni, the Kainai, the Tsuut'ina, and the Stoney Nakoda First Nations, including Chiniki, Bearpaw, and Wesley First Nations. The City of Calgary is also home to Métis Nation of Alberta, Region III. In Victoria, British Columbia, we acknowledge the Traditional Territories of the Lkwungen (Esquimalt and Songhees), Malahat, Pacheedaht, Scia'new, T'Sou-ke, and W̱SÁNEĆ (Pauquachin, Tsartlip, Tsawout, Tseycum) peoples.